A CENTURY OF CONFLICT

A CENTURY OF CONFLICT

1850–1950

ESSAYS FOR A. J. P. TAYLOR

EDITED BY
MARTIN GILBERT

ATHENEUM
NEW YORK
1967

Library of Congress catalog card number 66–25470
Printed in Great Britain by Morrison & Gibb Ltd.
London and Edinburgh
Bound by H. Wolff, New York
First American Edition

CONTENTS

LORD BEAVERBROOK
The Man Who Likes to Stir Things Up
page 1

SIR NORMAN ANGELL
History Teaching and the Voter
page 7

F. H. HINSLEY
Reflections on the History of International Relations
page 19

BETTY KEMP
Patriotism, Pledges, and the People
page 35

PROFESSOR FRANCO VALSECCHI
European Diplomacy and the Expedition of the Thousand: The Conservative Powers
page 47

ELIZABETH LONGFORD
Queen Victoria's Doctors
page 73

PROFESSOR MICHAEL HOWARD
William I and the Reform of the Prussian Army
page 89

PROFESSOR ALFRED GOLLIN
Asquith: A New View
page 105

JAMES JOLL
Rathenau and Harden: A Footnote to the History of Wilhelmine Germany
page 115

SIR BASIL LIDDELL HART
French Military Ideas before the First World War
page 133

PROFESSOR MAX BELOFF
The Special Relationship: an Anglo-American Myth
page 148
PROFESSOR H. N. FIELDHOUSE
Noel Buxton and A. J. P. Taylor's The Trouble Makers
page 173
GEORGES BONNIN
Les Leçons du Putsch de Hitler de 1923
page 199
PROFESSOR SIR ISAIAH BERLIN
Lewis Namier: A Personal Impression
page 213
PAUL EINZIG
The Financial Crisis of 1931
page 231
PROFESSOR HUGH THOMAS
Anarchist Agrarian Collectives in the Spanish Civil War
page 245
EDWARD CRANKSHAW
Revisionism and Reform in the Soviet Union since 1953
page 265

PREFACE

THIS volume of essays has been put together by friends, pupils and admirers of A. J. P. Taylor. Each essayist chose his own topic, and such is the range of Alan Taylor's interests that he has written on or taught every one of the historical problems discussed. The century of conflict which spans the nineteenth and twentieth centuries is one which, both as a teacher and writer, Alan Taylor has made very much his own. On his sixtieth birthday, as a tribute to his energy and enthusiasm, this volume is respectfully presented.

MARTIN GILBERT

Merton College
Oxford

LORD BEAVERBROOK

The Man Who Likes to Stir Things Up

LORD BEAVERBROOK

The Man Who Likes to Stir Things Up

ALAN TAYLOR is the finest historian writing in Britain today. I must make it clear that this is only an opinion. As I am not a historian myself, I am not qualified to make judgments.

I am a chronicler, which is a very different thing. Sometimes, in the words of Shakespeare, I may 'chronicle small beer' and sometimes I have chronicled the alarming effects of strong drink. I may provide raw material for historians, but the great sweep of history is beyond me.

It is not beyond A. J. P. Taylor. His numerous enemies would not deny that he is a brilliant historian. His knowledge is enormous. He is a master of documents.

He has the capacity to bring order and meaning out of a huge, confused mass of sources. He can burrow as effectively as any mole, but he is the opposite of the mole by nature.

His is not a world of darkness but of light. His prose style is lively and individual. Above all, it is clear.

The opinions which he freely expresses are combative and disconcerting to those who like a safe and quiet intellectual life. He has been accused of irresponsibility and even of deliberate mischief.

Certainly he is no respecter of persons or established reputations. He is openly sceptical of the notions which everybody accepts as gospel, simply because everybody else is accepting them at the same time.

He likes to stir things up. If a psychologist were to give him a word-association test, I am sure that the word 'pigeons' would provoke the word 'cat'.

Taylor has been teaching at Oxford, where there are plenty of pouter pigeons, but the cats appear mostly to be academic tabbies. Taylor had been at Bootham, the famous Quaker school in York. It was a curious background, for, whatever else Taylor may look like, he would be a most unconvincing Quaker.

I used to wonder what influence the school had on him, but after the publication of a Quaker tract on sex, I began to wonder what influence Taylor had on the school.

He was exposed to the earnest social philanthropy of the Rowntrees, and it is characteristic that he turned against it, not because he thought it didn't work, but because it worked far too well.

It distracted people's minds from Socialism, and Taylor preaches Socialism. Of the Taylor variety, of course.

Perhaps the school did influence him in one way. The Meeting, with its periods of silence, is the heart of the Quaker's religious life. I presume young Taylor had to sit silent along with the other boys. Maybe that is why he has never been silent since.

His learning and his brilliance are not in doubt, but he is far from being Oxford's favourite son. The reason is obvious. Taylor writes an enormous amount, and much of it is written for ordinary, intelligent people who make no claim to be scholars.

This is highly distasteful to the kind of don who writes a little monograph once every ten years to be read only by other dons and maybe a few young men who are trying hard to become dons themselves.

Writing for the millions is thought to be as vulgar as trying to throw the Athenaeum Club open to a big game of bingo. It is even worse if the writer is actually read by the millions.

Taylor takes the opposite view of his own function and the function of a university. He believes that a university must wither if it is not in the main stream of national life.

He believes that a university should contribute to the nation and try to meet the nation's needs. He believes that men of great knowledge should make the fruits of their knowledge as widely available as possible.

That is why he writes so much for newspapers. Of course, he gets paid for it, which doesn't make him any more popular. He frankly enjoys worldly success, but there are many who condemn him for that who would do the same if only they could.

But his worst enemies cannot say he has achieved his success at the expense of thankless, unprofitable academic work. His output even in that unrewarding field is equal to the output of two or three ordinary historians put together.

He has been in many an academic fight and has enjoyed them thoroughly without bearing any malice.

As a historian, he does not believe much in melodramatic villains or in deep and dark designs. He believes that many a great historical figure has been credited with long-term plans successfully carried out when, in fact, he was merely acting from day to day and responding to events as they came along.

His theory that even Hitler was not always sure where he was going or how far he meant to go provoked a really spectacular free-for-all. Many hard words were said and many academic bricks were thrown around.

Whether Taylor was right or wrong will remain a question unsolved till the end of time, but at least he reminded people that there are two sides to the question. That was the purpose of the exercise.

As a speaker he does not disappoint those who have formed such a high opinion of his writings.

At Fredericton, New Brunswick, I listened to an oration lasting more than one hour. Taylor had no notes and no manuscript, and possibly very little preparation.

For clarity, wit and polish his speech was equal to the matured orations of Winston Churchill, and with the fire and enthusiasm of Lloyd George at the height of his powers. That is why I am proud to write this introduction, even though I shall not be in a position to read it when it is published.

SIR NORMAN ANGELL

History Teaching and the Voter

SIR NORMAN ANGELL

History Teaching and the Voter

WHAT is the social purpose of history teaching in those schools whence come most of the millions who make up the electorate of the Western democracies? To put it more completely and concretely: Does the teaching of history of the kind which prevails in our State schools help to produce sound political judgment in those masses who as voters, electorates, have the power to replace one Government by another, and thereby determine the course of national policy and profoundly influence the international situation? If there is failure in this respect, can the content and method of history teaching be so modified as to make it more effective in the development of social and political wisdom?

These questions are here examined in the light of certain relevant historical facts which are obvious and indisputable and include these:

This is the most educated of all the centuries of which we have record; educated so far as Western democracies are concerned in the sense that school attendance for every child is now compulsory; that the school-leaving age is being constantly raised and the amount of education received thereby increased; that access to secondary education, and thence to University has been very greatly extended. The virtual abolition of illiteracy has resulted in a stupendous increase of printed matter in the shape of daily newspapers of immense circulation, periodical publications of all kinds, the provision of free libraries; to which, during the last few decades, has to be added the marvels of radio and television. Never before, in any century in any area have the masses been endowed with such abundant means of communication, of information, of greater access to learning, to education, to the 'wisdom of the ages'.

Yet the outstanding events of this century reveal on the part of the nations of the West a distortion of political judgment, a public opinion so blind to obvious fact and simple truth, so subject to the irrationalisms of violent national political animosities as to have rendered impossible the prevention of two world wars and many minor ones, all of which worsened the situation they were designed to remedy; as will presently be indicated.

Such verdict on the public mind of our century may be deemed extravagant, far too sweeping. Yet it is based on this author's contact with the reading public in Britain, America and to a lesser (but considerable) extent in France and Germany during some seventy years, either as journalist, pamphleteer, author, lecturer and, for a period, as Member of Parliament. And it also happens to be the judgment of other publicists of similar experience in their attempts to reach the public mind.

For fifty years Walter Lippmann, whose articles appear in scores of daily newspapers and thereby reach many millions of readers, writes in his book *The Public Philosophy* (Boston: Little, Brown, 1955):

> There is a deep disorder in our society which comes, not from the machinations of our enemies and from the adversities of the human condition, but from within ourselves. . . . Something had gone very wrong in the liberal democracies. . . . They were entangled in a vicious circle of wars that led to ever bigger and wider wars. Could it be denied that they were sick with some kind of incapacity to cope with reality, to govern their affairs, to defend their vital interests and, it might be, to ensure their survival as free and democratic states? . . . Mass opinion has acquired mounting power in this country. It has shown itself to be a dangerous master of decisions when the stakes are life and death.

To that might be added the view of Edward R. Murrow, who has in the sphere of radio and television the sort of authority Mr Lippmann possesses in the printed word. In a forceful lecture at the London Guildhall, Mr Murrow said:

> Of one thing I am sure. In the areas of political television we are all ignorant. . . . We don't know with any degree of accuracy how we sell or convey ideas. . . . I would doubt that under today's systems of communication a Lincoln or a Jefferson could be nominated or elected.

Note Edward Murrow's implication that the public mind, despite such miracles of communication as afforded by radio and television, is less competent for its political tasks than was the public mind of America a century or even two centuries since.

*

In that connection it is sometimes argued that government was easier and thus better when in the hands of a highly educated minority, an elite, than when, under a greatly enlarged franchise, it is exposed to such psychological risks as those of crowd-mindedness, and the herd instinct.

History of this as of previous centuries does not bear out such a conclusion. A minority, an elite, a dictatorship which possesses unchallengeable power, will be corrupted thereby, as Acton warned us. Great learning and profound philosophies do not protect men from such corruption.

More than two thousand years ago Greece produced a civilisation comparable to any which has existed since. It gave mankind some of its greatest philosophers and bequeathed an immortal political literature, still part of our heritage, still studied in our institutions of higher learning. But all the brilliance of the Athenian political philosophy did not prevent policies which engendered wars even with other Greek City States, wars which had their part in the destruction of the ancient Greek civilisation. Nor could the absorption of Greek learning by Roman leaders prevent the collapse of the Roman Empire.

Religious teachers, Western and Eastern alike, have a broadly similar record. Most have taught peace, and those they taught have gone incessantly, repetitively, to war. For nearly twenty centuries the Christian theologians have learnedly elaborated the message of the Prince of Peace and set before themselves the objective of carrying that message to all mankind. But very early the effort brought war, not peace. In the centuries of the Crusades the wars were mainly against the Muslims; and in the later centuries, the long and destructive religious wars were between the Christian churches and Christian nations, provoked largely by violent differences between the theologians in the interpretation of that message of peace, and of the doctrines of human brotherhood, upon which the message is based.

Much more than war is involved. Theologians of great learning managed to reconcile the doctrine which includes the Sermon on the Mount with the torture chambers of the Inquisition and the *auto-da-fé*. These latter features of Christendom endured for six hundred years and the theological philosophers who defended them were not ignorant men. They were profoundly learned, of great knowledge and complete sincerity.

We should not minimise or discount these features of history. For the forces which explain them—mainly forces deeply rooted in our human nature—are still active, still producing immeasurable miseries for uncountable millions of human beings. Indeed the victims of our modern political errors far outnumber those who suffered under the Inquisition or in the religious wars. Suffice at this point to remind the reader that the massacre of six million men, women and children carried out by the very efficient bureaucracy of the most educated nation of this most educated century, in conditions of calculated cruelty, exceeded in horror—as it certainly succeeded in crass political stupidity—anything of which the Inquisition was guilty.

The Hitlerian episode, though the most shocking in this century's record, does not stand alone.

The First World War was to be the war that would end war and make the world safe for democracy. The fact that it resulted very quickly in a second war, even more disastrous than the first, and in an epidemic of dictatorships the world over—including that of Stalin—was due to sudden changes in mood and opinion, to veritable political somersaults in all three major Western democracies. The American record, although fundamentally the same as the British and French, reveals this series of somersaults most clearly.

When the United States entered the First World War, President Wilson, in his speech to Congress of April 2, 1917, indicated the conditions of stable peace. He insisted that henceforth when major aggression occurred, neutrality would be impossible for a power such as the United States. It must co-operate with other powers in some system of collective defence so that no aggressor could apply what Churchill later called 'the simple and deadly plan of one by one'. The case was simple, clear, unanswerable. And when the President outlined the project of a League of Nations he received warm and widespread support.

But after the war, it all changed. Far from American neutrality being abandoned, it was made ironclad by a series of Neutrality Acts. Britain and France asserted their isolationism in the form of appeasement.

The internationalism warmly supported in 1917, rejected in 1920, was readopted twenty-five years later in the form of the United Nations. If the three democracies had done early what they did late, it is extremely unlikely that there would have been a second war, which Churchill christened 'the unnecessary war'. And note what followed that second war. Because the United States and Britain could not agree on the political purpose of the war and on the strategic situation which should follow it, Stalin was able to turn Hitler's defeat into the means of stupendous expansion of the Communist empire. Both wars aimed at destroying German military power. The Western Allies are now engaged in re-arming Germany as a condition of their own security.

What should most concern us of the new nuclear age about our post-political failures is that we now face a situation the like of which has never before confronted mankind. If, in this new age, men continue to behave politically as men always have behaved in every age of which we have record, then mankind will perish. Heretofore men have fought wars endlessly, fought as tribes, as clans, as races, as nations, as states, as parties within states. But through it all man has survived. We of this generation have survived two world wars and many minor ones and 'never had it so good'. But we are now beginning to realise that we would not survive a third world war, fought as it would be with nuclear weapons, given the blindnesses which war engenders, the degree to which men in war take leave of their senses. Technology—the skills which men manifest so competently in the manipulation and management of matter and so incompetently in the management of the psychological forces within ourselves—is rendering nuclear, chemical and biological weapons increasingly available to all and sundry, including those two-score new nations in Asia and Africa, some of which would be combatants. If the dictator of a Cuba could manage to secure possession of weapons with which he could in a couple of hours reduce New York and Washington, and other American cities of skyscrapers and traffic jams, to so much radio-active rubble, then other small states, Asian or African perhaps, will manage to secure similar weapons. In that connection it is well to remind ourselves that if Hitler had possessed the thermonuclear bomb he would have used it, even though it destroyed the German people as well as Germany's enemies. For that power which so corrupts mind and judgment had corrupted his mind to the extent of a more than incipient insanity. We shall be extremely lucky if during the next fifteen or twenty years we escape the emergence of more than one Asian or African Hitler, a contingency helped by the worsening of the colour problem in the United States which threatens to develop into a racial war with repercussions through the world. All of which makes it imperative to face starkly, without evasion or complacency, the universality and antiquity of the forces which make for the defeat of rationalism in politics, for the perversion of political judgment.

*

The feature of our cultural failure most worth the attention of educationists and which a different teaching of history might go far to correct, is this: The knowledge which would have enabled the West to avoid their most disastrous errors during this century was already in the possession of those who made the errors. The school education the masses receive, though it continues during ten years, does not give them the particular skill or habit of mind which might enable them, in making their political decisions, to use the obvious social truths in the work-a-day world about them.

More than thirty years ago I had occasion to restate that proposition in these terms:

> It is a very simple truth which I am trying to state; yet it is one which evades us, or which we evade. It is this: The greatest evils which devastate our civilisation and at times nearly destroy it, are not due in the main either to the wickedness or evil intention of man; nor to lack of knowledge, in the sense that we lack the knowledge to cure cancer. . . . Those evils are due to the failure to apply to our social relationships knowledge which is of practically universal possession, often self-evident in the facts of daily life and experience, and to derive from that already available knowledge the relevant social truth. We disregard knowledge which we possess though we are unaware of that disregard.

I went on to add that:

> if it be true that in the gravest decisions affecting the common welfare the great mass of men disregard what they already know, it would serve little purpose for education to endow them merely with further knowledge.

They could disregard the new knowledge as easily as they did the old:

> unless to the possession of knowledge are added skills which the organised education of our schools and colleges very inadequately develops, if indeed at times it does not tend powerfully to inhibit them.

This latter view has been vigorously expressed by several eminent educationists. Alfred North Whitehead deprecates 'the teaching of small parts of large numbers of subjects' the result of which is 'the passive reception of disconnected ideas not illumined with any spark of vitality'. He goes on:

> Let the main ideas which are introduced into a child's education be few and important and let them be thrown into every combination possible. The child should make them his own and should understand their application here and now in the circumstances of his actual life. . . . The understanding which we want is an understanding of an insistent present. The only use of a knowledge of the

> past is to equip us for the present. . . . There is only one subject matter for education and that is Life in all its manifestations.[1]

Another educationist, Sir Richard Livingstone, so far supports Dr Whitehead as to declare that what a schoolboy should get from the subjects he learns is:

> to argue a case and weigh evidence, to distinguish the relevant from the irrelevant, to seize the point at issue, to arrange his thought and marshal facts to support a theory, to discover when a statement is proved and when it is not, to reason logically and express himself clearly.[2]

*

It is useful at this point to relate our educational failure to the world situation now confronting us. That situation can be summarised thus:

There can be no peace, no security against nuclear annihilation save by the creation of a workable World Government. But that has been made impossible so far by certain basic assumptions and ideas embodied in slogans about the right to national independence, complete national freedom, state sovereignty. Yet obviously if every nation is to be completely independent there can be no World Government. Moreover, the slogans are largely meaningless. No nation can be independent of others. What Japan did at Pearl Harbor compelled America to go to war. That is to say, the lives of every man, woman and child in the United States were in some degree affected by the act of an Asiatic island state thousands of miles away. This is not independence, or freedom from foreign interference. Yet those words, so largely meaningless, have power to excite intense emotion, just as martial music, which has no precise meaning, excites emotion. A catchy marching song will induce thousands to go on marching without even *wanting* to know their destination.

These passionate demands for complete national freedom—which by a monstrous irony are the current coin of Moscow propaganda—ignore a social truth obvious in daily life: If everybody had complete freedom nobody would have any. If each motorist were allowed to drive his car as he saw fit there would not be more freedom on the roads, there would be none. All would go in danger of sudden death. The maximum of freedom demands a traffic code, and the time has come for a traffic code governing the relations of states.

In addition to the fallacies concerning 'the natural right to complete national independence' there is another which today has split the world into two rival political faiths, creating the gravest political problem now confronting us. It arises out of the assumption that in a world which changes almost from day to day by reason of new technological devices, political measures can be based upon a complete, closed, watertight 'doctrine' or dogma. What is at most an hypothesis that such and such measures will produce certain desirable

[1] *The Aims of Education and Other Essays* by Alfred North Whitehead.
[2] *The Future of Education.*

social and economic results becomes a sacred creed to be defended to the death against all heresies. Such tendency is fatal to all political rationalism, to toleration, to peace.

To assume, as in Russia and China it is assumed, that socialism is something completely incompatible with private property, the latter being an institution which must be fought to the death; to assume, as it was assumed by a large section of the American public during the McCarthy era, that any degree of socialism is fatal to a capitalist or a free society—such assumptions constitute a myth. There is no 'Capitalist' state in the world that has not adopted and does not go on adopting, measures that our grandfathers would have called socialism. And it would take the power out of much Communist propaganda if in our public discussions we made it clear that what Moscow calls a 'Capitalist' society—the British or, for that matter, the American—has already adopted a lot of socialism and is ready to adopt as much more as will prove workable in practice and not be destructive of the good life for the individual citizen. Public discussion along those lines would help to break down at least part of the barriers which divide the world.

Could history be so taught as to promote that purpose?

*

Space available will only allow of one or two examples of the way in which history teaching could help dispel some of the prevailing myths.

One of the most portentous events of the early nineteenth century was the coming of the railway and the steamship. The story could make it clear that the railroad as a means of public transport of persons and goods could not exist until the State had given its authority. Here, at one step, was an increase in the part played by Government in industry. But more was to follow. Many an old-fashioned squire declared he would have no Puffing Billy across his estate. He would assert the rights of private property. So the next step in State intervention was to invoke the State's Right of Eminent Domain and qualify the rights of private property. It was made plain that the public interest must come before any absolute right in private property and the squires who objected to a railroad crossing their estates were overridden. Nor was that all. At an early state the State fixed prices—fares and freight charges. Price fixing by the State was almost socialism itself. The laws heretofore governing the relations of debtor and creditor had to be modified if adequate capital for the construction of the railroads was to be assembled. Until the coming of the railways the personal property of any partner in a firm was subject to seizure if the firm became bankrupt, a fact made plain by many an early Victorian novel. So the principle of limited liability was introduced into investment. Then the railway became a means of the levelling of classes. Members of the working classes could not and did not use the older horse-coaches for travelling. Such means were confined to the well-to-do. But when the railway and steamship came the worker was able to use the means used by their 'betters' and the workers could travel to, say, America in great numbers. (The Duke of Wellington's objection to railways was mainly that 'it would enable the lower orders to wander about the country escaping all proper control'.) And steam began the work of making the whole world interdependent. A famine in China, by reducing the sale of cotton goods, could produce starvation in the working-class streets of Manchester. And increasing foreign trade made necessary increasing Government control in banking and finance. In almost every aspect of the economic life of the nation, the State, the Government, was playing an ever larger part; the 'Socialist' element was increasing in every Capitalist society of the world.

But while that part of the story could bring home the ever changing character of human society, the underlying fallacy of so many of the fanatical political doctrines and dogmas which divide us, there remains a more fundamental task in which history teaching could play a large role.

That task is to render the youngster more conscious of the psychological forces which underlie the worst features of political behaviour: the irrational, deep-seated animosities and hates which mark nationalism, the colour bar, anti-Semitism, opposing dogmas of all kinds. A whole great literature has been devoted to the analysis of these forces so largely unconscious, and that literature is valuable in its right place; but it will serve little purpose to give the youngster scraps of Freud or Jung. It will be more to the purpose so to present such features of the story of mankind as the long endurance of human sacrifice, the burnings and torturings by priests and religious authorities, the Ordeal, the fear of witches, the duel, that he will see in those practices manifestations of a human nature which is his as well as that of his ancestors; and that it is up to him now to beware of falling into those particular emotional traps.

To achieve this end history teaching should include even with the quite young some elementary anthropology—stories of how men in the Stone and subsequent Ages lived and behaved and thought. Above all how they thought. History should be made mainly the story of changing ideas, since it is ideas which determine behaviour. And it should be brought out that differences in behaviour of past and present mankind are not due to physical changes in the brain, but to changes in the way it is used, in ideas, perception; that changes in ideas can produce not merely transformation of conduct, behaviour, but of feeling; that the spectacle of a child being cut to pieces on a Holy Altar, which did not at all disturb people as civilised as, say, the Carthaginians in the time of Hannibal, would revolt and horrify the man of the twentieth century. That such changes of feeling are not due to physical changes in man is demonstrated by the survival of something similar to human sacrifice in quite modern times, such as the *auto-da-fé*, the burning alive of the heretic, sanctioned by an institution which was not brought to an end until the nineteenth century. The fact that men of different faith, Protestant and Catholic, can live peacefully side by side in pleasant social contact would have seemed utterly impossible to most of the Christian generations of the past. The achievement of that degree of toleration owes less to the learned theologian than to the unlearned layman. The process by which the latter has achieved even that degree of tolerance and rationalism should be better understood, should be made plain to teacher, to parent and to child, and applied more fully in our educational method.

The cost of failure so to do may now be the extinction of mankind.

F. H. HINSLEY

Reflections on the History of International Relations

F. H. HINSLEY

Reflections on the History of International Relations

SINCE the Second World War men have applied their intellectual resources as never before to the study of the international problem; and their researches have themselves been vastly expanded, in variety at least, as compared with any previous age. The historian of international relations should be the first to welcome the resulting invasion of his field by the methods of rigorous analysis and adventurous hypothesis which have originated in other branches of social study and proved so fruitful there. In adopting them for himself he cannot fail to advance his aim of writing history in the way in which it should be written—in prose, as Mr Raymond Aron has put it, and not in verse.[1] But it becomes increasingly necessary for him to insist in return that the historian still has a contribution to make, a contribution which he alone, perhaps, can render.

His task has, first of all, its negative side. Faced with the enthusiastic assault upon the international system from newer disciplines—from games theory and economic theory; from operational research and conflict research; from the sociologist, the political scientist and the lawyer—he must point out that the system is a political system, and that even among political systems it is a system *sui generis*. Games theory, conflict theory, even economic theory rest on assumptions which do not always apply in political contexts: it is not possible without serious distortion to use the soap-flake firm as our model or the game of 'Diplomacy' as our guide when analysing the international ways of the State. Perhaps the same warning needs to be extended even to the political scientist, the sociologist and the lawyer. There is a great future for both sides in a closer alliance between these disciplines and historical scholarship, but we must constantly recall—as, if we are awake, we will constantly find—that to cross from politics to international politics, from society to the international society, from law to international law, is to cross a considerable divide.

This is not to suggest that the historian alone can hope to understand international politics, but only to indicate that there is also a positive side to the historian's role. Any political system can usefully be studied by the

[1] Raymond Aron, introduction to Max Weber, *Le Savant et Le Politique* (1959), 23.

historical route. When a political system is *sui generis*, however, as the international system is, the study of its evolution, its history, cannot but be especially profitable; and the historical approach has perhaps the additional merit that, unlike some of the more novel approaches, it is more concerned with understanding the system than with finding a solution to its problems or an escape from its defects. Above all, there is this further and growing need for the historian's services. Even though he himself must profit by what he can learn from other disciplines, it is he who must reconstruct the history of the modern international system if the other disciplines, absorbing what he can reconstruct, are to be employed as fruitfully as possible in advancing our understanding of it.

*

If historians will reflect upon this task of reconstruction and this purpose in undertaking it—this need to make international history understood by other kinds of scholar—they must become aware that some further effort on their part is overdue. In their work on the origins of the First and Second World Wars, for example, the central controversy is still whether the First World War was caused by the Kaiser or by capitalism, the Second by Hitler or by the existence of separate sovereign states, when a little thought suffices to show that neither of these opposed interpretations can be wholly satisfactory. And if they will turn their minds from the task to the subject—to the history of international relations—they must notice that two things deserve more attention than they have generally received. The modern international system is of more recent origin than is usually realised. And in its brief history it has accomplished more than it is fashionable to concede to it.

International relations, systems of states, may be traced back to the beginning of recorded history—even if this is far from being true of what we now understand by the nation and the state. So can the whole range of diplomatic expertise—including, for example, the practice of the balance of power. The earliest extant document which we can call a treaty dates, it appears, from *c.* 2500 B.C.[1] When we move on to the ancient Greeks it is at once apparent that they were no less familiar with and adept in these matters than we are—or perhaps we should say that we are no more advanced. It was only comparatively recently, on the other hand, that the *modern* states' system had its rise. There is some evidence, indeed, that it did not begin until the eighteenth century. For it was not until then—and even then this was only the case in Europe; and even in Europe it was not to be the case without serious interruption—that men for the first time in history accepted over any wide area the wisdom of what we now term coexistence between contiguous separate communities. One indication to this effect may be seen in the change which took place from that time in the conception of the balance of power: it was in the eighteenth century that the balance of power first ceased to be merely an expediency device and became as well a principle to be upheld, a purpose to be served, an aim to be pursued. And there is another piece of evidence which

[1] J. A. Thompson, *The Ancient Near Eastern Treaties and the Old Testament* (1964), 9.

points in the same direction. It is back to the eighteenth century, and no further, that we can trace the marked alternation of periods of peace with periods of war which has ever since been a feature of the international history of the more advanced states.

Before the eighteenth century, it is not too much to conclude, the pattern of warfare in the whole history of the human community had undergone only two main phases: the phase associated with the stateless community and the phase associated with the primitive state. In and between stateless communities, which possess little or no central or state organisation, which consist of territorial segments cohering around local lineages, and which anthropologists thus sometimes term acephalous or segmentary communities, the notions of victory and defeat are absent. The weaker of two segments or communities prefers retreat to fighting; and if one segment or community does clash with another it does not attempt to establish political dominance over it. The pattern of conflict resembles that which operates in and between the species of the animals and the birds. Outside the Roman Empire the European communities were in this condition, and their warfare conformed to this pattern, until perhaps the fifth century A.D.; and some parts of the world remain in this condition to this day. With primitive states—communities which may remain highly segmentary but in which there has arisen a central authority of some kind—the pattern of warfare is quite different. It is dictated by the search of every state for the physical conquest of others; and if things go reasonably well for one of the states this search will not stop short of the consolidation of all the communities sharing with it some ritual or cultural or linguistic unity, or which are within practicable distance, into a single empire. The states of Europe were by this test primitive states until the eighteenth century; and outside Europe and its oversea offshoots many of the states of the world are still primitive states.

This is why, as Sir George Clark has reminded us, there were only seven complete years without inter-state war in Europe (1610, 1669–71, 1680–2) during the whole of the seventeenth century; and it is also why of late, since the withdrawal of European imperial control, there have been few years which have not seen some war in one or another of the areas outside Europe. Nor did this pattern which prevailed throughout the seventeenth century in Europe at once disappear when that century came to an end. It remained in force there, while beginning to show signs of losing its grip, until well into the eighteenth. It was not until the 1760s, indeed, and then only inside Europe, that a break of any significance took place—that an alternation of peace with war began to establish itself in place of the situation in which warfare had been for centuries a continuous activity exhibiting an unbroken if fluctuating rhythm, and one in which official and unofficial war, international and civil war, had been inextricably mingled. But after 1763 there were nearly thirty years of nearly total peace between the more advanced states before the wars that followed the French Revolution. And then there were forty years of nearly total peace between the major states between 1815 and 1854; forty-four years between 1871 and 1914; twenty years between 1918 and 1939. Since 1945, in the same way, there have by now been another twenty years of peace between the Great Powers.

Let us, by all means, avoid exaggerating the decisiveness of this shift of pattern. Some steps towards the canalisation of war were taken before the last quarter of the eighteenth century. In the subsequent history of relations between even the more developed states there have been during the phases of peace not only the danger of war but also actual conflicts—like that which arose out of the revolt of Great Britain's American colonies in the eighteenth century; or those which followed from the intensification of colonial expansion during the nineteenth century; or those which, as in Korea and Indo-China, have reflected the completion of violent strategical changes during the past twenty years. It is not to be expected that a shift of this magnitude could establish itself at some precise date or over any brief period of years. We should not be surprised to find that while a man like Grotius was pleading for a departure from primitive conduct as early as the first half of the seventeenth century, a man like Napoleon was attempting as late as the end of the eighteenth century to restore the primitive imperial pattern in which France had till recently been supreme and from which Europe had so recently escaped. But we shall not go far wrong if we emphasise that, nevertheless, a change of some significance in the history of the states' system took place during the eighteenth century in this respect. Nor can we overlook the fact that this was sensed by men at the time, and that this is one reason why the eighteenth century, as Émile Faguet once said, was 'un siècle enfant, ou, si l'on veut, adolescent'.[1] It is no coincidence that, as we shall see, not only the modern pattern of peace and war but also the modern attitude to International Law and the modern interest in peace began at this same juncture in the history of international relations; for these are further indications that it was then that the European states at last passed into a post-primitive stage in their relations with each other.

We shall not go far wrong, either, if we regard this change and the subsequent persistence of the new pattern of alternation as constituting a considerable achievement. If warfare was almost continuous up to the middle of the eighteenth century this was partly because war was an activity in which men and societies were disposed, not to say delighted, to indulge. It would be a great mistake to overlook another fact which stares us in the face when we study any subsequent war—the fact that even after the eighteenth century, even for the more advanced societies, war still remained a relevant if not always a rational mode of expression, an activity in which the majority of men were always avidly, often profitably, and sometimes nobly engaged. In these days a large number of men at last want to avoid war. They tend to think that at least in modern times a large number of men have always wanted to avoid it, and that wars have recurred in spite of this fact. This is almost

[1] Émile Faguet, *Dix-Huitième Siècle: Études Littéraires* (1890), p. xii.

the reverse of the truth. At least until the twentieth century the wish to avoid war was the wish of a tiny minority. The periods of peace have alternated with periods of war in spite of this, even if it was partly because of this that war continued to recur after every period of peace. No historian of modern international relations will dissent when I add that in the past two hundred years governments have wrestled successfully against this continuing social urge to war as often as they have exploited or given way before it.

Yet it must also be added that during this period governments have been more and more impelled in this restraining direction. For it is not merely the case since the eighteenth century that war has continued to recur after every period of peace. It we want to understand the mechanism of this alternation which has been so pronounced a feature of modern times we must seize on this further fact—that it has been an alternation of periods of peace with periods of war in which, as never before, warfare was always becoming more intensive and more extensive, more violent if more efficient, more disastrous in its consequences as well as more decisive in its outcome. And this fact seems to provide one clue to the explanation of this pattern to which the modern international system has so markedly conformed.

In its original replacement of the previous continuous rhythm of violent but limited conflict, no less than in its subsequent interior dynamics, it seems reasonable to suppose that this alternation reflects—that it is the outcome of—three basic developments of modern history in the more advanced areas of the world. Before the eighteenth century, even in the more developed area of Europe, internal social structures, systems of government, state frontiers, organisational and control techniques, attitudes to international problems—all these things remained insufficiently formed and consolidated to permit that degree of central regulation of a community's resort to war which has underlain the subsequent alternation of peace with war. Since the eighteenth century if only in the more developed areas—for it must be repeated that societies still exist elsewhere in the world which have little hope of achieving this degree of control in our time—the three basic developments I have in mind have made continuous inroads into that earlier situation in two main ways. The consolidation and centralisation of the political communities; the accompanying rise of organised government, of the modern state, in those communities; the underlying advance of technology and science—these three processes have produced, however slowly and painfully, an increasing control over the resort to war. And then, again, it is these developments which have produced yet another source of restraint by ensuring that war would become ever more devastating in its effects if ever more efficient in its conduct, ever more drastic if also ever more uncertain in its outcome, when control and restraint broke down. The consequence was that governments which were in any case becoming more competent at controlling the resort to war were also becoming more cautious in deciding whether to resort in it. We are not wrong to be reminded of the situation which obtained in Europe up to the eighteenth century when we read that in one of the Yoruba primitive states, in an area of nineteenth-century Africa in which there were some fifty separate wars or campaigns between 1817 and 1893, the ruler sent out his army every second year, partly for spoils and partly for military exercise, and that the senior general of this kingdom was required by his office 'to go to war once in three years to whatever place the king named and, dead or alive, to return home a victor or be brought home a corpse within three months'.[1] But the situation which began to develop in Europe from the middle of the eighteenth century was in this respect, and for these reasons, a wholly different situation.

Why, then, have control and peace continued to break down? Why is it that, despite the restraining effects of these developments and their power to produce the periods of peace, peace has nevertheless continued to dissolve in recurring periods of international war? I have already suggested two directions in which we should look for an answer. The developments themselves, in the first place, were of their nature slow developments whose influence could only slowly increase even after it had begun to get established. Thus the historian will ignore at his peril the extent to which, even in the second half of the nineteenth century, even the more developed states of Europe could not control their nationals beyond their immediate borders—could not prevent a Cecil Rhodes or the officers of France's Upper Senegal Command, let alone the Russian general in the trans-Caspian or the Manchurian areas, from fighting campaigns and creating large empires with almost as much freedom as had once been enjoyed by the Conquistadors. Then, again, in the modern history of even these states the deterring effects of these developments have had constantly to battle with the persistence of older habits by which men welcomed war and with the continuation of older conditions in which war could be regarded as an appropriate, not to say unavoidable, method of settling conflicts between communities. But these are not, I think, the sole answers to this question. There are two other features of modern history which deserve just as much, perhaps even more, attention in this connection.

The first is this. If the continuing technological revolution, the rise of integrated communities and the emergence of the efficient state have been most prominent features in history since the eighteenth century despite their slowness in registering a powerful effect, another has been the fact that these developments did not take place throughout the world, but only in some parts of it. Even where they did proceed moreover—even in the more rapidly developing parts of the world—they began at different times and proceeded at different speeds. In consequence, while the growth of science, the development of the state and the change in the character of the community were moving the criteria of international power increasingly towards scientific, industrial and organising ability and away from mere acreage or size of man-power or geographical advantage, the fact that the different communities were

[1] J. F. Ade Ajayi and Robert S. Smith, *Yoruba Warfare in the 19th Century* (1964), 10.

affected disproportionately by these developments, in a world consisting increasingly of inter-locked communities, was gradually placing a new and an ever-increasing strain upon the forces that were making for restraint. It was doing so by setting up a growing and a continuously shifting inequality of relative power between the states.

At first, it is true, the disproportionate rates of advance within the more developed areas created not instability but a greater stability than Europe had previously known. During the eighteenth century itself and during the first half of the nineteenth century if we exclude the prominent exception of the primacy temporarily achieved by Napoleon's France—a primacy which, paradoxically enough, arose because France enabled Napoleon to attempt a return to the imperial goal of the primitive days by becoming the first country noticeably to break through to the integrated community and the modern state of the post-primitive age—the greater rapidity of advance in some states than in others was having the effect of levelling up an old, traditional, dynastic and highly unequal and unstable distribution of power. It is to this consideration, as well as to the fact that the basic developments as yet proceeded slowly, that we may attribute the comparative composure, the prominent progress, of the modern international system during its first hundred years—to about 1850. After the 1850s, in contrast, accelerating rates of advance and increasingly disproportionate advance in the three processes I have singled out were beginning to produce distortions in that distribution of power which had been basically stable since 1815—were beginning to establish, indeed, a greater and more shifting inequality of relative power than men had ever had to contend with. This was occurring both as between the developing and the undeveloped parts of the world and as between the leading states within the more developed area. And it is to these facts that we may attribute first the great burst of modern oversea imperialism after the 1860s and then the grave international unsettlement of the more developed area after the closing years of the nineteenth century.

Now in such a situation we should not find it surprising that during the past hundred years, when the underlying developments have thus given rise to increasing incentives to the resort to war as well as to increasing deterrents against it, the incentives to war have continued to be stronger from time to time than the restraints—that the old belief in the profitability of war has continued to be more powerful, at least at intervals, than the new reluctance to unleash warfare's increasingly formidable and dangerous tools. Certainly the historian cannot fail to notice how often governments have been aware during these years that they were faced with this problem of disproportionate advance no less than with the persistence of this old belief. At the same time, we should not neglect another feature of modern international history which throws some light upon this struggle between the deterrents against and the incentives towards war. War went on alternating with peace not only for the reasons already outlined, but also because men went on failing to understand,

and thus to be able to control, the forces which were integrating their communities, producing their modern governments and issuing in their great technological advance.

*

This will seem to be an arrogant claim. As a historian, I must add that this failure was unavoidable, notwithstanding that these forces were forces which men were themselves unleashing—and notwithstanding, also, that this addition, while it may take the edge off the charge of arrogance, must call down upon me the charge of being determinist.

Against the determinism charge I must be content to say that I am trying to explain the recourse to war in a pattern of peace and war in which war did regularly recur; and that it is not inconsistent both to maintain that this recurrence of war was unavoidable and to believe, as I do, that no single one of the wars which recurred within this pattern was unavoidable. War was in general inevitable but no particular war was inevitable. This is the key to the character of international relations in what I have called their post-primitive stage. The different argumentations arise on different levels, according to whether one is studying the pattern from outside or investigating the outbreak of any given war within the pattern.

The charge of arrogance demands, perhaps, a more extended reply. Even when coupled with the statement that the failure was only to be expected, the statement that war has persisted partly because men have failed to understand their circumstances is sure to sound arrogant to the politician and the diplomat. Have not governments become increasingly well informed, as well as more efficient, during the past hundred years? Who but an academic, unversed in the difficulties with which practical men are confronted, could conclude that, even so, governments have remained incompetent at their jobs? To the professional opponent of governments, to the radical member of the peace movement, the statement will seem arrogant on the different ground that it makes a fine flourish with something he has always said. Is not his type as old established as modern war? Has he not always insisted that war would cease if men would mend their ways? Yet the historian must persist in making it in spite of these protests. The radical in the field of foreign policies has indeed never ceased to proclaim that war will only cease if men will learn to understand the forces they have unleashed; but he has not himself understood the nature of those forces. No amount of sympathy with the problems of government—and there is no historian worth his salt who does not have such sympathy in abundance—can hide the fact that governments have been little more proficient at understanding them.

The weakness of the radical peace movement from the eighteenth century to the present day may be fairly stated in this way. At a time when the increase in the power, the scope, the efficiency—and the necessity—of the individual state was the outstanding development in history, these men have concentrated their efforts to solve the problem of war—their hopes for permanent peace—

in schemes for the supersession or the suppression of the individual state. They have done so for two reasons. They have perpetuated a tradition established before the eighteenth century by copying medieval and early modern schemes for an international government—and have done so because they misinterpreted these schemes. The schemes were originally propounded before the individual state had emerged in its full proportions. They were originally advanced with the object of reconstructing that single empire of Europe which had been the logical, the inexorable, aim of international relations during the phase in which the participants in the international system were primitive states. More modern men have thought that they were aimed at achieving peace, and that they pointed to the only way of achieving it, between post-primitive states. In the second place—and this accounts for this misinterpretation—the coincidence of the rise of the post-primitive state with increasing international unsettlement and the increased destructiveness of war—conditions which were the product of the same developments as those which were forging the modern state itself—convinced men that the first of these phenomena was the root cause of the others.

Nor did this mistaken conviction cease to grow in intensity as the unsettlement and the destructiveness became ever greater after the 1890s. On the contrary, while most schemes for eliminating war in modern times have been schemes for international government in some form or another, schemes of this radical character have in the twentieth century been far more widely accepted as the ultimate wisdom than they had been in any previous age. For there had been earlier periods—all too brief—when some men—all too few—had recognised that this conviction was ill-founded, these schemes impracticable and inadequate. With Fénelon at the beginning of the eighteenth century and in a period of revulsion from the seventeenth century's wars, with Bentham and Kant at the end of the eighteenth-century Enlightenment and in the earliest of the modern periods of peace, and again in the second half of the nineteenth century with the rise of the International Lawyer and during another of the periods of peace, the suspicion dawned that the separate community and the centralised separate state, which had the deepest roots in the past, were also likely to have a long future; and the view developed that the elimination of war would only come, if it ever came, through an increase in the wisdom, the caution and the sense of responsibility of the separate communities and their separate governments. Perhaps Kant alone, the most percipient among these few men, went further still—to the point of suggesting not only that peace could be founded only on the relations between independent states, but also that the world would have to wait for the necessary increase in caution and responsibility until its separate communities and their governments had passed beyond what I have called the post-primitive stage and what he would have termed their pre-constitutional days. Even so, we cannot fail to notice how from time to time some men—while they were usually more confident of quick results than Kant, and while their confidence was indeed excessive—at least approached a degree of understanding from which the twentieth century has in general witnessed a sad retreat.

Governments themselves at these same times temporarily reached similar conclusions. If we look for the explanation of their achievements during the course of the modern phase in the international system—of their success in first discovering the modern conception of International Law during the second half of the eighteenth century; or in first developing in the shape of the Concert of the Powers in the first half of the nineteenth century the international machinery of which an international system in modern conditions stands in need; or in producing the first great expansion of modern International Law in the second half of the nineteenth century—we shall find that it lies in one thing. Even if it is also true that this recognition was on each occasion being forced upon them by recent experience of the increasing destructiveness of war and by their lively fear of the increasing risks of uncontrolled behaviour, it lies in their recognition of the need for individual caution as the basis of common collaboration in a multilateral system of states. But the conduct of governments since the end of the nineteenth century, in admittedly difficult and deteriorating conditions, has not been more encouraging than the history of the peace movement since that time. Unable by their very nature to implement the more radically internationalist schemes of that movement, they have paid lip-service to them while abandoning, if not universally then at least in sufficient numbers to ensure international disorder, the alternative and more fruitful effort to maintain responsibility and restraint.

*

I have said that in this behaviour we have one of the explanations of why peace has continued to break down at intervals. I have also insisted that it was inevitable that men would behave in this way. This is no mere playing with words. It is a conclusion imposed upon us by the true character of the international system in its post-primitive phase. Is there any evidence, then, that this phase is coming, or will ever come, to an end?

The historian should be the first to admit that on the basis of our present evidence there can be no guarantee that the victory of peace and restraint will be any more permanent in the future than it has been in the past. On the contrary, although substantial peace between the Great Powers has now lasted twenty years, and in spite of the basic character of some of the developments which seem to account for this latest interval of at least the absence of war, the historian should be the first to insist that men now stand at a point in international history at which either one of two outcomes may still ensue.

The alternation of periods of war with periods of peace which has run throughout the recent history of the more advanced area of the world may be prolonged; this present age of peace may once again terminate in a return to war between the leading states which would be conducted, as always before, at a previously unparalleled level of extensiveness and violence. Alternatively, this alternating pattern may at last be about to be destroyed. The phase of international history associated with the prevalence, in even the most advanced area, of the post-primitive community and state—the phase in the development of the international system which succeeded in the eighteenth century to a structure of relations between primitive states that had previously persisted for most of Europe's recorded history—this latest phase may now be giving way at long last to another in which international relations between advanced states, while continuing to be the relations of independent communities, would take their character from the fact that these communities had at last proceeded beyond their post-primitive years.

It is all the more the case that we cannot be certain which of these two forecasts is the more likely to prove correct because there is a gulf between the possibility of short-term and the impossibility of long-term prediction. I make so bold as to claim that we already know enough about the history of the international system to be able to say of the present period of peace between the Great Powers that, even if it is to be merely one more period of peace within the post-primitive alternation, it will still be at least as prolonged as has been any such period since the end of the eighteenth century. I base this confidence on the operation of a subordinate but significant theme in international history. The basic theme in that history has been the continually mounting process of revolution in technology, of integration in the community and of competence in the state. The important subordinate theme has been that this process has proceeded disproportionately in the various communities of which the international system is composed. During the second half of the nineteenth century, and even more intensely during the first half of the twentieth century, this disproportion produced a condition of increasing international instability within the post-primitive frame. Since 1945, on the other hand, as in the hundred years before the middle of the nineteenth century, the same disproportionate growth rates have combined with the results of the Second World War to produce a marked return to balance, to a stable distribution of power, among the world's leading states. The most prominent illustration of this fact may be seen in the way in which the more backward of those states, Russia and China, have begun to level up with those in Western Europe and the United States which were previously so much more advanced.

On this basis it was possible to conclude some years ago that the world balance of power is more stable since 1945 than it has been at any time since the 1890s; and it was possible to predict the end of the bipolarity of the super-Powers of Russia and the United States, the onset of a multilateral system of state relations closely similar to that which operated during the period between 1815 and 1854, and, within that system, the development of such features as the decline of the Russian-American ideological struggle and the rise of a close if cautious Franco-Russian alignment.

Nothing that has happened since has required any modification of these conclusions. Despite appearances to the contrary, the trend in international relations, as revealed in each succeeding crisis, is still away from tension and cold war to a more relaxed and more flexible condition. The evidence still suggests that stability has won over instability, peace over war, if only temporarily—if only for a period that will last for, say, the remainder of this century. But it is equally clear that there is nothing in this analysis that bears on the longer-term question whether we are now also witnessing the beginnings of a more basic transition from the post-primitive stage in the history of international relations to a wholly new phase—to the post-post-primitive stage.

At the same time, there is some evidence for the existence of a widespread sense that such a shift is taking place. It is impressive because it lies in a special direction. Preoccupation with the avoidance of war was always before the present age the preoccupation of a tiny minority of men. In one sense, on one level, it still remains so. Since 1945 there has been, perhaps, a great proliferation of the demand for peace among the more professional citizens of the more developed communities. But on the one hand this proliferation began to register itself as long ago as the end of the eighteenth century; and on the other hand the great feature of the public mind today in relation to this question is not this continuing proliferation of interest in it. On the contrary, it is the refusal of the ordinary man to countenance the possibility of further major war—his insistence on living his life without regard for this danger.

We may explain this by recourse to his irresponsibility or to the inability of his imagination to comprehend the size of the issue—or merely to human nature. But it is possible to suggest that the real explanation lies elsewhere—that it lies in the ordinary man's vague recognition that a major transformation has recently begun in the attitude of the men who control the more advanced states. For the other outstanding feature of the present situation is a marked determination to avoid war in precisely these circles at a time when, given the largeness of the issues which they think divide the Great Powers and the smallness of their understanding of these issues, this was least to be expected. It remains as true today as ever it was that statesmen will not, and perhaps cannot, abstain from the use of war or the threat of war in defence of the vital interests of their states. But it is still probable, I think, that a qualitative change of immense proportions has come about or is coming about in this respect. If the reluctance of governments to fight is not new, it now seems to have a quite unprecedented edge on it. If states will still go to war to defend their vital interests, they have significantly adopted a distinction between the use of force and all-out war and significantly reduced their conceptions of what their vital interests are—though they may still talk of them in traditional phrases.

If this is so, we do not have to look far for the explanation of the change. In the continually intensifying struggle between the restraining and the inciting implications of the main developments in modern history—the growth of the modern community, the rise of modern state, the advance of the modern technological revolution—the deterrents against the resort to war, after mounting continually since the eighteenth century, and especially since 1914, have at last, for the first time in history, become overwhelmingly strong as compared with the incentives to it; and these incentives have at last, for the first time in history, been seriously undermined. The rise of the integrated community and of the regulatory, all-competent state are processes with a long history; but they have made more advance since the 1930s than in all previous history. For all the earlier scientific revolutions in history, the increase in scientific and technical knowledge and power in all history before 1914 was but a trickle compared with the stupendous growth in this direction since that date. Since 1945 there has been a further huge leap in all these directions even as compared with the acceleration of the inter-war years. And how much this has on the one hand heightened the deterrents against war is obvious, especially in the field of weapons—in the shape of the nuclear achievement. On the other hand it has most noticeably reduced the attraction of warfare for developed societies—as is most obvious in the way in which the continuing alteration in the bases and criteria of international power has at last destroyed for such societies the rationality of such objectives as are best or only achieved by war. Nobody can now believe that war is a profitable means—or at least the most profitable means—of increasing the power of an advanced community, or that it is a sensible way of expressing the power which such a community already wields.

*

It will be said at once—I have conceded already—that this analysis, even if it is quite correct, is still only an analysis of straws in the wind. More than that, while some evidence suggests that this is the way in which the wind is blowing, there is evidence pointing in the other direction. If it is right to say that there had been a marked increase of restraint on the part of governments in the advanced communities, it is also necessary to admit that their caution is based as yet on fear rather than on understanding of the forces at work. If it is right to say that the main source of this fear is the new dimension given to the risk involved in war by the advent of the nuclear weapons, it would be wrong to ignore the persistent efforts of governments and their advisers to circumvent this formidable obstacle to their old freedom of action by evolving such techniques as the so-called tactical nuclear weapons and such self-styled sophisticated policy procedures as 'crisis management'. Then again, while there are no grounds for believing that the immensely heightened deterrents against war can be much reduced by these means—any more than there are for thinking that they will lose much of their restraining power or that men can succeed in preventing the spread of the weapons to more governments in these days when technological development is so rapid and so much reduced to proven formulae—there can be no guarantee that international instability will not return, or that men in their folly will not be tempted to exploit it or to guard themselves against it by the resort to war.

On the contrary, if the world is to make a transition of proportions comparable to that which completed itself about two hundred years ago, if it is to move from the post-primitive to a more advanced form of international relations, men must begin to learn more than they have so far learnt from the study of international history. One thing it can teach us has already been mentioned: before instability can be expected to return we have some time, if not eternity, in which to reflect on another of its lessons. It is safe to say that, when unstable conditions do return, the only thing that will guard us against a reversion to post-primitive ways will be the fact that we have come to understand in sufficient numbers that the character of the states' system, apparently dependent on underlying developments beyond our control, is in reality dependent on developments which men have created for themselves and against which they must also continually contend.

BETTY KEMP

Patriotism, Pledges, and the People

BETTY KEMP

Patriotism, Pledges, and the People

PATRIOTISM, pledges, the people: the words are written, large and often, on the banners of eighteenth-century dissenting politicians, pamphleteers and poets. To explain the juxtaposition is more than an exercise in semantics. 'Patriotism', in the special sense of reform, or restoration, or rescue from corruption, linked the other two. 'Pledges', solemn promises by members of parliament to their constituents, seemed a means to an end, the achievement of the patriot programme. The object, the promised beneficiary of the patriot programme, was 'the people'. There was, here, a hint of the idea of the people as the 'origin of all just power', of the old Whig view of the prince as the servant of the people, of the older view of the prince who could do no wrong but might be prevented by evil counsellors. At the end of the century 'patriotism' broke away from the trio,[1] shedding its domestic meaning and keeping only the more obvious one of concern for one's country abroad, in the world. In this sense it was a word more often used by governments than by oppositions, though 'unpatriotic' was a label pinned to dissenters in foreign policy, from Fox onwards. A generation or so later 'the people' was also claimed for the establishment, though the word did not cease to be used by their opponents. Used by both sides, it gradually lost its sting, and could mean, indifferently, either the electorate, or the political nation, or those who were excluded from it. The government used the word 'people' in 1832, though their Representation of the People bill bore little resemblance to the bill demanded in the 1780s to satisfy Granville Sharp's 'Claims of the People'. It was used by the Benthamite Roebuck, who in 1837 described the Radicals as the only 'representatives of the people' in the House of Commons, and by the Chartists, who called their Six Points the People's Charter. It provided governments with the title of all later Reform bills. Pledges were left, suffering neither metamorphosis nor adoption, and outliving the old, classical, pre-Reform

[1] Of the trio, patriotism was the one most favoured by poets, and of course not only dissenting ones, and with them it was much concerned with love of the actual countryside. But cf. B. Dobrée, *The Theme of Patriotism in the Poetry of the Early Eighteenth Century* (*Proceedings of British Academy*, vol. xxv) for a contrast between the patriotism of this period (care for the good name of one's country) and the later 'my country right or wrong' variety. The first was an easy spring-board for criticism.

political world. They were, indeed, stronger in the new world than in the old, because of the stimulus and encouragement seemingly given to them by the Reform bill.

As with other evocative political abstractions—democracy and liberty for example—one expects patriotism and the people to have different meanings at different times and in different circles.[1] What is surprising is that in the eighteenth century patriotism should have acquired, in political circles, a meaning so precise that it could be defined in terms of specific legislation. This legislation was regarded as anti-government, and the adjective has stuck to its sponsors. Nevertheless, the programme they advocated was constitutional, not political. They believed, as many English reformers have done, that the constitution was being perverted, and they wished not to introduce new principles but to resuscitate principles which seemed, to them, to have been submerged.

Shaftesbury's country party in the 1670s were, of course, patriots, standing for the interests of their country against the machinations of a misguided king and his evil counsellors. But their patriotism did not stop at dislike of Charles II's pro-French policy, and James II's popery. They also believed in limited kingship, and in some sort of implicit contract between king and people[2]; they demanded frequent and free parliaments, and they believed that these had once existed. The country-court antithesis continued to have force until the monarch was clearly no longer able to choose his own servants, perhaps after 1867. The use of 'patriot' as an alternative to 'country' was firmly established in the 1730s. Bolingbroke's patriot king was simply a king who would restore the constitution by putting into practice the 'country' programme: independent parliaments; frequent elections; no placemen; non-party government; a militia instead of a standing army. The chief patriot organ, *The Craftsman*, had the alternative title '*or Countryman*'. The label patriot was pinned, over the next half-century, to a series of opposition groups, all of them with some constitutional aims, and all of them seeking their justification in the past. There was the patriot opposition to the Excise bill in 1733, and the boy patriots' denunciation of Walpole's system. There was patriotic nostalgia for the two repealed clauses in the Act of Settlement—the clause forbidding placemen to sit in the Commons and the clause making privy councillors accountable for the advice they gave—and the patriot demand for a militia, at last successful with Pitt's Militia Act of 1757. There was the patriotic programme of 1770, centring round Wilkes and the Society for Constitutional Information, and that of 1780, centring on economical reform,

[1] One could perhaps claim that in the eighteenth century the word patriot was, both in England and in France, in the process of acquiring its modern sense. Earlier, it generally either meant 'compatriot', 'fellow countryman', or was qualified (e.g. 'good patriot', 'bad patriot').

[2] Cf. Dryden, *Absalom and Achitopel*, 965:

> Gull'd with a Patriot's name, whose Modern sense
> Is one that wou'd by law supplant his Prince.

county associations, petitions to parliament. Of course the use of the word patriot in all these cases was challenged, but the challenge showed that the use was both well-understood and dangerous. 'Many People think', wrote William Arnall in 1735, 'that there is an inherent Virtue in Opposition, nay, a Sort of Divinity in it.' To disabuse them he gave a list of occasions when '*Patriotism* was on the side of the Government, and the *Opposition* repugnant to Patriotism'.[1] Forty years later Dr Johnson tried, with rather laboured ridicule, to make the same point, drawing a distinction between true and false patriotism and warning the unsuspecting that place bills, agitation for short parliaments, and 'an acrimonious and unremitting opposition to the court' were not infallible signs of patriotism.[2]

This use of the word patriotism as synonymous with love of the true constitution, and therefore with zeal for constitutional reform if not with opposition, was dead before 1832, and probably died during the Revolutionary wars. Although it was not killed by the association of patriotism with sympathy for the American rebels, it could hardly survive association with the French *patriote* party, and after 1792 few used the word in the old sense.[3] Something of this old sense was echoed, perhaps, by Peel's refusal to engage in consistent party opposition after 1832, because he thought the constitution in danger, and by his non-party stand in 1846, though head of the government. 'He believes the country generally, as distinguished from mere party, is in favour of the measures proposed,' he wrote to the Queen.[4] He called his attitude not 'patriotism', as Pitt would have done, but 'public duty'. Even so posterity, following Disraeli, has judged it anachronistic.

Since its death, patriotism as a constitutional creed has suffered neglect and ridicule. Historians and politicians alike have scoffed at its confusions, as Dr Johnson did, and have damned it as impracticable: its protagonists are dismissed as fools, idealists who did not know how things work, or as knaves, place-seekers who had no intention of implementing, when in power, the programme they preached in opposition. Even if it be too late to rehabilitate the patriots,

[1] *Opposition no Proof of Patriotism* [1735], pp. 6, 7; and see G. Berkeley's *Maxims Concerning Patriotism* (*Works*, ed. A. C. Fraser. 1901).

[2] 'The Patriot' [1774] in *Works* ed. A. Murphy, viii (1792). 142 *et seq.*

[3] See, for example, John Gifford, *A Letter to the Earl of Lauderdale* (1795). Gifford attacks the 'patriotic addresses . . . from disaffected societies in this country to the convention in France . . . replete with reflections on the constitution of England', their pretended concern with political liberty and their belief that it was to be found in France. He cites Lauderdale's 'friend', the *patriote* Brissot, with his 'factious paper Le Patriote François', and his opinion that 'the English had no political liberty'. Three years earlier, Oldfield had called for 'a patriotic and disinterested resolution, in all, to recur to the first principles of our constitution . . . and remove those [members of parliament] who, thus, prove themselves unworthy of their delegated power . . . they are the public servants, and are, therefore, liable to dismission when they betray the trust they are hired to guard.' (*History of the Boroughs*, i. 3, 203).

[4] February 11, 1846. C. S. Parker, *Peel from his Private Correspondence*, iii. 339. Peel did, in 1837, use the word 'patriotic' to mean something like 'love of the constitution', that is the 'old constitution' (see *Annual Register*, 1837, p. 17).

one can at least question the pretended realism of their critics. The patriot Pulteney, after all, was realist enough to do this at the time, urging patriots not to be duped by the 'Artful Attempt' of their opponents to persuade them of the

> Uselessness and Folly of these high-flown Notions. You will be told they are romantick, impracticable, the Bane of all Business, and the Contempt of every Man of Sense . . . [And] an Opinion [will be] inculcated, that the Dispute *on either Side*, is only for Power, not Principles.[1]

Pulteney was not a very successful politician, and his warning impressed neither his contemporaries nor their successors. Yet there is no good reason why the patriot programme should not be taken as seriously as any other plan of constitutional reform: charges of impracticability and insincerity are based simply on the fact that the plan was never tried, and on the fact that the unreformed system worked. Of course annual parliaments, a House of Commons barred to placemen, non-party government, would have vastly altered the shape of constitutional government, but this is not proof that the new shape would have been unworkable. It is true that under the patriot programme 'the modern party system' could not have developed, in so far as its pre-requisites were placemen and patronage. But to regard the modern party system as the logical and beneficial 'end' of the constitution is, even now, no more realistic than to regard it as a perversion of the constitution. This is what the patriots did. The idea that a government ought to have a safe majority in the House of Commons was, they thought, 'the most profligate sentiment in politics that ever was conceived'. Members of parliament who subscribed to it would be

> in a worse condition than galley slaves—their servitude has the baseness of being voluntary. To effect this dishonourable purpose, they must abuse every power and violate every trust which the Constitution hath reposed in them; they must encroach upon the rights, and weaken and diminish lawful authority of the Crown, by wresting and perverting the whole institution of a House of Parliament.[2]

Whether or not one agrees with the patriots, one begins to see that another reason for the death of patriotism was its apparent alliance but real incompatibility with pledges. This incompatibility was disguised, for a time, by the fact that pledges were regarded as a means and patriotism as an end, but it could not be disguised for long. Patriotism stood for independent parliaments, and uncommitted members of parliament, and saw these as a restoration of the good old constitution. The principle which underlay pledges, the direct sovereignty of the electorate, was the antithesis of this. Pledges were stronger than patriotism. They were too concrete to be re-defined, too radical to be adopted by any government. So they survived, not as a means to patriotism but as an end in themselves.

[1] *Address to the Knights, Citizens and Burgesses elected to represent the Commons of Great Britain in the Ensuing Parliament. By a Freeholder* (London, 1734), p. 6.

[2] *A Letter to a Country Gentleman* (London, 1784), pp. 41–2.

Pledges denote the acceptance by members of parliament of a dependence on their constituents over and above the mere elective one, an obligation tying them more tightly to their constituents than to the Commons. It is often assumed that this dependence had been normal in the fourteenth and fifteenth centuries. I am inclined to doubt this, and to suspect that the orthodox theory of representation in the eighteenth century—that members of parliament were representatives not delegates—was, in a sense, always orthodox. The classical definition of the right relationship between members and constituents, given by Algernon Sydney in the 1680s, by Speaker Onslow in the 1740s, by Blackstone in 1769, by Burke in 1770, is a clear echo of a passage found in 1669 in Chamberlayne's *Notitia Angliae*:

> Although every member of the Commons House be chosen to serve for one particular County, City, or Borough, yet he serves for the whole Kingdom . . . his Power absolute to consent or dissent without ever acquainting those that sent him, or demanding their Assent, as the States General of the United Netherlands are obliged to do in many Cases.

Chamberlayne's phrase in its turn echoes that used by Coke in 1623: 'Though one be chosen for one particular county, or borough, yet when he is returned, and sits in parliament, he serveth for the whole realm.' Moreover, the words of the writ of summons to parliament, which Blackstone used as proof that 'the end of their [members'] coming thither is general not particular', had been used in the same way by Coke[1] and could equally have been used in, or with reference to, the fourteenth and fifteenth centuries. There was, of course, a change in the eighteenth century, a disposition to place more and more emphasis on the corporate nature of the Commons, and on the fact that each member served 'for the whole Kingdom', not for a particular constituency,[2] and to leave the constituents with no right save that of election.[3] This is, however, a difference of degree, not of kind, and it is explicable partly at least as a response to the growing challenge of pledges. The fact that there was, in the eighteenth century, an increasing awareness, and dislike, of the constitutional theory implied in the giving of pledges, does not prove that pledges and instructions had once been normal.

Opposition to this constitutional theory often took the form of protests against particular instructions, petitions or other attempts to bind members

[1] *Fourth Part of the Institutes of the Laws of England* (1797 edn.), p. 14. Coke quotes an instance (Rot. Plt. 9 Ed. III) of a 'subsidy . . . of a new kind' to which the Commons said they dared not agree 'without conference with their counties' (*ibid.* pp. 14, 34). But this is clearly, for him, the exception not the rule, and hardly justifies the 1780 reformers in citing him as approving of instructions in general.

[2] The end of payment of members by constituencies had broken one bond between them; the Commons' Resolutions forbidding the reporting of debates were an attempt to prevent the forging of another.

[3] In and after 1716 *Notitia Angliae* (then *Notitia Magnae Britanniae*) omits its earlier phrase 'Yet are they to make it their special Care to promote the good of that County, or Burrough for which they serve'.

to a course of policy favoured outside parliament. Sometimes the policy advocated was political, as with the Kentish Petition of 1701 which urged the House of Commons to support the king's foreign policy, or with the instructions of 1733 ordering members to oppose the Excise bill. More often the policy was constitutional: members were urged to press for short parliaments, free elections, place bills, a militia bill. This was the patriot programme. But, although many authors of instructions were clearly concerned primarily with the particular policy they recommended, it was not easy for them to confine the argument to this. Instructions were normally prefaced by some sort of explanation or justification for their issue, and, however temperately this was phrased, it could hardly avoid all echo of Defoe's description of the Commons in 1701 as the 'inferiors' of 'the People of England, . . . as the person sent is less than the sender'.[1] To de Lolme, at least, not an actor but an observer, the content of instructions was irrelevant: whatever their content, they revealed a misconception of the nature of the constitution, a wish to substitute the direct sovereignty of the electorate for parliamentary sovereignty, and to turn the House of Commons from an independent deliberative body into an assembly of delegates. Representation, as de Lolme defined it, had enabled the House of Commons to achieve greater power than any popular assembly: in particular, initiative in legislation.[2] This could not co-exist with instructions.

Pledges, the other side of the coin, were more dangerous than instructions, simply because they showed that some members of parliament shared this misconception of the constitution or, more probably, did not understand the implications of pledges. Certainly the eighteenth century saw fewer pledges than instructions, and not all members who received instructions were bound by them. Some of them, in any case, were little more than rather general statements of public feeling, and some, more precise, were openly repudiated. The content of the pledges demanded and given in the 1740s, both before and after Walpole's resignation, linked them firmly with the patriot programme. Yet, even then, proof that patriots did not want pledges for their own sake is found in the patriot Egmont's condemnation of them in 1743.[3] After all, the independence of the House of Commons was one of the patriots' chief concerns: they could not really subscribe to the theory on which pledges were based.

Perhaps this was where radicalism differed from patriotism, and why patriotism suffered from its association with pledges. The patriots who drew up pledges in the 1740s were concerned primarily with their programme,

[1] Legion letter, 1701, printed in *Parliamentary History* v, 1256.

[2] J. de Lolme, *The Constitution of England* (London, 1775), pp. 210, 214. Cf. *Rise and Fall of the Late Projected Excise Impartially considered by a friend to the English Constitution* (1733) for an earlier view that instructions were subversive of the constitution.

[3] *Faction detected, by the Evidence of Facts* (1743), especially pp. 96–7. Algernon Sydney, another patriot or countryman, had condemned instructions.

though they asserted the people's 'right' to bind their members. When Wilkes offered pledges, twenty years later, he took the right for granted and asked his constituents to give him 'instructions on every event of importance and respecting my parliamentary conduct'.[1] Pledges were, for Wilkes, an end in themselves, the expression of popular sovereignty as opposed to parliamentary sovereignty. After this it became clearer that the content of pledges was not of prime importance, and this put the emphasis so squarely on their constitutional implication that some Radicals, harking back to patriotism, refused to give them. Romilly, for example, in 1811 refused a demand from the Middlesex Freeholders' Club for 'an explicit declaration of your opinion on the subject of a reform in Parliament, and, to remove all misunderstanding, we desire to have it in writing'.[2] In July 1832 John Stuart Mill attacked pledges in the *Examiner*, and even Joseph Hume failed to clear himself from Cobbett's charge of not supporting the demand for specific pledges.[3] In December Burdett and Hobhouse refused to pledge themselves at Westminster.

Yet, in spite of these Radical doubts, the Whigs' chief argument for parliamentary reform in 1830–2 seemed a clear endorsement of the principle on which pledges were based. 'The public voice', it was said, demanded reform; therefore there must be a Reform bill and it must pass. The general election of 1831 followed a request from the King to be informed of the sense of his people on the subject of the Whig reform proposals, and this, a quite unprecedented appeal for a mandate on a specific issue, endorsed the same principle. After the election, in place of the customary handful of pledged Radicals, it seemed that Whigs, monarch and 'everyone' was pledged. When the Reform bill was passed, it was so clearly the product of pledges that it could hardly help being an encouragement to them in the future.

The belief that pledges would become more common, perhaps even normal, as a result of the Reform bill was widespread. It was asserted that the Whig government's introduction of a reform bill on the grounds that it was demanded by 'the people' had changed the constitution: pledges would in future be the mainspring of parliamentary action, the House of Commons would dwindle into a mere legislative body, and policy would be decided outside parliament, by the electors.[4] Members of parliament would lose their independence, and the government, faced with a House of instructed and committed members,

[1] Address to the electors of Middlesex, March 29, 1784, printed in *Annual Register*, 1784–5, pp. 275–6. The Address begins by referring to the 'solemn engagement' with his electors which he signed in 1774.

[2] *Memoirs*, ii. 421–5.

[3] Cobbett insisted that pledges must be specific and detailed. A general pledge 'to do all they could for the benefit of the country' was worse than useless: Peel, Croker, even Wellington, could subscribe to this. (*Political Register*, lxxvii. passim.)

[4] Cf. *Quarterly Review*, July 1831. 'If the people, even in the present state of the representation, have an *omnipotent* voice, on the subject of Reform—if its mandates are to be obeyed as the final decision of the last resort on a *theoretical* question—how can it be resisted on any practical question?' (vol. xlv, p. 539.)

would have no hope of winning support for its measures. These arguments were never answered, but they cannot be discounted on the grounds that they were put forward by opponents of the Reform bill.[1] They are, indeed, strongly reinforced by the fact that supporters of the bill, far from defending pledges, tried hard to disassociate them from the Reform bill, and even claimed that the bill would discourage pledges. Grey, for example, believed that the Reform bill, by restoring confidence in the House of Commons, would decrease the need for pledges, and therefore their number. Russell saw no possibility that the Reform bill might do anything but strengthen the eighteenth-century theory of representation. The *Edinburgh Review*, on the eve of the first general election under the Reform Act, deplored the 'jealousy and suspicion' which had in the past led electors 'to exact pledges', and urged them to show their confidence in the new system by not demanding pledges.

> To send a man into Parliament fettered by pledges is neither more nor less than to prevent him from discharging his duty of consulting for the common good . . . [In this way] the greatest violence has, without any doubt, been done to the principle of representation, and the relation between the constituent and the member has been completely changed.[2]

Of course Grey and Russell were wrong and the *Edinburgh Review* urged in vain. The number of pledges increased, and, more important, members began to feel obliged to uphold their constituents' views, even if they had not in fact pledged themselves. Hobhouse's retirement from parliament in April 1833 because his constituents disagreed with the government's policy was seen, said Greville, 'with a sort of grim satisfaction' by the Tories, who 'point at it as a happy illustration of the benefits of the Reform bill'. 'I point too,' he added wryly, 'but I don't rejoice.'[3] Even more worrying to constitutionalists was the retirement of about two dozen members of parliament, in January and February 1846, because they had come to agree with the government's policy of repealing the corn laws but thought their constituents had not. Most of these members had not made specific pledges; nevertheless, they thought it right to follow their constituents' opinions, not their own.[4] In other ways, too, the post-1832 electorate showed that it was not willing merely to elect. Petitioning, like pledging, grew more instead of less frequent; so did deputations to the House of Commons. Extra-parliamentary associations like the Chartist Association and the Anti-Corn Law League, formed to exert pressure on

[1] The 'constitutional' critics of the Reform Bill are, in fact, often discounted by the use of arguments which, like those employed against the patriots, really take success—or 'what works'—as their criterion. The constitution, it is said, 'worked' after the Reform Act, as it 'worked' in the eighteenth century: therefore the critics both of the old world and of the new are discredited.

[2] *Edinburgh Review*, lvi (October 1832), p. 255.

[3] *Journals of the Reigns of George IV and William IV*, ii, 370.

[4] See C. S. Parker, *Peel from his Private Correspondence*, iii, 337, for Peel's criticism of the principle on which these retirements were based.

parliament, seemed the direct heirs of the Political Unions formed in 1830 to press for parliamentary reform. Self-styled progressives like Disraeli asserted that great issues of policy—the repeal of the corn laws, for instance—should be submitted to the people for their decision, as reform had been submitted to them in 1831.[1] Weak government, too, which seemed a corollary of a pledged House of Commons, was present after 1832. Indeed, 'the problem of the executive' haunted every government in the period between the first and second Reform Acts. Peel's government was the exception to the rule of weakness, and it may be that he only achieved success because he was so aware of the problem.[2] In 1856 the *Quarterly Review* thought the 'paralysis of government' worse than it had ever been: no government, it seemed, would ever again have a stable support in the House of Commons.

There can be no doubt of the reality of the problem of the executive between 1832 and 1867,[3] but there is considerable doubt about its connection with the Reform Act. The problem was not new. It was felt acutely in the twenty or so years before 1832, and it was then attributed primarily to the decline of patronage which began in the 1780s. Indeed, early nineteenth-century complaints of the weakness of the executive, the difficulty of winning elections, the impossibility of managing the Commons, are so similar to complaints after 1832 that unless one thinks the early complaints greatly exaggerated one can hardly allow to the Reform Act even an intensification of the difficulties felt before it. Here, without doubt, the Reform Act was at most another step in a process which had set in long before.

This was true also of other developments commonly associated with the Reform Act: the problem is whether, or how much, reform hastened them. The Reform Act was, after all, the result of pledges, not pledges of the Reform Act. The break away from the old constitution was well advanced by 1830, and die-hard Inglis deserved more consideration than he was given for his claim that this was an argument against reform. The precedents set in 1830–2 came to be inseparably linked, in people's minds, with reform: a general election lost in 1830; a dissolution in order that 'the people' should decide the issue of reform in 1831; a House of Commons elected solely in order to pass a Reform bill; a House of Lords forced to pass it or be overridden. Even so, these precedents were not the result of the content of the Reform bill; like the bill itself, they grew out of and were signs of pre-1830 inroads on the old constitution. Croker wrote in 1833 of 'the late constitution',[4] killed by the Reform

[1] Russell agreed with Peel that the House of Commons, not the electorate, should decide the issue of repeal, and quite failed to see that this was inconsistent with his views in 1831–2 (*Hansard*, 3rd Series, lxxxiv, 464).

[2] Cf. Lansdowne's insistence in July 1847 that the weakness of Russell's government, and its inability to pass measures, must be blamed not on its own shortcomings but on 'the inevitable tendency of the Reform bill' (*Annual Register*, 1847, p. 182).

[3] But Gladstone's opinion that England was never better governed than in these years makes one pause before equating 'weak government' with 'bad government'.

[4] *Quarterly Review*, xlix (April 1833), p. 270.

Act; Russell believed that the Reform Act would 'preserve' the constitution. In fact the old constitution had been dying for some time before 1832, and the Reform bill crisis proves it. Croker's prophecies, of course, were more accurate than Russell's, even if the things he prophesied were not caused by the Reform Act. The last word, however, should be Cobbett's, for he was one of the Radicals who not only understood but also vehemently welcomed pledges. Cobbett described the Reform bill, notwithstanding its many imperfections, as 'the commencement of a mighty revolution', the beginning of an era in which the people would choose governments and decide policies. Then, having made this pronouncement, he at once rejected the causal relationship it implied. 'We all know that if the House of Commons had not been pledged, we should have had no Reform bill', he wrote.

> The Reform Bill is a striking instance of the advantages of adopting that system [of requiring pledges] . . . The Reform bill would never have passed into a law unless a complete revolution had already taken place in the minds of the people.[1]

Perhaps Cobbett was right. Pledges, in the last analysis, were more important than the Reform bill. One of the reasons which made them so had already made them more important than patriotism and the people. It is, that pledges are based on a clear and unequivocal principle. Critics of the Reform bill believed that it pushed the constitution along the road which led to direct popular sovereignty. Nearly all the friends of the bill denied that it had this purpose. Some of them feared that it might have this effect; only a few both believed that it would and were glad of it. There could be none of these doubts about pledges, once they were recognised to be more than a mere instrument: they are based on the principle of the direct sovereignty of the electorate whatever its size. Although this principle was, after as well as before the Reform Act, incompatible with the constitution as most people understood it, in practice pledges had won too many victories, even by 1832, to be turned back.

[1] *Political Register*, lxxvii, pp. 2, 26, 27 (July 7, 1832).

FRANCO VALSECCHI

European Diplomacy and the Expedition of the Thousand: The Conservative Powers

FRANCO VALSECCHI

European Diplomacy and the Expedition of the Thousand: The Conservative Powers

IT was not only Piedmontese intervention which made the Crimean war the curtain-raiser of diplomatic events which were to lead to the unification of Italy. It was also, and mainly so, the repercussions of the conflict on European policy and the consequences deriving therefrom, in the arrangement of the pawns on the international chessboard.

The 'second restoration' following the 1848 revolution had reconstituted, at least outwardly, what in the Chancelleries of that time was called 'the conservative alliance of the three Northern Courts', Vienna, St Petersburg and Berlin: the 'Conservative Front', in which the tradition of the Holy Alliance was perpetuated for the protection of the established rule. This was a powerful barrier, which barred any attempt at undermining the existing order and thus prevented any possible extension of the Italian problem into the international field. The Crimean war, the first great European conflagration since 1815, marked the collapse of this barrier. The conservative front was shattered. The estrangement between Vienna and Berlin, separated by the discord of their rivalry in Germany, was revealed in all its importance. The conflict of interests between Vienna and St Petersburg, exasperated by the Russian bitterness over the Austrian 'betrayal', showed itself in all its gravity.[1]

The way was opened for Napoleon III to make full use of the breach in the conservative bloc, by playing on the Austro-Prussian rivalry and the ill-feeling between Austria and Russia. At the Peace Congress in Paris he held out his hand to the old enemy, forming with Russia an *entente cordiale* which was to become a precious instrument in his future plans.[2]

[1] See A. J. P. Taylor, *The Struggle for Mastery in Europe*, 1848–1918, Oxford 1954. Valsecchi, *L'alleanza di Crimée*, Milan 1948. In the wide literature in argument, see, in general, Vicomte de Guichen, *La guerre de Crimea et l'attitude des Grandes Puissances européennes*, Paris 1936. On the Russian attitude see L. Thouvenel, *Nicolas Ier et Napoléon III*, Paris 1891. On the Prussian attitude, see K. Borries, *Preussen im Krimkrieg*, Berlin 1931; on the German problem, see F. Eckart, *Die deutsche Frage und der Krimkrieg*, Berlin 1931, and H. von Srbik, *Deutsche Einheit*, vol. 2, Munich 1935.

[2] See Charles-Roux, *Alexandre II, Gortschakoff et Napoléon III*, Paris 1913; E. Schüle, *Russland und Frankreich vom Ausgang des Krimkrieges bis zum italienischen Krieg*, 1856–59, Berlin 1935.

The results were seen in 1859. What Napoleon really expected from the Czar was a cloak for his Italian enterprise: St Petersburg was to immobilise the German Confederation with the threat of intervention and keep Austria under the sword of Damocles of Russian hostility. True, the secret Franco-Russian treaty of March 3 remained only an instrument of collaboration: the Czar avoided committing himself in precise terms.[1] But it nevertheless represented a Russian approval of Napoleon's plans in Italy. The consequences were immediately felt during the diplomatic campaign preceding the war, in the Russian proposal for a European Conference, prompted by the Tuileries in order to thwart the insidious English mediation. And during the war, the Russian support of French policy contributed, with its weight, to curb the German impulse to intervene, and determined the Prussian attitude.[2]

In Berlin Russian pressure counteracted Vienna's call for solidarity. Prussia was prepared to run the risk of a war at the side of Austria only on one condition: this was that Vienna should satisfy Prussian aims in Germany and share with Berlin the position of pre-eminence in the German Confederation. But Vienna refused to compromise on this point and, at Villafranca, preferred a compromise peace in Italy to a loss of supremacy in Germany. On the other hand, Austrian pride rejected the idea of appealing for help to a rival at a time when the fortunes of war were against the Empire (not to mention the impact this would have had on the prestige of the Hapsburgs).[3]

At Villafranca Franz Joseph deceived himself into thinking that he could achieve a balanced solution in the Italian Peninsula. In the Austrian Emperor's view the renunciation of Lombardy was balanced by the clause providing for the reinstatement of the deposed rulers of Central Italy.[4] Vienna was struck with the idea of reaching a stable agreement with France on the strength of the Villafranca settlement, which would have enabled Austrian policy to emerge from its isolation and which would have represented a solid guarantee of stability and preservation in Italy and in Europe.

These diplomatic combinations were soon to be upset by events. The blow inflicted on Austrian power in Italy, on the battlefields of Lombardy, had opened the breach to the forces of the Italian national movement, which with irresistible impetus gained the upper hand and swept aside the diplomatic

[1] See B. H. Sumner, 'The Secret Franco-Russian Treaty of March 3, 1859', in *English Historical Review*, 1933.

[2] See, on international policy in regard to the Italian question in 1859, F. Valsecchi, *La mediazione europea e la definizione del l'aggressore alla vigilia della guerra del* 1859, Rome 1938; and of the same, 'Europa 1859', in *Atti del XXXVIII Congresso di Storia del Risorgimento*, Milan 1959.

[3] See, on the Prussian attitude during the war of 1859, the recent work by B. Malinverni, *La Germania e il Problema Italiano nel* 1859, Milan 1959.

[4] See, on the developments in the austro-French negotiations at Villafranca and Zurich, W. Dentsch, *Il Tramonto della Potenza Asburgica in Italia*, Florence 1960; on the significance of Villafranca see, A. J. P. Taylor, 'European Mediation and the Agreement of Villafranca', 1859, *English Historical Review*, January 1936; F. Valsecchi, 'Villafranca ovvero la fine della Diplomazia', *Nuova Antologia*, September 1959.

obstacles. The Villafranca provisions remained a dead letter, as did the peace treaty of Zurich, which was to have been the confirmation and approval of the preliminaries of Villafranca. The dream of an Austro-French collaboration remained an empty one. When put to the test, Napoleonic policy revealed all its contradictions and ambiguities. The French Emperor could not and would not approve the ever-increasing expansion of the Italian national movement, by giving it his support. The unification of Italy was neither in his interest nor in his plans. But he could not, nor did he wish to, oppose the liberation movement as an enemy, having himself set the movement in motion, and he could not repudiate the costly and glorious heritage of Magenta and Solferino. Faced with a dilemma from which there was no way out, he exhausted all the resources of his diplomacy in an impossible attempt at conciliation, destined to deceive the hopes of Austrians and Italians alike. Vienna saw its illusion vanish one by one. It could not build its policy on the unetady foundationss of Napoleonic good faith. For Franz Joseph, the outcome of the much desired alliance with Bonaparte is summed up in the bitter comment: 'The Emperor Napoleon is, and remains, a scoundrel' ('Kaiser Napoleon ist und bleibt ein Schuft').

The possibility of following a new course directed towards the Tuileries having thus been ruled out, the *Ballhaus* had no option, as *ultima ratio*, but to revert to the old order, to resume the old alliances which had been interrupted, to reconstitute the conservative front which had been shattered by the Crimean war, to oppose the spread of the revolution in Italy with the united forces of order and preservation and to oppose the French and English 'intrigues' in Italy with the solid bloc of a renewed Holy Alliance between Vienna, St Petersburg and Berlin.

*

In effect, the turn of events in Italy after Villafranca was certainly such as to warrant concern for the established order and a reversion to the conservative solidarity invoked by Vienna. The failure of the compromise reached at Villafranca marked the end of diplomacy in the unification of Italy, the end of the diplomatic phase which began with the Paris Congress and the Plombières Convention. The Italian national movement eluded the control of official policy. What was happening in Italy, in Emilia, Romagna, in Tuscany, was a fully fledged revolution, even if it did not assume the violent and dramatic aspects of one. It was the type of revolutionary initiative which gains the mastery of and imposes itself on the initiative of governments. The Garibaldine enterprise in Sicily was merely the confirmation and the completion of this new course in Italian politics. A spontaneous development, it followed its own course with an ostentatious independence of governmental intervention and without heed for the sacred rules and strictures of diplomacy.

The reaction to these events was inevitable in the capitals of the Holy Alliance. At St Petersburg the Czar made no attempt to hide his indignation over the events in Sicily. It was the spectre of the revolution, exorcised in

1849, which had reappeared; it spelt danger for the dynasty of the Bourbons, which the Russian Court had always protected. Berlin was more cautious, but no less alarmed: its rivalry with Austria and its hopes in Germany balanced in part its conservative and dynastic apprehensions. The policy of Piedmont, involved as it was in the revolution, appeared to the European Courts as an 'act of piracy'.[1] Then there was the general fear of France, of Napoleon's obscure ambitions. In a dispatch to the Prussian representative at Turin, Brassier de Saint Simon, the Prussian Foreign Minister, Schleinitz, declared that Piedmont, in pursuing her Italian aims, risked not only furthering the aims of the revolution, but also the French aim of supremacy in Italy.[2] 'I am as little French as Austrian'—replied Cavour to the Prussian diplomat. 'France has rendered us great services; but the day when her support should degenerate into pressure and the interests of Italian independence are threatened, I shall be as anti-French as I have been anti-Austrian.' As to the charge of connivance with the revolution . . . in regard to Garibaldi's enterprise, Cavour protested his innocence and denied all responsibility. 'If Garibaldi has left, and of this I am not aware (the talk took place on May 6), he has deceived me and behaved "comme un mauvais drôle" .' Piedmontese policy was aimed not at stirring up the revolutionary fire, but rather at putting it out, and at putting it out in the only possible way, by doing justice to the legitimate hopes

[1] See the letter from the Prince Regent of Prussia to the Czar Alexander II, dated May 23, 1860: 'C'est pour moi un vrai bonheur que nous nous soyons rencontrés dans les mêmes vues à l'égard de la coupable entreprise de Garibaldi; et je ne puis qu'applaudir de tout mon coeur à l'attitude énergique que, suivant vos ordres, le comte de Stackelberg a prise à Turin. J'ai muni mon ministre à Turin d'instructions tout-à-fait analogues, et je ne doute pas qu'il ne s'en soit acquitté avec tout le zèle que la situation réclame. J'ai éprouvé une grande et rare satisfaction à voir par votre manière d'agir à Turin, qu'a travers toutes les vicissitudes de la politique les grands et nobles principes de l'honneur et de la justice trouveront toujours en nous défenseurs zélés', in 'Die auswärtige Politik Preussens 1858–71', *Diplomatische Aktenstücke*, Oldenburg 1938, vol. II, part I, n. 176. In reality, the instructions of Berlin to the Prussian representative at Turin vigorously condemn the Piedmontese conduct: 'Le principe que nous nous proposons de soutenir ce n'est autre chose, que le maintien des bases fondamentales du status quo territorial que les traités de 1815 on crée dans l'intérêt de l'équilibre européen et qui se trouvent modifiées mais pas encore renversées par les événements d'Italie; ce n'est autre chose que le respect dû au droit des gens et aux institutions consacrées par l'histoire et destinées à conserver à l'Europe les bienfaits d'une civilisation qui doit succomber si les attaques des révolutions frivoles ou des ambitions sans frein remportaient la victoire'. Schleinitz to Brassier, May 21, 1860, ib. n. 175. At Vienna however they complained that the Prussian representative at Turin, notedly sympathetic towards Piedmont, did not execute with sufficient energy the instructions of his government: 'Bei den bekannten Sympathien des preussischen Gesandten für die italienische Sache ist wohl zu erwarten, dass die Ausführung dieser Instruktion wesentlich geschwächt worden ist'. Kàrolyi to Rechberg, May 26, 1860, ib. n. 4.

[2] Schleinitz to Brassier, April 27, 1860, in *Politik Preussens*, cit., n. 151. 'En admettant même la possibilité d'une révolution à Naples qui vienne à renverser la dynastie régnante peut-on se faire illusion sur le résultat d'un tel changement? Serait-il réellement en faveur de la Sardaigne qu'il s'accomplirait, et ne faut-il pas prévoir, au contraire, que d'autres puissances, également intéressées à empêcher un nouvel agrandissement de la Sardaigne, interviendraient pur réclamer des compensations ou des garanties?'.

of the people and by protecting them from the arbitrary actions of the oppressor.[1]

This is the note which Cavour struck time and time again. He countered the accusations of subversion by vindicating the stabilising function of Piedmontese policy. Only by presenting to Europe the monarchy of the House of Savoy as the most suitable instrument for dealing with the disorder in Italy could he hope to allay the fears and suspicions of the Powers and avoid the danger which threatened the successful outcome of the struggle in Italy: the reconstitution of the conservative front and the formation of a new Holy Alliance. It was an obsession which weighed on Paris no less than on Turin. For Napoleon III it would have meant the failure of his entire policy, it would once more have cast doubts on the results achieved at Sebastopol and Solferino at such heavy cost. In his relations with the Russians, the French Emperor felt relatively safe in his knowledge of the persisting rancour and contrast of interests separating Russia and Austria in the East. He had met the Czar at Warsaw in October 1859. He knew that the Czar, despite increasing reservations, had no intention of renouncing his understanding with France; there were too many reasons which prevented the Czar from doing so, from his need for French support for his Eastern policy, to the fear of driving France into the arms of England.[2] The great question mark was Berlin rather than St Petersburg. Prussia was tied to Austria by federal bonds in Germany and was subjected to the pressure of German public opinion, suspicious of the Italian upheaval, and suspicious above all of French ambitions. It was essential, therefore, for him to play on the persistent rivalry between Vienna and Berlin, to widen the gulf between them.

[1] Brassier to the Prince Regent, May 7, 1860, in *Politik Preussens*, cit. n. 161. See also Brassier to Schleinitz, June 2, ib., n. 183: 'Si V.E', replied Brassier to Schleinitz's observations, 'me dit avec une haute raison que les institutions consacrées par l'histoire sont destinées à conserver à l'Europe les bienfaits d'une civilisation qui doit succomber si les attaques des révolutions frivoles ou des ambitions sans frein reportent la victoire, cette verité incontestable dans toute monarchie gouvernée avec intelligence paraît d'une application douteuse à l'Italie où l'opinion générale, loin de voir dans les anciens gouvernements et nommément dans ceux de Naples et de Rome les conservateurs des bienfaits de la civilisation, les accuse au contraire d'y oppose des entraves infranchissables autrement que par la révolution, et, si un déchaînement général devait résulter de cette compression, les en désigne comme les auteurs responsables. Quant aux ambitions sans frein, je n'entreprendrai certes pas la tâche assez difficile de laver le roi Victor Emmanuel et son premier ministre des reproches qu'on peut leur faire à cet égard. Loin de là, j'ai saisi jusqu'ici toutes les occasions que se sont présentées pour leur rappeler les principes du droit des gens qu'aucun gouvernement ne saurait violer impunément. Mais j'a finalement dû comprendre comment, le courant une fois établi, les conseils on bien peu de poids, lorsque populations et gouvernements sont entrainés par la force des choses, résultat inévitable d'une crise historique. Le roi Victor Emmanuel et ses ministres profitent du vent qui leur est favorable dans l'intérêt du pays. On peut le blâmer, on peut le regretter, mais on ne saurait s'en étonner, surtout si l'on n'a ni la volonté ni le pouvoir d'y mettre le hola avec des coups de canon'.

[2] See Bismarck to the Prince Regent, June 14/2, 1860, in *Die Politischen Berichte des Fürsten Bismarck aus Petersbourg und Paris*, Berlin 1920, I, p. 113 and ff.

Napoleon had one aim in mind: the attainment of the so-called 'natural frontier'. He thought of bargaining for Prussian concessions on the left bank of the Rhine in exchange for his approval of an extension of Prussian territory in North Germany, and for an eventual assertion of Prussian supremacy in Germany;[1] in other words, to favour Prussian ambitions to his own advantage and to the detriment of Austria. On more than one occasion he expressed to Wilhelm, the Prince Regent of Prussia, his desire for a private talk in order to sound his feelings.

Vienna became alarmed, convinced that this desire had a well-defined aim: "To separate Prussia and Austria and thereby bring about the conquest of Veneto by Italy."

> At this prospect [Vienna felt] the French Emperor would not be opposed to a strong and united Italy, which would completely paralyse Austria. Having achieved this aim, France would turn against Prussia and Germany in the certainty that Austria, paralysed by the Italian menace, would no longer be able to come to the aid of her German confederates. The success of Louis Napoleon's policy consisted exclusively in his ability to isolate the Great Powers at the right moment. He put these tactics to the test by provoking the Crimean War against Russia and subsequently the war in Italy against Austria. He was undoubtedly thinking of doing the same thing with Prussia and Germany in order to realise the so-called natural frontier on the Rhine.[2]

Vienna was not alone in thinking on these lines. The opposition circles in Paris also connected Napoleon's Italian plans with his plans in Germany. Drouyn de Lhuys, the ex-foreign Minister who was forced to resign because of his reservations in regard to the policy of the Tuileries, expressed to the Prussian Ambassador Pourtalès his conviction that Bonaparte would give free rein to the revolution in Italy. After Naples would come the turn of Rome and Venice. Following the creation of a Kingdom of Italy of 26 million inhabitants, the French Emperor would feel entitled to ask for a reward, which could only be Belgium and the left bank of the Rhine. Only close solidarity between the European Powers could foil such a move.[3]

What was needed was collaboration between the Powers, and above all between Russia and Prussia, in order to cause Napoleon to desist from his plans to subvert the European situation. At St Petersburg it was hoped that Napoleon, impressed by Russian and Prussian firmness, would be induced to retreat and join the conservative front. The Czar's pet idea was to create a

[1] See Srbik, cit., p. 314. See regarding the talks between Napoleon and the Prussian ambassador Pourtalès, J. von Grüner, Rückblick auf mein Leben, in *Deutsche Revue*, 1901. On the Rhine policy of Napoleon, see H. Oncken, *Die Rheinpolitik Kaiser Napoleons III*, Berlin 1906, vol. I, p. 15 ff.

[2] Werther, Prussian ambassador in Paris, to Schleinitz, June 12, in *Politik Preussens*, cit., n. 195.

[3] Pourtalès to Schleinitz, June 19, ib., n. 202.

Franco-Prussian-Russian alliance, which would contain Napoleon and force him to collaborate with the cause of law and order.[1]

It is understandable that Berlin, faced with such a prospect, tried by every means to elude Napoleon's request for a meeting, which seemed not only insidious, but also compromising. But Napoleon refused to be discouraged. On hearing that Prince Wilhelm was going to Baden-Baden, he announced his intention of paying a visit, and this could not be refused.[2] However, Wilhelm immediately took precautions. He made it known to all that he would never allow the integrity of German territory to be impaired. He also stated publicly during a visit to Saarbrücken that Prussia would never yield a square inch of German soil.[3] The Prince Regent had only one concern: to behave like an uncompromising German patriot, a faithful and scrupulous member of the Confederation.[4] But this was not all: in order to cover himself and create an alibi, he insisted on a certain number of German Princes being present at the meeting; these were the Kings of Bavaria, Würtemberg, Saxony and Hanover, who were joined by the Grand-Dukes of Baden, Hessen and Saxony-Weimar, and by the Dukes of Saxony-Coburg-Gotha and Nassau. At Erfurt a 'parterre de rois' awaited the new Napoleon, as it had awaited the old one. 'What an affair—commented the Emperor Franz Joseph at Vienna—I do not envy the Prince Regent and the other German Kings and Princes who must present their respects to that mighty scoundrel [dem mächtigen Spitzbuben].[5] In the event, however, the German Princes were not called upon to pay their respects. It was the 'mighty scoundrel' who was forced to put on an easy countenance and say: 'I am happy to find here such a great number of Sovereigns, to be able to express to them personally my desire to be at peace with them.'[6]

[1] Bismarck, Prussian ambassador in St Petersburg, to the Prince Regent, June 14, in *Die Politischen Berichte Bismarcks*, cit., p. 113 ff. Bismarck refers to the words of the Czar: 'Le évènements qui se passent en Italie sont d'un trop mauvais exemple pour l'Europe entière et servent d'encouragement à toutes les tendances subversives; il est du devoir de tous les souverains de se cautionner. Il paraît que l'Empereur Napoléon aussi en a senti le besoin . . . Je vous dis franchement, que je désire établir une alliance entre la Prusse, la Russie et la France, parceque j'y vois en ce moment le moyen le plus simple et le plus efficace pour assurer le repos de l'Europe. . . . Si faire se peut, il vaut mieux d'approvoiser la France, que de lui faire la guerre; je répète qu'il vaut au moins la peine d'en faire l'expérience. Si les mots d'alliance et de garantie ne vous conviennent pas, parlons d'une entente à établir entre les trois puissances, à l'effet de fair rentrer l'Europe dans les conditions regulières d'une paix assurée'.

[2] 'Einige Notizen des Herzogs zu Nassau über die Zusammenkunft des Kaisers der Franzosen mit dem Prinzen von Preussen und einigen anderen deutsche'. Fürsten in Baden-Baden am 16, 17, 18 Juni 1860, in *Quellen zur deutschen Politik Oesterreichs* 1859–66, Berlin 1934, vol. I, n. 178.

[3] La Tour d'Auvergne, French ambassador in Berlin, to Thouvenel, June 3, in *Politik Preussens*, cit., n. 185.

[4] Schleinitz an die Missionen in London, 'Wien und bei den grösseren deutschen Höen', June 6, ib., n. 187.

[5] Billet des Kaisers Franz Joseph an den Grafen Rechberg, s.d., in *Quellen*, cit., n. 152.

[6] 'Einige Notizen', cit.

Bonaparte fell back on the tactics of conciliation. According to Drouyn de Lhuys, he had a two-fold aim:

> To lull German suspicions; and, in case of failure, to be able to say that he had done everything in his power to overcome an unjustified distrust. If he succeeded in dissipating the suspicions his policy had aroused, he would continue his intrigues in Italy; if, on the other hand, he saw that he was still being watched and distrusted, he would loudly accuse the Germans of ill-will and, according to circumstances, take advantage of the resentment which German hostility never failed to arouse in French public opinion.[1]

In the event, he multiplied his reassuring declarations. At the first meeting on June 15 he began by declaring that 'he had wanted the meeting in order to provide evidence of his peaceful intentions and to put an end to the alarm being displayed in Germany about his alleged designs on German territory'. To this the Prince Regent replied that he had agreed to the meeting because of the very fact that he was certain that his assent would be interpreted as 'un gage du maintien de la paix'.[2] And so it went on during the following meetings held on June 17.[3]

Nothing was achieved; and Wilhelm was pleased with himself for 'having given proof, by the presence of so many German Princes, of how united Germany was when threatened with danger'.[4] In a note to diplomatic representatives abroad Schleinitz expressed satisfaction at the fact that the meeting had achieved its purpose: 'To receive the personal assurances of the French Emperor in regard to his peaceful intentions, which provided Germany with a guarantee against the complications and dangers which had seriously perturbed public opinion.'

> The Emperor Napoleon [continued Schleinitz], in the two political talks he had with the Prince Regent on June 15th and 17th, disavowed in the most formal manner all ideas of expansion and aggressive tendencies which public opinion had attributed to him.[5]

Still, nothing was in fact achieved, except a clarification of Prussia's German 'orthodoxy'. On the one hand, Napoleon's hopes of playing on the antagonism dividing Germany came to naught. On the other hand, there was no trace of the Franco-Prussian *entente*, which St Petersburg had hoped might form the foundation of the future alliance.[6]

[1] Pourtalès to Schleinitz, June 19, cit.

[2] 'Bericht des Prinzregenten Wilhelm von Preussen über seine Unterredung mit Kaiser Napoleon III', in *Quellen*, cit., n. 170, Beilage. 'Privatschreiben des Prinzregenten an den Kaiser Franz Joseph', June 27, ib., n. 195.

[3] Eigenhändige Aufzeichnung des Prinzregenten, Baden, Juni 15, in *Politik Preussens*, cit., n. 199.

[4] Ansprache des Prinzregenten an die in Baden versammelten deutschen Bundesfürsten am Juni 18, 1860, in *Quellen*, cit., n. 195, Beilage.

[5] Schleinitz an alle Missionen, June 25, in *Politik Preussens*, cit., n. 206.

[6] Bericht des Grafen Trautmansdorff, June 19, in *Quellen*, cit., n. 173. 'Die erste Befürchtung des kaiserl. Kabinetts war gerichtet auf die Möglichkeit, es dürfte die Zusammenkunft

At Baden the Italian situation was discussed at length. It was the most important topic, the test of Napoleonic policy. The Prince Regent carefully sounded the French Emperor.

> I asked him [we read in his diary] for news about Naples. 'Bad news', he replied: 'Sicily seems lost.' In that case, I said, an attempt must be made to save the rest of the Kingdom, and for that purpose the only safe means seems to be for all to bring pressure to bear on Sardinia, to ensure that the Garibaldini are not allowed to cross over to the Continent and to ensure that there is no intervention at Naples should disorders break out there. Napoleon replied that the situation at Naples was extremely serious and that he would continue to work on King Vittorio Emanuele in the manner I had indicated. However, he said, it was impossible to deny that the Government of Naples certainly did not deserve the approval of Europe. I do not deny this, I relied, but if a Government is far from praiseworthy in many respects it does not mean that it should be overthrown when the means still exist for protecting it.[1]

Referring to this conversation afterwards, the Prussian Ambassador in Paris, Pourtalès, went as far as to comment on the 'favourable and most conservative impression [*sic*] which the Prince Regent's speech made on Napoleon'. 'If the Northern Powers could agree on combined measures in favour of the King of Naples—he concluded—the probability of success would be greater than it was a few days ago.'[2]

The Austrian thesis was as follows:

> Austria can do nothing as far as the present situation in Italy is concerned [said Rechberg to the Prussian Ambassador Werther] if Prussia and Russia maintain a completely passive attitude. These two Powers must raise their voice in favour of the Two Sicilies: the task of mediation cannot be left entirely to France'[3]

This was also the Russian attitude. Gorciakoff favoured a direct Prussian and Russian intervention at Turin, 'which would carry considerable weight'. It was merely necessary for Berlin to follow the example of St Petersburg, whose representative at the Sardinian court had been instructed to leave Turin immediately in the event of the Piedmontese Cabinet declaring itself for the annexation of Sicily and thereby identifying itself with Garibaldi's expedition.

---

des Prinzregenten mit dem Kaiser der Franzosen für Preussen eine Politik der Annäherung an Frankreich eröffnen, die Grundlage einer Allianz zwischen diesen beiden Mächten werden. Solches hat nicht stattgefunden: der Prinzregent hat gegen seine deutschen Bundesgenossen die grösste Offenheit gezeigt und gegen den Kaiser Napoleon eine vollkommen korrekte Sprache geführt, in welcher weder der Keim einer Annäherung zwischen ihm und dem Kaiser, noch der einer Trennung Preussens von Deutschland liegen kann'.

[1] Eigenhändige Aufzeichnung des Prinzregenten, cit.

[2] Pourtalès to Schleinitz, June 21, in *Politik Preussens*, cit., n. 199, n. 6.

[3] Werther to Schleinitz, June 12, 1860, in *Politik Preussens*, cit., n. 195.

The King of Sardinia [continued Gorciakoff] has given numerous assurances that he has nothing to do with the Sicilian affair. This is not altogether unlikely. It calls to mind the proverb 'qui trop embrasse, mal étreint'. The Sardinian conquests extend to the farthest limits which the Savoy dynasty is capable of absorbing without being pushed into the background of the Italian national movement. The conquest of Sicily would represent an embarrassment which would once more threaten to call in question the acquisitions of Northern and Central Italy. Even prior to the expedition Vittorio Emanuele had defined Garibaldi's existence as 'un embarras'; and Count Cavour, the shrewdest mind among the Piedmontese statesmen, fondly cherished the hope that during his expedition the bold liberator of Sicily would find a glorious death in the cause of Italy. A firm attitude on the part of Russia and Prussia could induce the Turin Cabinet to keep out of the Sicilian affair. And it should not be impossible to convince France to take a similar line.[1]

But in Berlin not everybody shared Pourtalès' optimism about the effect which the Baden-Baden meeting had been able to exercise on the French Emperor's frame of mind. As Bismarck pointed out to Gorciakoff: 'Napoleon tends to change his allies just as Monarchs change their residence, according to the season.'[2] And Berlin was not anxious to pursue a policy which would lead to the Russo-Franco-Prussian triple alliance which the Czar was cultivating. A less compromising collective step by all the five Great Powers was preferred.[3] However, even this was a course of action which was not so easy to carry out: 'How was England to be convinced?', was the question which was asked at St Petersburg.[4]

*

One of the results of the Baden-Baden meeting was a certain relaxation in Austro-Prussian relations. The declarations of Germanic patriotism and federal loyalty by the Prince Regent had kindled Vienna's hopes of being able to reconstitute the old conservative front, or at least the alliance with Berlin. (Gorciakoff still showed himself reluctant to renew the ties with Austria, though he was not against an Austro-Prussian reconciliation.[5]) The wheels of Austrian diplomacy began to turn. The Austrian Ambassador in Paris, Richard von Metternich, repeatedly drew the attention of his colleague, Pourtalès, 'to the need and the urgency for a close understanding between the two Courts': and he explored the ground in regard to the possibility of a meeting between the two Rulers.[6]

This was Austria's answer to Napoleon's move at Baden-Baden. Franz Joseph personally advanced the proposal.

[1] Bismarck to Schleinitz, June 15, in *Die Politischen Berichte*, cit., pp. 123–4.
[2] Bismarck to Schleinitz, June 21, 1860, in *Die Politischen Berichte*, cit., p. 125.
[3] Schleinitz to Pourtalés, July 12, in *Politik Preussens*, cit., n. 216.
[4] Bismarck to Schleinitz, June 15, cit.
[5] Bismarck to Schleinitz, July 14, in *Die Politischen Berichte*, cit., p. 133.
[6] Pourtalés to Schleinitz, July 3, in *Politik Preussens*, cit., n. 211.

> It appears to me no less important than comforting that the Baden meeting with the French Emperor should have ended with a proclamation to Europe of German solidarity. . . . The firmness with which Your Royal Higness vindicated the inviolability of German federal territory filled me with satisfaction. . . . The situation seems to be ripe for a closer union between the two Courts: and I would be doubly pleased if this healthy development could be consolidated by a personal and confidential exchange of views between the two of us.[1]

Wilhelm was prepared to accept and fixed the meeting for July 26 at Teplitz. But this time it was a meeting between two: he considered it neither necessary nor desirable for other German Princes to be present.[2]

Berlin thought the time had come to show Europe that the Germanic solidarity proclaimed at Baden affected not only the minor States of the Confederation, but extended to the two major, and rival, German powers.[3]

> Personal contact between the two august personages [declared the Prussian Ambassador at Vienna on instructions from Schleinitz] will serve to put an end to past recriminations and lay the foundation for joint action in matters relating to European policy . . . so as to strengthen the defensive powers of Germany to such an extent that the prospect of a war against a mighty enemy can be faced without concern.[4]

The anti-Napoleonic slant is obvious. Berlin always regarded Napoleon as the potential enemy of Germany.

At Teplitz it was a question of defining the extent of the threat, the terms of common defence and the conditions underlying Austro-Prussian collaboration.

> Now that it has been clearly shown at Baden that H.R.H. The Prince Regent does not propose under any circumstances to align himself with French policy [observed Schleinitz in a memorandum prepared in anticipation of the Teplitz meeting] the compass of negotiations with Austria has been considerably reduced. Whereas before it was still possible to obtain concessions from Austria by playing on the danger of a Franco-Prussian alliance, now there is no denying that even Prussia regards French policy as a threat to her security. However, Prussia's relations with France are substantially different from those of Austria. Should France again attack Austrian possessions in Italy, or support an attack by Sardinia, there can be no doubt that in the situation now prevailing in Europe, Austria would have to fight alone if Prussia failed to come to her aid. On the other hand, a French attack on the borders of the Rhine, Belgium, Holland or Switzerland would probably, if not inevitably, bring about an English intervention, and subsequently that of Russia. If at the Teplitz discussions Austria and Prussia

[1] Privatschreiben des Kaiser Franz Joseph an den Prinzregenten, July 10, in *Quellen*, cit., n. 213.

[2] The Prince Regent to Schleinitz, July 14, in *Politik Preussens*, cit., n. 217.

[3] Schleinitz to the Prince Regent, July 16, ib., n. 219.

[4] Schleinitz to Werther, July 17, ib., n. 221.

> were to establish the contingencies which are to be regarded as a *casus belli* against France, it would not be possible to admit that any pledge given by Austria to defend Belgium or Holland could be considered, by the same standard, as a request to Prussia to reply with a declaration of war to a direct or indirect French attack on the Veneto. The purpose of the negotiations is rather to recognise that if Prussia concludes an alliance with Austria which guarantees the Veneto, she will be entitled to an adequate reward for the services rendered to the European cause and above all to the need of defending Austria. It is as well to be clear that it is Austria who needs help, whereas Prussia can easily find allies and is not dependent on Austrian help. In this connexion it is better to leave it to the Austrian negotiators to define the various *casus belli*, and then to put forward our own claims in the event of an attack on Belgium, Holland or Switzerland. If on the other hand Austria asks us to regard an attack on the Mincio as an act of war, then we would have to explain the reasons which prevent us from complying with this request, if our aspirations in Germany are not taken into account.[1]

Those were Berlin's plans. And Vienna's? The Ballhaus had prepared a detailed memorandum for Emperor Franz Joseph. There can be no doubt—it declared—about Napoleon's plans: The French Emperor is out to conquer the frontier of the Rhine and exploit the Italian revolution as a means to this end. How would he try to achieve this aim? The memorandum listed in detail the various possibilities and the agreements that must be reached, in consequence, between Vienna and Berlin.

> (1) Sardinia, with all the Italian forces that can be mustered, attacks Austria, and France remains in the background for the time being. In that event an Italian success would merely pave the way for a French triumph on the Rhine and also impair the integrity of the Federal territory in the Tyrol and on the coasts. Prussia should assume the initiative in proposing or in supporting in the Diet, the despatch of Federal troops to defend the frontiers of the Germanic Confederation. (2) France sends troops to Italy to support the war against Austria. This should represent a *casus belli* for Prussia and the Germanic Confederation. Austria, engaged in Italy, could send to the Rhine only the contingents provided for in the federal pact. (3) The French attack on the Rhine takes place at the same time as the Italian attack on the Mincio. In that event a situation similar to the one described in paragraph (2) would arise. (4) France attacks on the Rhine without Austria being committed to a war in Italy at the same time. In that event Austria should intervene on the Rhine not only with the federal contingent, but with far superior forces. (5) Austria, Prussia and the Germanic Confederation attack France in order to prevent Belgium and the French part of Switzerland from being annexed by Napoleon's empire. The only problem would be that of arranging for a suitable distribution of commands.
>
> If a definite agreement cannot be reached at Teplitz in regard to these contingencies [concludes the Memorandum] a meeting of generals should at least be decided upon to draw up a military pact.[2]

[1] Memorandum from the Minister for Foreign Affairs, July 20, in *Politik Preussens*, cit., n. 224.

[2] Denkschriften des Freiherrn vonBiegeleben, d. about July 22, in *Quellen*, cit., n. 234.

There remained—and this was the delicate point—the question of the rewards. Werther, the Prussian Ambassador at Vienna, made it clear that the question of the concessions which Austria would be called upon to make to Prussia in exchange for the Prussian guarantee over the Veneto would be raised at Teplitz. And he presented a detailed list of requirements. But Vienna was prepared to ask, not to give.

> It is obvious [was Vienna's line of thought] that Prussian diplomacy is not prepared to forego any attempt to wrest concessions from Vienna. It is to be hoped that in a frank and friendly talk the Prince Regent will be persuaded to waive claims of a type which would seriously damage Austria. Has not the Prince Regent declared publicly that internal German questions take second place when solidarity against the foreigner is involved? He cannot demand internal advantages in exchange for the help to be provided against an external enemy. The Prince Regent must understand that the Imperial Court, even with the best will to further the influence, the prestige and the very power of Prussia, cannot but feel the most legitimate reluctance at this juncture in sacrificing its rights and its position in Germany. Austria has fought honourably against Germany's hereditary enemy, has suffered losses and money, has had to sacrifice a province in Italy, has seen the minor branches of the Imperial House being illegally dethroned in the peninsula: and now she is expected to retrace her steps in Germany too! The Prince must understand, as a friend of Austria, that he cannot ask such a thing, which would have a disastrous effect internally for the Hapsburg Monarchy and cause it to lose face throughout Europe.[1]

Vienna and Berlin thus approached the Teplitz meeting with opposing intentions and sentiments. During the talks of July 26 and 27 the two merely developed the arguments which had been fixed by their respective Foreign Ministers.[2] In the event, in the first place the principle was established that Prussia and Austria 'would face together the dangers which threatened them both'. This meant 'joint resistance to a French attack on the two States'; and an undertaking 'to oppose jointly, and if necessary by force of arms, any French attempt to incorporate Belgium or parts of Swiss or Dutch territory'. In other words, complete solidarity in the face of a hypothetical French attempt to achieve the 'natural frontier'. But as regards Italy and the taking of an immediate stand in the face of the Italian events, nothing definite and binding was agreed. In the event of a Sardinian attack on Austria, only the violation of Federal territory could be regarded by Prussia as a *casus belli*. Berlin refused to agree to the dispatch of German troops to protect Austrian territory, because this would have represented a provocation to Sardinia and brought about a break with France. Moreover, it was inadvisable to split the German

[1] Ib.

[2] Eigenhändige Aufzeichnung des Prinzregenten—Unterredung mit dem Kaiser Franz Joseph am Juli 26–27 in Teplitz, August 1860, in *Politik Preussens*, cit., ns. 229 and 230. Eigenhändige Aufzeichnungen des Prinzregenten über zwischen Oesterreich und Preussen abzuschliessenden Vertragspunkte, July 26, in *Quellen*, cit., n. 237.

army, as this would have seriously impaired the defence of the Rhine. As to Prussian aims in Germany, Vienna merely made a vague promise to come to an agreement with Prussia on German affairs.[1]

In the end Berlin was prepared to exchange reciprocal assurances with Vienna against the dangers inherent in Napoleon's policy, but not to go beyond that. As had already happened in 1859, Vienna refused to make concessions in Germany, and so Berlin had no intention of running any risks for Austrian interests in Italy. This was what Schleinitz hastened to communicate to Turin. For one moment Cavour had been alarmed. Austria seemed to be adopting an aggressive attitude and had increased her armaments in Italy. Was not this resumption of Austrian belligerence—they asked at Turin—a consequence of the Prussian promises given at Teplitz? 'Prussian policy—declared Schleinitz—will never be the result either of blind deference to one Power or of a feeling of hostility towards another.' All rumours concerning commitments entered into by Prussia 'have no foundation whatsoever'.

> Nevertheless [he continued] the position of the Prussian Government, while enabling it to remain an impartial and unconcerned spectator up to a certain point, at the same time demands the maintenance of its freedom of action to watch over its interests and those of Germany, which are indissolubly linked.

Schleinitz wanted to dot his i's.

> It is true [he wrote to his representative at Turin] that the new positions attained by Sardinia in Italy do not immediately affect Prussian interests. It is true that the national sympathies and tendencies, to which King Victor Emmanuel is attached, should not in general encounter any feeling of hostility from us. But it is no less true that neither we nor any established Government can regard with indifference the way in which recent events in Italy have come about. A Government which is based on justice, on the observance of other people's rights and of the law of nations cannot be asked to approve the methods chosen by the national movement in Italy to achieve its aims. I do not conceal from you that in this disapproval we are fully in agreement with Austria, and we have no doubt that it will be shared by the majority of European nations. The most sacred principles have been called in question by the excesses and by the flood of sentiment, legitimate in itself; and no Government can escape its duty to be on guard to ensure that the propagandist influence of new principles, dangerous in their application, does not threaten the very foundations of social structure.

This was the conservative reserve towards the Piedmontese 'piracy' and towards the revolutionary threat which was making itself felt. To this was added the German reservation.

> You know Germany too well not to realise that a large and intelligent part of the nation regards the territorial changes which must be the ultimate consequence of Italian tendencies [meaning the Italian claim to the Veneto], as a threat to

[1] Aufzeichnungen des Prinzregenten über zwischen Oesterreich und Preussen abzuschliessende Vertragspunkte, mit zur Mitteilung an den Prinzregenten bestimmten Gegenbemerkungen des Kaisers Franz Joseph, in *Quellen*, cit., n. 239.

Germany's legitimate interests and to the security of her frontiers. The Prussian Government cannot but take serious account of this opinion, which is shared by men of great political and military standing. On the other hand, it is impossible to ignore the fact that the development of events might produce in Germany tensions and excitement, which might make it impossible for Prussia to maintain a negative and passive attitude incompatible with that very duty of which King Victor Emanuel is so rightly jealous, i.e. that of guiding and directing the national movement.[1]

Having made this clear, Schleinitz multiplied his assurances to the effect that the Teplitz meeting, 'while favouring a certain agreement of views between the Prince Regent and the Emperor of Austria, has not led to the conclusion of a formal treaty. There has been [he stated] only an exchange of ideas and good feeling'. Schleinitz was also able to give an assurance that Austria 'has absolutely no thought of intervening in Italy, and even less of taking the initiative by attacking Piedmont. Austria is merely resolved to defend herself in the Veneto if attacked; and she is convinced that it will not be long before she is attacked'.[2] Meanwhile Prussia—as Schleinitz had already declared in Paris on the eve of Teplitz—did nothing but preach abstention to Vienna 'as the best and only possible policy, thereby giving the Emperor of Austria to understand that no attempt at aggression in Italy would find any support in Berlin'.[3] The fears of Turin were allayed. The reports about Austrian arms in Italy had been grossly exaggerated.

It is untrue that Austria has 200,000 men in her Italian possessions. I believed so myself for a while. But now I know with certainty that the Austrian forces are not anywhere near this number. I shall not tell you the exact number, for fear of encouraging you.[4]

To sum up, what Berlin wanted was that Piedmont should not attack Veneto; the Neopolitan question was already a foregone conclusion.[5] Cavour realised this. He too was very explicit.

Do you want my profession of faith, my innermost thoughts? [he asked Brassier, the Prussian Plenipotentiary.] Here they are: if Austria attacks us, we shall defend ourselves with the help of those who will consent to be our allies. If in the course of a general war, whatever the reason which may have caused it, we have the opportunity of acquiring Veneto, we shall not hesitate to do so, because sooner

[1] Schleinitz to Brassier de Saint Simon, August 22, in *Politik Preussens*, cit., n. 245.

[2] Thus Schleinitz to the French ambassador La Tour d'Auvergne. See, La Tour d'Auvergne to Thouvenel, July 29, in *Politik Preussens*, cit., n. 235. And thus the Emperor Franz Joseph spoke to the Prussian ambassador. See, Werther to the Prince Regent, August 26, in *Quellen* cit., n. 260.

[3] La Tour d'Auvergne to Thouvenel, July 19, in *Politik Preussens*, cit., n. 223.

[4] Launay, Piedmontese minister at Berlin, to Cavour, July 28, in *Politik Preussens*, cit., n. 231.

[5] 'L'ambassadeur d'Autriche m'a parlé d'ailleurs lui-même avec un certain détachment de l'issue probable de la révolution tant à Naples quà' Rome. Il vaudrait peut-être mieux dans les circonstances actuelles porter les regards au delà de catastrophes qui paraissent inévitables'. Pourtalès to Schleinitz, July 17, in *Politik Preussens*, n. 222.

> or later this must come about in the natural course of events. Otherwise we shall not move until Italy is sufficiently strong to conquer the Province by herself, which according to our belief belongs to her. Should this moment arrive and France offer us her aid, we shall request her politely but firmly to stay at home, because we have no desire to alarm Europe nor to suffer the inconveniences of any sort of patronage when we are strong enough to stand on our own feet.[1]

The language was proud, but reassuring on the whole. Piedmont would not attack Veneto for the time being. But there was another point—Naples. Here Cavour claimed complete freedom of action.

> I am tired of being diplomatic [he told Brassier]. I will tell you plainly what we are going to do. We shall wait until the King of Naples defeats Garibaldi and destroys his army, or until Garibaldi dethrones the King. In the first case, things will sort themselves out. In the second, we shall see what happens at Naples; if Garibaldi, as victor, after completing his mission were to lay everything at King Victor Emanuel's feet as promised, then the King would accept, in his own interests and in the interests of all monarchist governments; because only by taking the reins offered to him and by governing with strength and wisdom will he be able to subdue the elements of disorder, destruction and revolution which are threatening humanity and which experience has proved cannot be overcome by repression; on the contrary, they have always gained in strength whenever the legitimate hopes of nationalism have been frustrated.

It was always on this reference to Piedmont as the guarantor of law and order that Cavour continued to dwell, in order to justify the Piedmontese 'piracy'.[2]

There nevertheless remained, as the outcome of Teplitz, a new air about Austro-Prussian relations. A new cordiality, including the form of address. The cold and distant Franz Joseph had offered the Prince Regent the use of the 'thou' of confidence. A circular from Schleinitz to all Prussian representatives abroad stressed that

> the most significant result of the Baden meeting has been rounded off by the Teplitz meeting. . . . The conviction that all differences in regard to Germany and the federal structure must be subordinated to the common duty of maintaining intact the integrity of German territory; this conviction has found expression in the personal contacts between the two greatest German rulers in the most binding form.[3]

In a circular to its envoys in Germany, the Government at Vienna emphasised, in turn, the identity of view of the two courts in regard to outstanding questions of general policy, 'an identity which will not fail to have an extremely beneficial influence on the development of German politics.'[4]

*

[1] Brassier to the Prince Regent, August 1, ib., n. 236.

[2] Brassier to the Prince Regent, August 3, ib., n. 239.

[3] Schleinitz to all the Prussian Legations, July 29, ib., n. 232.

[4] Rechberg to all the Austrian Legations in Germany, August 2, in *Quellen*, cit., n. 248.

Meanwhile, events in Italy followed their course. On September 12 a Sardinian memorandum informed the Powers that the Turin Government 'had ordered its troops to cross the frontier of the Papal State and enter the Marche and Umbria, with the task of re-establishing order there and enabling the population to give free rein to its feelings'. To re-establish order in freedom; this is how Cavour justified his entire policy to the European Chancelleries, and this is how he justified this latest bold step. The state of unrest in the Marche and Umbria caused by the excesses of the Papal troops could have had untold consequences: the Papal State could have been reached by the 'flot de revolution provenant du midi'. The Government of the King was in duty bound to protect the Italians from the dangers of anarchy; and to maintain, before Europe, the promise to fight the revolution. With its latest decision it was merely fulfilling this dual task.[1]

This was a new bomb, which troubled the waters of European diplomacy. Gorciakoff, the Russian Chancellor, was of the opinion that the two Courts of St Petersburg and Berlin should act in unison and with the utmost energy; to recall their representatives at Turin and hand the Piedmontese representatives their passports. Since the French Emperor had already taken a similar step, this would have had the advantage of aligning his policy with that of the conservative Powers. St Petersburg was still pursuing the idea of a Russo-Franco-Prussian alliance.[2]

For this reason Berlin was disinclined to subscribe to the Russian proposal. There was also another reason. 'Prussia's and Russia's diplomatic break with Sardinia, which would probably be imitated by other continental Powers, while Austria and France had already preceded them, would amount to overwhelming proof of England's isolation.' This was what Gorciakoff wanted. But not what Schleinitz wanted.

> However much we disapprove of English policy in Italy, we must carefully guard against aggravating existing differences unless circumstances absolutely compel us to do so. And we must force ourselves above all, in anticipation of events which are far more important to us than the Italian problem, to maintain our relations with the English Government on such a footing as to rule out the complete estrangement of the two Cabinets and not prevent a close and effective collaboration in the future.[3]

Here lies the complete answer to the Prussian attitude towards the situation in Italy. The Italian problem as such was only of minor interest to Berlin; it was merely a means, a game of chess 'in anticipation of far more important events'. It was towards Germany that Prussia was looking: and for her

[1] Sardinian memorandum, September 12, draft signed by Cavour, in Carteggio Cavour-Nigra IV, *La Liberazione del Mezzogiorno*, n. 1109.

[2] Schleinitz to the Prince Regent, September 26, in *Politik Preussens*, cit., n. 258. See also Bismarck to Schleinitz, September 18, in *Die Politischen Berichte*, cit., p. 170.

[3] Schleinitz to the Prince Regent, October 2, in *Politik Preussens*, cit., n. 262.

German policy, starting with the question of Schleswig-Holstein, she had need of England.

Schleinitz was of the opinion that the best solution lay in a vigorous reply to the Piedmontese memorandum, to be worded in the strongest language ('mit den schärfsten Ausdrücken') and publicised.[1] And he did in fact explain to Turin, even though without undue haste, 'what the Prussian Government thinks of the Sardinian Government's most recent steps and the principles outlined in the memorandum'.

> All the arguments contained in the memorandum [he said] refer to the sacred right of nationality. Far be it from us to dispute the high value of the nationalist idea, which is the main and openly avowed motive of our policy. Nevertheless, while giving the principle of nationalism the importance it deserves, we cannot allow it to be used as a justification for a policy which repudiates every principle of law. We feel, on the contrary, that only by having recourse to the legal method of reforms, and by observing the existing laws, can a normally constituted Government be permitted to achieve the legitimate aims of a nation. According to the Sardinian memorandum, everything ought to be subordinated to the exigencies of the national aims; and whenever public opinion declares itself in favour of these aims, the established Authorities should merely relinquish their powers. A principle so diametrically opposed to the most elementary rules of the law of nations could not be applied without seriously endangering the peace of Italy, and the equilibrium and the peace of Europe. Upholding this principle means abandoning the method of reform and rushing headlong into revolution.[2]

Cavour refused to be put out by the Prussian rebuff. He pleaded necessity. He frankly admitted having acted against the law of nations 'as at present conceived in theory and in practice'. But he had no other choice.

> The peace of Villafranca had created for Piedmont and for Italy a situation which could not be solved except by means of a violent crisis. After Villafranca there were only three possible alternatives: either a reaction, which would inevitably have caused new disorders and upheavals, to the detriment of the Monarchist cause and the peace of Europe; or the triumph of the revolution pure and simple, with a Republic; or the French in Tuscany and at Naples.

These alternatives were neither in the interest of Piedmont nor of Europe. 'What else could we do? True, we have hurt some feelings, we have violated principles regarded as sacred. But we have saved the Monarchy, which other Italian States had led to ruin.' Look at Naples! It was essential to avoid a Republic or the setting-up of a dynasty owing allegiance to Napoleon. Piedmont acted in the only possible way to avoid both the danger of revolutionary anarchy and the danger of foreign domination.[3]

Schleinitz did not insist. On the contrary, he stressed that his Government 'had acted completely independently, both towards Austria and Russia, as

[1] Ib.

[2] Schleinitz to Brassier, October 13, ib., n. 268.

[3] Brassier to the Prince Regent, October 16, ib., n. 270. In a report of the same date to

well as towards England'; that it had abstained from associating itself with the Russian and French step of breaking off diplomatic relations. For his own part, he asked for understanding:

> Do not ask us to do anything which implies indirect recognition on our part of the changes which are taking place in the Peninsula. You would cause us considerable embarrassment. If one day the other Powers are prepared to approve the new order of things, we will not be the ones to object, but for the time being we want to have our hands free.

What Piedmont had to avoid at all costs was to raise the burning question of the Veneto. 'I would not like the same state of necessity which you have invoked over Naples to cause you to take action against the Veneto. It is in your interests to mark time.' Let the question come to a head: as things stand at present, a spark in the Veneto could cause a European conflagration.[1]

This was the crux of the whole problem. If Piedmont attacked Veneto, the stage would be set for every sort of trouble. Austria did not want to attack, was unable to attack. Her internal situation and the impending financial crisis prevented her from doing so. But neither could she, for this very reason, adopt indefinitely a wait-and-see attitude, with the heavy burden of military preparations this involved. Only with the support of St Petersburg and Berlin could she take the initiative; and St Petersburg and Berlin were inclined to curb rather than encourage her. However, they also meant to hold back Turin. But behind Turin there was Paris. What would Paris do if Turin attacked Veneto? Even if Paris stood aloof from the conflict, how far would Austria be allowed to go? Could Napoleon stand by while the results of the 1859 victory were being destroyed?[2]

The answer was to prevent a Piedmontese attack. And if it did happen, to prevent the conflict from spreading. The need was to find a point of agreement between Austrian claims and French demands. For the Courts of St Petersburg and Berlin, the problem was reduced to these terms. Neither Court was prepared to risk a war over the Italian question: neither was prepared to revive the conservative front, a new Holy Alliance, which would have been the signal for a European war.

Schleinitz, Brassier says: 'En lisant le passage de la dépêche de V.E. où il est question de la nationalité allemande et de la protection de ses intérêts dans laquelle la Prusse nel e cède à personne, mais qu'elle ne peut pas protéger par la violation du droit, le comte Cavour s'écria: Mais, mon Dieu, moi aussi je ne suis pas révolutionnaire de ma nature; j'âi été, il n'y a pas longtemps, sur la même ligne en Italie, moi aussi j'ai fait alors les mêmes réserves; mais la force des choses nous a démontré l'impossibilité de trouver une solution de la question italienne sans être obligé à trancher dans le vif et à violer le catéchisme international. L'histoire marche, les hommes, les individus ne peuvent pas l'arrêter.' Brassier to Schleinitz, October 16, ib., n. 270, note 3.

[1] Launay, Piedmontese plenipotentiary in Berlin, to Cavour, November 11, ib., n. 285.

[2] Pourtalès to Schleinitz, October 11, ib., n. 266.

In order to solve the problem, it was essential for the various countries to clarify their position. Prussia had already played her part, at Baden with Napoleon, at Teplitz with Franz Joseph. It was now up to Russia to assume her responsibilities. The climax of Baden and Teplitz was to be a meeting between all three Sovereigns of the conservative Courts. The Prince Regent of Prussia, the Emperor of Austria and the Czar of Russia agreed to meet at Warsaw on October 22.

The Czar of Russia, however, was opposed to a coalition against France. At the very most, he might contemplate a display of solidarity which would serve to curb Napoleon's ambitions. Let the Master of the Tuileries be aware of the consequences if he went beyond certain limits. But St Petersburg was not prepared to forgo its understanding with Napoleon which had come into being after the Congress of Paris and which was expected to favour Russian policy in the East; still less was St Petersburg prepared to play into the hands of Austria. The Czar and his Chancellor hoped to be able to deflect Napoleon from his revolutionary course, which had caused him nothing but disappointment; they were anxious to make it easy for him to return to normality, to return to the fold of conservative Europe. Gorciakoff was still obsessed with his project for a Franco-Russian-Prussian alliance.[1]

The Prince Regent of Prussia had no such illusions. Napoleon's ambitions on the Rhine affected Prussia too closely not to arouse in Berlin 'an unbounded suspicion and a deep hatred of Napoleon'.[2] Prussia's 'German Mission' caused her to assume the role of champion of the integrity of German soil; and she was affected by the threat to the Veneto because of the repercussions this would have in the German Confederation. On the other hand, the very fact of this German mission prevented her from taking any risks, to the exclusive advantage of her Austrian rival. At Baden the Prince Regent had shown Napoleon 'a Germany united, as has not been the case for a long time'. At Teplitz he had promised the Emperor of Austria his solidarity against the common dangers in Germany, but he had also warned him not to rely on his support in Italy; he had obtained from the Emperor an assurance that he would do nothing without prior warning; he had warned him that in Italy he would have to act at his own risk and peril; and he had formally ruled out any possibility of a conservative coalition, the reconstitution of a new Holy Alliance. Now, at Warsaw, he warned the Czar that he was not prepared to join any other coalition nor to give any formal undertakings. The sole purpose of the meeting was 'to avoid misunderstandings by means of a direct and personal exchange of views and to strengthen the unity of purpose which already existed in regard to numerous problems'.[3] Schleinitz was not anxious to fall out with Paris, nor was he anxious to fall out with London. His aim was not

[1] Bismarck to Schleinitz, September 7 and 13, in *Die Politischen Berichte*, cit., pp. 154 and 167.

[2] Chotek to Rechberg, September 24, in *Politik Preussens*, cit., n. 257.

[3] Schleinitz to Bismarck, September 21, ib., n. 254.

so much to reconcile Austria and Russia as to reconcile Russia and England, thereby isolating both the Austrian rival and the French enemy.[1]

And so the Warsaw talks began. The first and only meeting took place on October 25. The sudden worsening health of the Czarina Mother compelled the Czar to leave at once. The meeting was attended by the Russian Chancellor, Gorciakoff, and the Austrian Foreign Minister, Rechberg, together with their respective Sovereigns. Schleinitz, on the other hand, was absent, because of a real or feigned illness. The Prince of Hohenzollern deputised for him.[2] Only one meeting was held and symptomatically enough it was devoted to the examination of a memorandum presented by Napoleon to Russia, which Russia had forwarded to the meeting.

The memorandum contained the proposals of the Tuileries concerning the policy to pursue in regard to the Italian situation, which was summed up in four main points.

> (1) If Austria were attacked in the Veneto, France was determined not to support Piedmont in any way. The binding and lasting nature of this undertaking was based on the assumption that the attitude of the German powers would be one of abstention. (2) It was understood that the state of affairs which had given rise to the last war would not be re-established. The guarantee against a return to this state of affairs was to be the maintenance of the bases agreed at Villafranca and stipulated at Zurich. The transfer of Lombardy should not therefore be called in question: Italy was to be organised on a national and federal basis under the protection of European law. (3) All questions concerning the territorial boundaries of the various States of Italy and the authorities which are to govern them will be examined at a European conference in the light not only of the rights of the Sovereigns at present in possession[3], but also of the concessions which are necessary in order to ensure the stability of the new order of things. (4) Should Piedmont lose the territories acquired outside the agreements of Villafranca and Zurich, the treaty whereby Nice and Savoy had been made over to France should not be the subject of discussion at the Conference.[4]

In short, the Tuileries were trying to 'cover themselves' in case of an Austro-Sardinian war over the Veneto, barely concealing the hope of taking advantage of Piedmontese difficulties in order to return to the original programme of Villafranca. As Rechberg observed immediately, however, the purpose of a conference, if anything, should be to avoid a war, not to tie Austria's hands in the event that a war did break out.[5] This was more or less

[1] Belcastel to Thouvenel, September 22, ib., n. 256.

[2] Schleinitz to Werther, November 1, ib., n. 279, note 1.

[3] Thouvenel said later to Pourtalès that the Russian copy contained an error of transcription in place of 'droits des souverains actuels à posséder' it read 'droits des souverains actuellement dépossédés'. Pourtales to Schleinitz, December 14, in *Politik Preussens*, vol. II, 2, n. 298.

[4] Memoire, S.K.H. dem Prinzregenten vorgelegt in Warschau, in *Politik Preussens*, cit., n. 274.

[5] Werther to Schleinitz, November 1, in *Politik Preussens*, cit., n. 280.

Prussia's opinion also. The Prince Regent subjected the four French points to a minute examination. There were no objections to the first point concerning French and German neutrality. The difficulties began with the second point. What if the military operations led the Austrian army into Lombardy? What if Austria, after occupying Lombardy, dictated her own terms for peace? What would France do in that case? There was another question: Would a victorious Austria be able to accept a 'federal and national system' in Italy and thereby limit her victory? As to the third point, what was the meaning of the sentence concerning the right of the Conference to define the territories of the various States and the authorities which were to govern them? Its vagueness and ambiguity not only left Austria in the dark about the purposes for which she would have been called upon to fight; it might even be regarded as an invitation to Sardinia to take up arms. Even in case of a defeat, the Conference would have organised Italy on a national and federal basis, which would ensure the predominance of Sardinia. In regard to the fourth point, Nice and Savoy, the Prince Regent did not and would not commit himself. His conclusions were completely negative:

> If neutrality were made subject to these conditions in the event of an Austrian war of aggression in Italy, one might perhaps discuss the matter. But to limit in this way Austria's right to defend herself against an unprovoked attack, to pose conditions for the convening of a Conference which are entirely in her disfavour even if she won the war would signify the adoption of a hostile attitude towards the attacked, to the exclusive advantage of the aggressor.[1]

Berlin was decidedly of the opinion that the French proposals were completely unacceptable. But it was necessary to take Russia into account; for even though she had not advocated the adoption of the French proposals, she had been a benevolent intermediary. There were also other considerations: what would be the impression in Europe if the Warsaw talks were to be an obvious failure? It was essential to avoid giving the enemies of law and order the impression that the Powers representing the bulwark of conservatism were unable to find a point of agreement.

> The rulers who go to Warsaw—warned a memorandum preceding the meeting—must realise that if they limit themselves to straightforward and harmless discussions, the general expectation will be so deluded in its hopes that an extra-Governmental solution will be sought to the problems now stirring public opinion. The time for words is past, the time for action has come. It is natural that the feelings and sympathy of the masses are for the men of action, even if from a moral viewpoint they are undeserving. It is essential, indeed imperative, to take this frame of mind into account. Let not the difficulties of an understanding and the conflict of interests be invoked. All conservative Governments have at this time a common interest which takes precedence over all others: this is the maintenance of their very existence against the attack of the common enemy, the principle

[1] Memoire, cit.

> of revolution. This principle appears under the most varied guises: here as the defender of national rights, as the apostle of freedom, there as the tamer of anarchy, the protector of society. Little perspicacity is needed to recognise this principle in its various disguises: it is the duty of the conservative Governments to unmask it wherever it appears and solemnly to proclaim the opposite principle, the principle of the observance of the law. The conservative Governments whose sovereigns are to meet at Warsaw are expected to agree on a common programme to ensure that the commitments entered into before the whole world are observed.[1]

Not all these aims were achieved at Warsaw. There therefore remained, as always, the need to conceal failure; there remained the desirability of not rejecting out of hand a proposal presented and supported by Russia. This could be achieved by declaring 'that the Warsaw negotiations have failed to reach an agreement and that the three Courts look forward to a further exchange of views'. The sudden departure of the Czar was given as the reason.

> This was a solution—commented the Prince Regent—which would compel the French Government to clarify and complete their proposals; it would also have the advantage of compelling France to give the three Powers a further explanation, whilst Prussia, Austria and Russia maintained, at least for the time being, a relatively united front against France.

There was no risk involved; Austria would never agree to the French terms. Prussia could therefore assign to Austria the task of opposing Russian pressure, and limit herself to affirming 'that the proposals advocated by St Petersburg require developing; and that they represent at all events an effective contribution towards the cause of peace, for which the Government of Berlin is grateful to Czar Alexander'.[2]

Everything worked out according to the Prussian plan. The Warsaw talks were followed by a long series of discussions: an endless repetition of the proposals advanced by the Sovereigns and Ministers during the meeting. Academic discussions, aimless repetitions.

When the Warsaw meeting was announced, Cavour was worried in case Vienna should succeed in 'protecting her rear' by re-establishing the solidarity of the conservative triple alliance, and thus leave herself free to intervene resolutely in Italy and halt Piedmont's military and political offensive in the Papal State and in Southern Italy. On October 13 he wrote to Farini, who was in the King's retinue at Grottamare with the Army: 'Get moving. Beg the King not to allow the troops to rest for a single moment. Time is precious. They must reach Naples before the Warsaw talks produce something to our

[1] The written statement of October 1860, emanating from the Grand Duke of Baden, See, H. Oncken, *Grossherzog Friedrich I von Baden und die deutsche Politik* 1854–71, Stuttgart: 1927, vol. I, p. 225 ff. The Prince Regent recommended it to Schleinitz, with the comment. 'I find these views very equitable.' The Prince Regent to Schleinitz, October 6, in *Politik Preussens*, cit., n. 264.

[2] Memoire, cit.

disadvantage.'[1] But the 'Warsaw talks' produced nothing. If anything, they laid for all times the ghost of the Holy Alliance which Vienna had in vain tried to evoke; they did more to paralyse than to support Vienna's attempt to resume the initiative. The outcome of Warsaw was, once again, 'nothing'. It was, as Gorciakoff wittily remarked, merely the blow of an olive branch on water, 'un coup d'olivier dans l'eau'.[2]

[1] Cavour to Farini, October 13, in Carteggio Cavour. *La Liberazione del Mezzogiorno*, vol. III, p. 101.

[2] Bismarck to Schleinitz, November 24, in *Die Politischen Berichte*, cit., p. 177.

ELIZABETH LONGFORD

Queen Victoria's Doctors

ELIZABETH LONGFORD

Queen Victoria's Doctors

WHO would rule Queen Victoria? This question naturally agitated the politicians when a girl of eighteen came to the throne in 1837. They were on the alert to prevent another Court physician from dominating the young Victoria as Sir William Knighton had ruled King George IV.

Curiously enough, Knighton and Sir James Clark, the Queen's first physician-in-ordinary, had both begun as naval surgeons; but whereas Knighton rose to be George IV's all-powerful private secretary, Clark never became more than Queen Victoria's 'dear old friend'. The fact is that Victoria, whether in youth or age, was not the type to be enslaved by a bedside manner. She spent a minimal fraction of her long life laid up in bed. At nineteen she confided to Lord Melbourne her great dislike of consulting doctors: 'Don't carry that too far,' warned the Prime Minister.[1] In her later years she did in fact see her doctors frequently. On returning from Balmoral or Osborne to Windsor her first act would be to visit the Mausoleum in which Prince Albert was buried, her second to summon her physician for a check-up. By that date, however, it was the doctors who were in bondage to the Queen and not vice versa.

Having got over the fear of childbirth, which was due to Princess Charlotte's appalling experience, she treated her accoucheurs with just the right mixture of obedience and levity. One of her favourite tricks was to keep her doctors on tenterhooks by moving, as she was required to do, from Windsor to London for the birth of a child, at the very last minute. After the birth of the Prince of Wales in 1841 she recorded her view that of all the doctors who had attended her (including the famous accoucheurs, Doctors Locock and Ferguson) the least conspicuous—a Dr Brown—was the best. She liked his 'quietness of manners & reasonableness'.[2] In other words, he did what she wanted without arguing.

So much for the Queen's opinion of her accoucheurs. And now for the

[1] Royal Archives, Queen Victoria's Journal, January 28, 1839: I have to acknowledge the gracious permission of Her Majesty the Queen to make use of this and other papers in the Royal Archives.

[2] Royal Archives, Queen Victoria's Journal, December 8, 1841.

opinion of her best-known accoucheur, Doctor—afterwards Sir Charles—Locock, about the Queen. As we shall see, the Queen showed herself to be far less 'Victorian' than her doctor.

Mr Arbuthnot was writing to his friend, the Duke of Wellington on October 27, 1840; the Queen's first baby, the Princess Royal, was to be born on November 21. The following story had been told to Arbuthnot by Lady Mahon, a mutual friend of himself and Dr Locock.[1]

> Locock seems to tell Lady Mahon everything [began Mr Arbuthnot]. He says that having a good while ago wished to go to his Country Place in the North of England, & fearing to be called back, he told Prince Albert that he really ought to see the Queen.
>
> This caused an interview, at the commencement of which Locock says he felt shy & embarrassed; but the Queen very soon put him at his ease.
>
> Every Medical observation which he made, & which might perhaps bear two significations, was invariably considered by Her Majesty in the least delicate sense. She had not the slightest reserve & was always ready to express Herself, in respect to Her present situation, in the very plainest terms possible.
>
> She asked Locock whether she should suffer much pain. He replied that some pain was to be expected, but that he had no doubt Her Majesty would bear it very well. 'O yes,' said the Queen, 'I can bear pain as well as other People.'
>
> It was a subject [commented Mr Arbuthnot at this point] going so near the wind of delicacy, that I could do no more than listen without asking questions. A good deal was told me by Lady Mahon to the same effect; but the results of the whole was that Locock left Her Majesty without any very good impressions of Her; & with the certainty that She will be very ugly & enormously fat. He says that Her figure now is most extraordinary. She goes without stays or anything that keeps Her shape within bounds; & that She is more like a barrel than anything else.

Lady Mahon next told Arbuthnot that there was to be nobody at the delivery except Locock, Prince Albert and a maid, and how she had said to Locock that no doubt the Queen would be very relieved at this privacy—'upon which he (Locock) remarked he verily believed from Her manner that as to delicacy, She would not care one single straw if the whole world was present'.

Locock and the Prince then retired to the Prince's apartment. 'The Prince,' continued Arbuthnot, 'remarking upon what the Queen had said with regard to pain, told Locock that he did not think She could bear pain well at all, and that he expected She would make a great *Rompos*.'

Arbuthnot added that the Queen had refused to get any baby linen ready until Locock made her, for which Baroness Lehzen was very grateful. 'The result of the whole', concluded Arbuthnot to the Duke, 'has been that Locock has been not a little disgusted with the Queen's manner; & he said to Lady Mahon that he should take no more interest in Her doing well, than he should

[1] I am indebted to the Duke of Wellington for permission to quote from the Stratfield Saye MSS.

in respect to any other Person. He is charmed however with Prince Albert. . . .'

This strange male then let it be known that the Queen would be brought to bed between December 5 and 15. It is pleasant to recollect that he was between fourteen and twenty-four days out.

*

Throughout her life, Queen Victoria's physique was excellent, apart from rheumatism often brought on by falls, but even before her widowhood she sometimes suffered from her nerves. There was always an amateur psychotherapist at hand, however, to treat her—the Prince Consort. (Doctor Albert informed his eldest daughter that ladies' nerves were only a polite word for lack of self control.) For a decade after the Prince's untimely death in 1861 the trouble became increasingly 'my nerves'. Unfortunately Sir William Jenner, who succeeded Clark as her physician-in-ordinary in that year, stoutly maintained that the patient's state of mind was none of his business. If he saw to it that her appetite was good, her sleep normal and her desk-hours lengthy—as indeed they were—what right had the country to ask more of him? That Gladstone did ask more of him during the 'seventies only increased Jenner's loathing of everything Liberal, and did nothing to create a tougher attitude among the Queen's medical men towards the Queen's nerves.

Queen Victoria, unlike her uncle King George IV, with his poor debauched body, had no cause whatever to surrender herself to a Knighton. All she desired, even during the most morbid years of her widowhood, was a hedge planted by her doctors to exclude the politicians. Jenner kept the hedge thick and prickly with snippets to *The Lancet*, emphasising Her Majesty's imperative need for 'repose and rest'. Many of these communications were composed and dictated by the royal patient herself. A memorandum addressed by Jenner to Lord Russell from 8 Harley Street on February 18, 1866, was sent by the Queen with a hasty covering note referring to her 'nervous temperature [*sic*]'.[1]

The man who perhaps came nearest to playing the part of a Knighton in Queen Victoria's early life was not her doctor but Baron Stockmar. It is true that Stockmar had been trained as a doctor; but he was careful never to practise his medical skills, such as they were,[2] in England. He did no more than hold Princess Charlotte's hand on her death-bed in 1817; twenty-four years later, when the baby Princess Royal was feared to be dying of some digestive complaint, Stockmar wrote out one prescription only—the dismissal of the Queen's interfering ex-governess, Baroness Lehzen.

Queen Victoria detested oiliness. None of her doctors was an exponent of the regular bedside manner, though she liked men to be good company. If her more famous physicians had any social gift in common it was a talent for telling racy stories. Sir Charles Locock, who made an international name for himself through his obstetric services to Queen Victoria and her nine babies, seems to

[1] Royal Archives, L25/65.

[2] The Duke of Cumberland, one of Queen Victoria's 'wicked uncles', used to say that the little eminence from Coburg was nothing but a barber.

have finally unbent, for he kept the lying-in apartments of the Continent in a happy titter with his jokes. Clark made room in his private diary for many a brisk anecdote about public men, including a story of Napoleon III in 1852. Napoleon III said to the Marquess of Hertford that when people asked him if he would invade England he always answered, 'Yes! but I shall not come till I am invited by the Queen which I think it is very likely I shall; to enable her to put down the democratic spirit which is increasing so much in England.'[1] He was invited in 1854, but to help put down the Russians in the Crimea.

Jenner was popular for his jovial wit even with those, like Sir Henry Ponsonby, the Queen's private secretary, who deplored the bellow of rage with which he greeted any mention of Gladstone. On hearing that two mountains in Guinea were to be named after Gladstone and Disraeli, Jenner remarked that the latter would doubtless be called 'Ben Disraeli'.[2]

As for Sir James Reid, Queen Victoria's physician-in-ordinary from the early 'eighties until she died, his sparkling humour was responsible for getting him elevated from the rank of an upper servant to that of a member of the Household. So irresistible were his stories that the Household, barred by royal protocol from inviting him to tell them at their own dinner-table, found themselves listening to them at his. Ultimately the Queen was obliged to scrap protocol and admit Jimmy Reid to the Household dinners. Having made use, as one supposes, of this privilege to propose to one of the Queen's ladies, he once more forfeited royal favour, but again recaptured it by swearing with a cheerful smile never to repeat the offence.

To say that none of Queen Victoria's doctors attained the position of a Knighton does not mean that they were unable to make any impact upon her outside their own medical domain.

Clark occasionally offered her political advice. On December 28, 1852, for instance, his diary states that during a ministerial crisis he criticised the suitability of both Lord Derby and Lord Aberdeen to form a government, advising her to send for Lansdowne.[3] (She did so, but Lansdowne declined on grounds of failing health.) Being a Liberal, Clark seems to have had a vaguely progressive influence, though he was not a strong enough character to achieve much. He was responsible for introducing Florence Nightingale to Queen Victoria and for fostering a royal interest in the new model profession of nursing. There is some slight evidence also that he disbelieved in the obscurantist attitude of the mid-nineteenth century towards sex education. At any rate, his diary severely castigates King Leopold I of the Belgians for his 'timid cautiousness, which led him to bring up his boys in ignorance of

[1] Royal Archives, Y206, Sir James Clark's Diary, 1852.

[2] Ponsonby Papers, Sir Henry Ponsonby to his wife, September 14, 1874: I am indebted to Lord Ponsonby of Shulbrede for permission to quote from this and other letters written by his grandfather.

[3] Royal Archives, Y206, Sir James Clark's Diary, December 28, 1852.

everything boys ought to know'.[1] On the other hand, Clark approved of Prince Albert's decision to give his backward eldest son a good whipping, for Clark's diary recorded in June 1849, 'The effect of the whipping was excellent'. Nor did Clark manage, if indeed he tried, to secure for the English Princes, including the Prince of Wales, a better education in the facts of life than their young Belgian cousins had received. At lunch one day Prince Arthur, aged fifteen, observed that he had never seen such an ugly crinoline as his aunt's, Princess Leiningen. 'She is expecting an addition,' whispered a lady-in-waiting. 'What for?' demanded the Prince.[2]

Diet was Clark's first line of defence against both physical and mental impurity. He tried in vain to cure the nineteen-year-old Queen Victoria's spinsterish vapours with light diets from which tea, though not wine, had been eliminated. The Prince of Wales's deep indolence, broken by energetic teenage rages, was treated by Clark with punitive diet sheets. Like Lady Macbeth's doctor, Clark said of Prince Albert's disturbed nights, 'It is the mind'; he was nonplussed to find that diet would not effect a cure. His patience and inventiveness over milk for ailing royal babies was inexhaustible: he changed from cows' to asses' milk, from a Scottish to a Hampshire wet-nurse; but he failed to discover that the Princess Royal was being starved or that what was wrong with little Prince Leopold was not diet but haemophilia. All the same, Clark's training must have helped Queen Victoria herself to resist the temptations of twelve-course dinners, to which her eldest son so spectacularly succumbed. Many gentlemen were later to complain of the horrible plain food served up to the Queen at Balmoral: flabby scones, wine tasting of resin and *potage* so nasty that she sometimes had to send it away. On one such occasion she got a repellent cabbage soup instead.

Sir James Clark's devotion to diet was surpassed only by his obsessional enthusiasm for fresh air. As a young medico he had offered a thesis entitled *De Frigoribus Effectis*. The effects of cold upon consumptives he afterwards verified, during various continental travels, as being wholly beneficial. On Queen Victoria the effects of Clark's enthusiasms were at first beneficial but later excessive. She gradually came to endow *Frigor* with almost divine properties, dogmatically asserting that cold was always good for people, warmth bad. She ruthlessly sacrificed on its altar the convenience of her less hardy husband and courtiers, establishing as its priesthood a vast array of wall thermometers. All this uncomfortable magic derived, like the austere food, from Clark, though some of his own rules had been eminently sensible. One of his earliest instructions to Princess Victoria's attendants still survives. Having taken up his position as her mother's physician in April 1835, in May he was insisting that the Princess's window must always be opened whenever she was out of the room. This was at Kensington. In Buckingham Palace Clark pored over stubborn problems of ventilation without ever quite solving them.

[1] Ibid., June 4, 1854.

[2] Royal Archives, Vic. Addl. MSS. X/2.211, Journal of Mrs Walter, 1865.

Years after his disappearance we find the Palace staff still racking their brains about how to ventilate the overheated ballroom. Whenever the ladies-in-waiting wished to sit out they had to sit on the air-vents, thus effectively blocking them. Ponsonby suggested that since M.P.'s so much prized their invitations to Court balls, Parliament might safely be asked to vote money for modern ventilation. 'Oh, no,' said Queen Victoria, who dreaded asking for money, 'Open the windows.'[1]

From Clark she learned to take an interest in public hygiene, especially in army camps and city streets. It seems likely that Clark originally inculcated her sensible view that epidemics must be stopped by giving more support to the medical profession, rather than by simply ordering churches to hold 'Days of Humiliation' for the nation's sins. From Jenner she learned to keep the clock back.

It is arguable that Queen Victoria would never have favoured women entering the medical profession, Jenner or no Jenner. There were certain reasons, however, why she might have made an exception at least for female obstetricians. She always regarded this branch of medicine as not necessarily a male preserve. She definitely encouraged female doctors in India—after Jenner's retirement. She was herself brought into the world by Dr Davies and a woman doctor. In one of his few surviving letters, Queen Victoria's father, the Duke of Kent, had asked his equerry to arrange for the Duchess of Kent, just before the birth of Princess Victoria, to travel back to England with a Fraülein Siebold in case of 'accident'—

> The Medical Lady whom her family and herself wish to attend her, in conjunction with Dr. Wilson . . . not only is an accoucheuse, but also practises as a Physician in all Ladies' complaints, having gone through the regular course of Anatomy, Physics, etc., at Göttingen.[2]

'Frau' Siebold or Dr Heidenreich, names under which Fraülein Siebold later practised, remained much in favour with German royalties. In 1842 one of Queen Victoria's foreign relatives wrote to her that Dr Heidenreich had more sense than all male doctors put together.

Queen Victoria probably never contemplated employing Frau Siebold herself. But for Jenner, however, she might conceivably have offered some encouragement to the training of English female obstetricians in the 1870s. There is a somewhat confused reference in Sir Henry Ponsonby's letters to an occasion when the Queen caused a sensation in medical circles by giving a profeminist professor the impression that she supported a move to admit women into medical schools.[3] The professor apparently passed on this glad news to the Queen's daughter and son-in-law, Princess and Prince Christian, who promptly announced it at a public meeting. Consternation among the

[1] Ponsonby Papers, Sir Henry Ponsonby to his wife, August 6, 1877.
[2] Royal Archives, Geo. Addl. MSS. 7/1353, Duke of Kent to General Wetherall.
[3] Ponsonby Papers, Sir Henry Ponsonby to his wife, November 8, 1870.

medical high-ups followed. Jenner must have contradicted similar rumours earlier in the year, for in the Royal Archives there still lies a note[1] from the head of the General Medical Council expressing his profound relief that Her Majesty was against 'mixed classes' even though some people thought she favoured them.

If Jenner exerted a reactionary influence on the Queen over women's rights, his influence on vivisection and the rights of animals was a moderating one. Queen Victoria was inclined to write off all doctors as 'butchers' when it came to scientific experiments on animals. She favoured legal action to prevent cruelty to animals; she opposed stag-hunting and sealing; when a courtier sent her a huge turtle as a present to make into soup she promptly had it put into a fountain and when it had sufficiently recovered from its experiences, sent it to Brighton Aquarium. She sometimes took a Whitmanesque view of the superiority of animals over human beings. One day a performing dog was placed on the table in the Council Chamber at Windsor and ordered to form from a collection of single letters any word which Her Majesty might care to name. She chose the capital of Austria, *Wien*. Nothing could have been more perfect than the animal's performance. It did what it had to do 'correctly, expeditiously and without the least fuss'.[2]

At each stage of the various laws dealing with vivisection which were passed during Queen Victoria's reign, she was on the point of vetoing it altogether. Thanks to Jenner, her more sweeping instincts were channelled into work for humane methods. There are few instances of Jenner giving the Queen political advice, but as a violent anti-Catholic he seems to have held some strange views on Ireland. One of his favourite solutions was that all Catholic landlords should be shipped to Ireland and Protestant landlords brought back to England.

Of all the Queen's doctors, Sir James Reid seems to have been the least afraid of her. For this reason he was partially successful in putting a curb on her whims. They had their tiffs, but she always forgave him, once she had 'had it out'. He in turn was preternaturally discreet, refusing to publish any memoirs of a period of royal service which must always have been interesting and sometimes dramatic.

Medical quarrels about royal illnesses, though all too frequent,[3] deeply

[1] Royal Archives, L13/34, April 30, 1870.

[2] Queen Victoria, however, was not absurd about animals, like some Victorians. The story of a friend's dog whose dinner had been forgotten and who therefore trotted up to his mistress with a spray of forget-me-not in his mouth, made the Queen smile.

[3] There is a note in the Royal Archives (C65/90, November 7, 1877) by the Queen saying that Dr Marshall was very clever despite the fact that Dr Clayton decried him. She added that Jenner said '*no one* can diagnose typhoid at first'. Ponsonby also mentions this 'row' between the 'Abergeldie and Balmoral doctors' in a letter to his wife, saying that he is determined not to be involved in it. Five years later he wrote: 'At dinner last night the Queen was rather amusing with some of her stories—one of Oscar Clayton, who since he had been knighted, said that he wd. now give up practice "if it were not for that dear royal family, indeed I am almost one of them".' (Ponsonby Papers, June 9, 1883.)

shocked Queen Victoria, who liked all human activities, including death, to be conducted like the dog's word-making, without 'fuss'. When Napoleon III's doctors quarrelled about his final illness and then went into print, she automatically denounced them all as 'butchers'.

Without doubt foreign doctors in her view were more likely to behave as 'butchers' than English ones. Her diaries abound in tributes to British methods and criticisms of those favoured on the Continent. Whenever one of her nearest and dearest fell ill, her first thought was to dispatch Clark, Jenner or Sir William Hoffmeister, to the German court in question. News that this or that foreign royalty had died suddenly, whether in childbed or of some rampant fever, provoked in the Queen the same thought: they had been neglected by their foreign doctors. Prince William of Prussia's withered arm she felt sure could be cured by British treatment, perhaps with the assistance of 'magnetism'. She implored his mother not to let the German doctors operate. Childbirth above all became in her eyes a mortal danger when handled by continental accoucheurs, with their dreadful 'relaxing treatment'. In the Queen's opinion her favourite cousin, the Duchess of Nemours, died during her confinement because of this treatment, which involved airless rooms, blood-letting, weakening diet, lack of exercise and long weeks in bed.

Queen Victoria probably regarded the Scots as the best doctors in the world, as well as being the noblest characters. Reid, Clark, Locock and Ferguson were all trained at Scottish universities; it was to Clark's contact with the Scottish doctors, Simpson and Snow, that she owed the boon of chloroform during the birth of her two youngest children. Sir James Clark, however, for all his Scottish loyalty, did not share Reid's resolute abstention from press comment. It was fear lest Clark should defend himself publicly, if dismissed from the Queen's service, which caused Lord Melbourne to reject that obvious course after the Flora Hastings scandal in 1839. Even so, Clark did finally go into print. Mention of this tragedy—the most shocking in which Queen Victoria was ever involved—brings up the question of her doctors' medical skill in an acute form. Was Sir James Clark's, in particular, the best that the profession could offer?

There is a school of thought which insists that royalty will always get the doctors it deserves, usually the worst. As applied to Queen Victoria, this pawky point of view is largely based upon two notorious events and two famous remarks: the deaths of Lady Flora Hastings in 1839 and of Prince Albert in 1861, Lord Clarendon's remark that the Prince Consort's medical attendants were not fit to nurse a sick cat, and Gladstone's announcement in 1871 that if Jenner were his own doctor he would get rid of him at once.

It has often been suggested that Clark's weakness was as a diagnostician. While looking after the dying Keats in Rome, Clark is said to have diagnosed the poet's consumptive condition as stomach trouble, until Keats actually had a severe haemorrhage.

This slur on Clark seems to be based upon a passage from Keats's letter to his friend Charles Brown, written from Rome two months before Keats died.

'. . . Dr Clark is very attentive to me, he says there is very little the matter with my lungs, but my stomach, he says, is very bad. . . .' From the context of Keats's letter, however, it is quite clear that Clark was simply doing his best to cheer his patient; and for the next fortnight Keats's devoted friend Joseph Severn did indeed report an apparent improvement, until 'his malady roused and sunk its claws into him again'.[1] *Again*—for Keats had already had a terrible coughing fit and haemorrhage on the day the friends landed at Naples. Severn must certainly have told Dr Clark about this attack, and in fact Clark's encouraging words were typical of his life-long kindness, coupled with a strong belief in psychological treatment. When it came to physical treatment, Dr Clark's decision to bleed his patient in proportion to his haemorrhage sounds insane to us, but then it was customary. Thus we cannot argue that Clark failed to diagnose Keats's disease. What of Prince Albert's and Lady Flora's? Neither Clark nor Jenner were thought by many to have recognised the Prince Consort's disease as typhoid until the week before his death. As for Lady Flora Hastings, that a malignant tumour was causing the swollen stomach for which she had consulted Clark, apparently struck him as only a remote possibility; he frequently observed, on the contrary, that the report about Lady Flora being with child might well be true. Moreover, the number of minor cases where Clark gave an opinion regarding the health of some friend or servant of the Queen's, only to be proved absolutely wrong, were legion. Again and again Clark would cheerfully predict recovery a few hours before the sufferer died. Among well-known people can be mentioned Sir Robert Peel (Peel's own doctors, unlike Clark, warned the Queen to expect the worst), Queen Louise of the Belgians and Prince Albert's private secretary, Sir George Anson.

There is no doubt that Clark had a record of false predictions. This does not prove, however, that his private opinions were always wrong. The fact that his prognosis so often erred on the side of optimism, provides the clue to his real weakness. Sir James Clark was too eager to please. He consistently gave pleasure by looking on the bright side. When the Queen's young niece, Princess Adelaide Hohenlohe, was thrown head first off her pony at Balmoral, Clark announced radiantly, 'She could not have fallen upon a better part of her head.'[2] It must not be forgotten that Clark had attended on Prince Leopold of Saxe-Coburg (afterwards King of the Belgians), a notable hypochondriac, before he was recommended to Princess Victoria's mother. A hypochondriac would be better suited by a kind doctor like Clark than by one whose diagnosis was always a meticulous distillation of the facts.

Returning to the case of Lady Flora Hastings, Clark's unforgiveable fault lay in deliberately bringing his verdict on Lady Flora's condition into line

[1] See *Illustrious Friends* by Sheila Birkenhead, 1965, for a glowing tribute to Clark by Keats's friend Joseph Severn.

[2] Royal Archives, Queen Victoria's Journal, September 23, 1852.

with what he knew were Queen Victoria's own suspicions. His chief purpose was to please the Queen rather than to discover the truth. Lady Flora's initial refusal to permit something as low as a doctor to examine her under her clothes, only made Clark's evasion of his duty the easier.

After the anguish and death of Lady Flora, Clark's income fell precipitously through loss of patients, and Queen Victoria's intensely loyal character drove her to favour this 'poor' physician as she was to favour no other. 'Clark dined' became a fairly regular entry in her Journal. No other physician shared this privilege at the time. For she held at least one belief in common with Lady Flora Hastings: that doctors were at best a species of upper servant.

In thus favouring Clark, she also remembered that as a young girl she had been well served by him. He was a glutton for vaccination and had his royal patient vaccinated twice more after her original vaccination as a baby, before she came to the throne. Queen Victoria inherited from Clark her passionate desire to get every one of her subjects safely vaccinated, and it took all Lord Salisbury's ingenuity to convince her that the introduction of a conscience clause would actually increase the rate of vaccination—because people would find exemption so expensive. At the age of sixteen she was nursed by Clark through a severe attack of typhoid. More than that, he seems to have been primarily responsible for dispelling a rumour put about by her mother's sinister major-domo, Sir John Conroy, that the future Queen was mentally sub-normal. According to Clark's son, Sir John Clark, there was a race to reach the Prime Minister's ear between Sir James Clark and Sir John Conroy during the last hectic days before Victoria came to the throne. Clark somehow got wind of Conroy's plot to persuade Melbourne that a backward young Queen would need a regent (her mother) and a private secretary (Conroy himself). Immediately Clark set about contradicting this lie with letters to Melbourne of his own.

Clark's appreciation of Queen Victoria's 'Coburg temperament', based upon his experience of three generations of Coburgs, completely satisfied his royal mistress. He steered a course mid-way between Conroy's and Stockmar's anti-Hanoverian view that Queen Victoria had inherited a tendency to George III's madness,[1] and Gladstone's that there was nothing wrong with her but feminine selfwill. (During the 'Bedchamber Plot', Stockmar had regaled the Continent, where he was travelling, with his theory about the Queen's unbalanced mind. Since Stockmar happened to be employed as Prince Albert's social tutor on this occasion, it seems more than likely that he passed on his

[1] According to Lord Clarendon, Dr Ferguson held similar views: 'I had some talk with Ferguson about her', wrote Clarendon in April 1861 when the Queen was greatly upset by her mother's death, '& his private opinion about her mind (founded on his attendance upon her years ago when she was in a strange state) is far from satisfactory.' (*My Dear Duchess*, p. 148.) The phrase 'years ago', quoted by Clarendon, may refer to a domestic upheaval at Buckingham Palace, following upon the birth of the Prince of Wales in November 1841 and lasting until January 1842. Ferguson was one of the accoucheurs, while Stockmar acted as peacemaker between Victoria and Albert. (See my *Victoria R.I.*, pp. 159–62.)

foolish fears to the young Prince. At any rate we know that the Prince Consort always believed that a prolonged emotional crisis might affect the Queen's sanity.)

Clark's more agreeable analysis of the Queen's temperament ruled out madness from the beginning, but recognised her to be highly strung and conceded her duty to pay attention to her 'nerves'. This was exactly what she wanted. Before his retirement he must have given Sir William Jenner, his successor, a synopsis of the 'Coburg temperament'—a concept which included various degrees of 'nerves' and applied to both the Queen and Prince Consort. A few months after Jenner's appointment, the Queen was widowed. Her overwhelming grief, her obstinate seclusion, her own insistence that if disturbed she might go mad, helped to drive Jenner away from Clark's more moderate position towards that of Conroy and Stockmar. By the early 1870s Jenner had completely swallowed the Stockmar thesis and was actually informing Lord Halifax that Queen Victoria's high colour after a meal was 'a species of madness'. The common sense of her Court ladies stalwartly resisted these masculine aberrations, some of the ladies regarding Jenner's attitude as madder than his patient's. An added trouble with Jenner was that he had done his distinguished work in hospitals and possessed no training in the subtle, lengthy techniques required to influence a recalcitrant individual patient. Sir Philip Magnus's account of Sir Francis Laking's success in persuading King Edward VII to have his appendix out before his Coronation, shows what a skilful Court doctor could do.

It has been suggested, notably by Dame Edith Sitwell, that Queen Victoria's culpable failure to dismiss Clark in 1839 brought its own nemesis in her husband's death at the hands of the same incompetent physician.

It would be a mistake to say that the Prince's death was caused by an error in diagnosis on the part of Clark comparable with that of 1839. Prince Albert died of typhoid. Jenner, Clark's colleague, was a leading expert in this disease. He was not unduly slow in suspecting the truth. What Clark almost certainly failed to provide was proper nursing. The Prince was nursed by his doctors, valet, daughter and wife. It took another ten years and another royal Prince with typhoid to convince the Mrs Grundys that nursing should be done by professional women.

Why did Clark go out of his way to jolly Prince Albert along instead of sending him firmly to bed? The answer must be found in his interpretation of the 'Coburg temperament', as shared by the Prince and his wife. Clark somehow hoped to keep the sufferer going simply by refusing to let him lie down and die. The reverse side of the Prince's ability to face death bravely was his inability to put up a plucky fight against it. Queen Victoria, on the contrary, was considered unable to bear anxiety, and her doctors therefore refrained from *stating* the nature of the Prince's disease long after they had *diagnosed* it. It was all very psychological and not very successful. For the Prince was not saved from death nor the Queen from what the Victorians might have called 'suppressed alarm'. (The lay reader of Victorian obituaries is surprised by the number of people who apparently died from 'suppressed' illnesses, 'suppressed measles' and 'suppressed gout' being among the favourites.)

Queen Victoria afterwards blamed none of her doctors. When Jenner informed her that death was due to the heart being over-strained by the Prince's heavy frame, she believed him. When Clark told her that three things had proved fatal—overwork, worry about the Prince of Wales's love affair and exposure to chill when already sick—she believed him. When Jenner assured her that reviewing the Eton Volunteers (a duty which she herself had forced upon the ailing Prince) had made no difference whatever, she was glad to believe him. There is one hint and one only that in retrospect she did not consider the Prince's illness to have been perfectly handled. When her eldest son recovered from the same fever, she wrote that his life had been saved by the nursing.

Sir James Reid took over from Jenner in 1883 when Queen Victoria's 'nerves' were no longer a problem. He told the daughter of Lord Stamfordham after the Queen's death that he had never once seen her in bed until she was actually dying. Though she sent for him every morning promptly at 9.30 a.m. she was always up and dressed. Nor was she much interested in unconventional forms of medicine. Queen Adelaide and several of her German relatives went in for homoeopathy, but not Queen Victoria. Prince Albert was attracted to phrenology; there were no phrenologists at Windsor after his death. Queen Victoria's medicines seem to have been of the simplest. We know that she took pills only because her grand-daughter, Princess Victoria of Prussia, tells us that she was late for dinner one day through swallowing a pill the wrong way. Dr Locock gave her a prescription to make her sleep after her first baby and years later she told the Princess Royal that she would never travel without it. The famous prescription was simply camphor. In later life she was sometimes given chloral as a pain-killer and sedative. Chloral was indeed a potent Victorian drug; it killed, for instance, the poet Rosetti. The Queen's doses, however, were so minute that they often did not work at all.

Queen Victoria's relations with her doctors reflect the transitional state of the medical profession, socially, during her century. Despite a few mental blocks, her views obviously progressed greatly from the Flora Hastings period to the Jimmy Reid period. She was always courteous to doctors, fond of them, dependent on them; but domineering and snobbish towards them. She treated them with meticulous respect as regards fees and titles, but though she liked them personally far better than, say, cavalry officers, she never regarded them as the officers' social equals. When short of a man for a ghillies' ball she once sent for an eighty-year-old doctor from the estate rather than call up some young officers from her Guard at Ballater. After the birth of her first child she was insistent that Dr Locock should get his fee of £1,000, Dr Ferguson his £800 and Mr Blagden his £500 'as soon as possible'.[1] In 1863 she wrote

[1] Royal Archives, M 11/6, Prince Albert to Sir Henry Wheatley.

to Lord Russell saying that no physician-in-ordinary got less than a baronetcy, therefore a knighthood would *not* do for Jenner.[1]

Apart from tradition, it was probably the subject matter of the medical profession which caused Queen Victoria to rank her doctors a little lower than the Household. She once warned her eldest daughter against 'too gt. intimacy with *Künstler* (art) as it is very seductive & a little dangerous!'[2] The study of anatomy seemed to her a good deal more dangerous and less seductive. As she informed her second daughter, it was 'disgusting'. Thus, though Queen Victoria was far more interested in illness than in sculpture, she frequently visited studios while never putting her head inside a laboratory. Her nearest approach to medical research occurred when one or other of her dear ones died. Then she would wring from the doctor of Prince Leopold, Prince Albert Victor or Prince Henry of Battenberg excruciating accounts of their last moments, which she admitted were too 'painful' to be entered in her Journal.

It was only when ladies were able to regard the doctor's subject matter with the same absence of squeamishness which they have always, surprisingly, brought to the soldier's, that doctors succeeded in severing the last historic threads which connected them with butchers, body-snatchers and barbers.

Meanwhile the Queen sat serenely at Balmoral on a Sunday in 1875 and listened to her Presbyterian minister poking fun at her doctors. 'Think of how much she must have suffered', intoned the Reverend Campbell, speaking of the woman in the New Testament who had been ill for ten years, 'both from nature and from physicians . . .' Dr Robertson and Dr Marshall, who sat behind the Queen, were furious.

[1] Royal Archives, M11/17.

[2] Royal Archives, Kronberg Letters, Queen Victoria to Crown Princess Frederick William of Prussia (Princess Royal), May 21, 1878.

MICHAEL HOWARD

William I and the Reform of the Prussian Army

MICHAEL HOWARD

William I and the Reform of the Prussian Army

FROWNING down the Middle-Western bustle of the Kurfürstendamm in West Berlin, a grotesque reminder, in the middle of the *Wirtschaftswunder*, of an older, grimmer age, stands the mutilated stump of the Gedächtniskirche; that hideous memorial to the Emperor William I and to the founding fathers of the Second Reich. The noble, heavily whiskered countenance of the Emperor himself dominates the surviving bas-reliefs; the better-known figures of Roon, Moltke, even Bismarck sink to the status of attendant lords.

And well they may. Roon may, as William himself acknowledged in 1871, have forged the sword with which Germany cut her way to triumph and unity; Moltke may have wielded it; but it was William who set them their tasks and, in Roon's case at least, defined meticulously what was to be done. Bismarck may have rescued William from constitutional deadlock, if nothing worse, and devised the expedients to get him what he wanted for his Army; but it was William's stubborn demands which precipitated a crisis which only Bismarck could solve. Lesser figures, Edwin von Manteuffel and Gustav von Alvensleben, may have stiffened the royal resolution during the months of crisis between 1860 and 1863, when abdication seemed to offer escape from a conflict more serious and far reaching in its implications than William could ever have foreseen; but the opinions which they reinforced and the programme which they supported were his own, and he had worked them out many years before the illness and death of his brother, Frederick William IV, put him in a position to give them effect. These men may have been the architects of the German Empire, that anachronistic edifice whose inherent instability was to have such disastrous consequences for the Germans themselves and for their neighbours; but they worked at the behest of a royal patron who supervised their work in detail and would allow little deviation from the pattern which he had laid down. The genius of the servants must not be allowed to conceal the fundamental responsibility, for good or ill, of the master.

Of this responsibility, William himself was constantly aware. It lay with him to decide, in 1861–2, whether Prussia should go like England, France and the Netherlands, along what Roon called in April 1861 'the path of monarchy by grace of the People ... [and] compete with Belgium in the material blessings of an unhistorical existence'; or whether it would be led in another direction by 'the assertion of the legally justified Royal will! It unleashes the eagle;' went on Roon rhapsodically, 'the King by the grace of God remains at the head of his people, the centre of the State, the ruler in the land, uncontrolled by ministerial guardians or parliamentary majorities . . . The way is rough at first, but leads, with all the splendour and all the armed magnificence of a glorious struggle, to the *commanding heights* of life. It is the only way for a Prussian King!'[1] William is unlikely to have been impressed by these Nietzschean visions; but he saw quite clearly that in nineteenth-century Prussia, as in seventeenth-century England, sovereignty lay with the control of military power.[2] The radical majority which was returned to the Landtag by the elections of December 1861 and May 1862 saw it too, and their attacks on the Government's military proposals were as consciously devised as blows at the old political and social order as those proposals were consciously devised to defend it. So significant indeed had the issue become by the autumn of 1862 that although there remained virtually no points of substantive disagreement between the leaders of the Landtag and the military specialists in the Ministry of War; and although both Roon and Bismarck saw that the conflict could be resolved by one simple concession which the Prussian War Ministry had been prepared to make from the very beginning; that concession could not be made, not only because the King himself was adamant, but because to yield would have been to strike the royal colours before the new, victorious vessel of parliamentary sovereignty. Better that parliamentary government—anyhow planted as precariously in Prussia, as one liberal bitterly remarked, as 'foreign rice'[3]—should come to an end altogether than that the *altpreussisch* tradition should be so shamefully abandoned.

The concession in question was the reduction of the period of compulsory military service from three years to two, or the *de facto* recognition of a situation which had prevailed in Prussia for forty years past. The proposed reduction affected infantry regiments only. It was generally accepted that three-year service with the cavalry and artillery must remain. Virtually all other matters of conflict had already been resolved. Opposition to the transformation of the independent Landwehr into a first-line reserve trained by regular soldiers had rapidly dwindled after the sweeping defeat of that institution's principal defenders, the Old Liberals, in the elections of December 1861. The financial cost of the new reforms, which had appalled even the officials of the Kriegsministerium, were swallowed up in the new prosperity of Prussia. Even the action of the King in using the Landtag's provisional grant of 1860 to create thirty-six new infantry and eighteen new cavalry regiments as cadres for the new Army, and marking their very unprovisional character by presenting them

[1] Albrecht von Roon, *Denkwürdigkeiten* (Berlin, 1905), vol. II, p. 48.

[2] See Erich Marcks, *Kaiser Wilhelm I* (Leipzig, 1900), p. 189.

[3] Eugene N. Anderson, *The Social and Political Conflict in Prussia* (University of Nebraska Press, 1954), p. 47.

with regimental colours as the first official act of his reign—even this might have been accepted, as it was accepted four years later, if the monarch had been prepared to give way over two-year service. His own officials in the Kriegsministerium were prepared to accept it. Bismarck was prepared to accept it. Even Roon was prepared to accept it. Manteuffel, of course, delighted at anything that provoked a conflict with the Landtag, was not prepared to accept anything, but General Stosch reflected a fairly general opinion in a letter of September 28, 1862, when he wrote 'Manteuffel must go, then Bismarck will advise the King to accept two-year service in the infantry, and at last we shall have peace'.[1] In fact Stosch was too optimistic. It took Bismarck two years to ease Manteuffel out of the royal entourage, and his disappearance made no difference whatever to the King's views. For him any proposal to reduce the length of service was simply, as he gloomily minuted on a famous memorandum of October 10, 1862, 'a death sentence on the Army'.[2]

In view of the importance which this issue assumed in the constitutional crisis of Prussia—and in view of the fact that within five years of William's death the German Army reverted to two-year service without any noticeable decline in its efficiency—it is worth examining this issue a little more closely. It was one on which William had very early made up his mind, as much on political grounds as on technical. Like so many men of his class and generation, he believed that in 1815 the ghost of the Revolution had been very inadequately laid. In his *wanderjähre*, in the early 1820s, he had travelled in Italy during its spasmodic revolts; he had visited Russia while the reverberations of the Decembrist conspiracy were still echoing through the corridors of St Petersburg; and he lamented the failure, in 1831, to settle with the new French revolution while opportunity offered. '[War] will now become a bloodier matter', he prophesied gloomily, 'as French armaments increase and as her erroneous teachings spread more widely.'[3]

Thus the Prussian Army, into which he had been commissioned in 1807 on his tenth birthday and in which he was to hold active command uninterruptedly until 1848, had to be considered not only as an effective fighting force but as a bulwark of the established order; and he did not need Roon and Manteuffel to tell him how necessary it was, if the Army was to be preserved, that the nobility from which it drew its officers should be cherished as well. As early as 1843, fifteen years before Roon's famous memorandum of 1858, he was stressing the need to encourage the Junkers by providing free places for their sons in gymnasia and cadet schools. This concern for the officer corps was a sensitive nerve on which both Manteuffel and Roon were, during the crisis, quite mercilessly to play. Manteuffel warned him, in 1861, that if he yielded to the Chamber 'the Army will gain the impression that Your

[1] Albrecht von Stosch, *Denkwürdigkeiten* (Stuttgart, 1904), p. 52.

[2] *Militärische Schriften weiland Kaiser Wilhelms des Groszen Majestät* (Berlin, 1897), vol. II, p. 479 (hereafter referred to as *Militärische Schriften*).

[3] Marcks, op. cit., p. 43.

Royal Highness is no longer in control of its destinies but has abdicated this privilege of the Crown to the Chamber'.[1] Roon was still more explicit. Surrender to the Chamber, he warned, would have the gravest effects 'on that part of the Nation which leads Your Majesty's armed forces and which the All Highest himself has always found to be the staunchest pillar of his throne'; to which the All Highest minuted desperately 'That *I* would never survive!'[2]

It would however be quite wrong to see in William simply a royal political soldier. His attention to military matters was minute and expert, and the respect with which his views on military questions was greeted came not just from his august status, but from his thorough knowledge of his profession. However little he knew about anything else, he knew his army and its problems very well indeed. The problems, throughout his period of active service, were those which had bedevilled and to some extent shaped Prussian military organisation since the days of his great-great-grandfather, Frederick William I. Almost all could be traced to the basic one: how to maintain an army of the size which had won Prussia her place among the Powers of Europe on so Spartan an economy. In solving them the Prussian Government in the early nineteenth century adopted many of the expedients of the eighteenth. Although the traditional liability of all young males to military service had been flamboyantly reasserted in 1814, it was a liability of which the Army, in order to keep down expenditure, took only very limited advantage. In 1852 it was calculated that out of an age-group of 66,000, 28,000 young men escaped altogether. The notorious situation resulted, when the Army was mobilised in 1859, that some 150,000 reservists, most of them married men, were recalled to the colours, leaving their families as a burden on the rates, while 100,000 young men were left undisturbed.[3]

As a further measure of economy, the traditional expedient was adopted of sending men on unpaid furlough after their initial training and recalling them only for the autumn manoeuvres. First revived in 1820, this system became firmly established in 1832, when the Army settled down again after the mobilisation of 1830–1. Formally, the obligation to three-year service with the colours remained. In practice the recruit was furloughed after sixteen and a half months, at the end of his second summer's training, and in his third year he was recalled for six weeks in August and September.[4] Against this decision William, then commanding III Army Corps, energetically rebelled, deploying arguments which were to remain fundamentally unchanged for thirty years. Some of them, indeed, can still be heard today.

> I will not say [he wrote to his royal father in April 1832] that one cannot complete a man's military training in two years; but in such a short period of

[1] Gerhard Ritter, *Staatskunst und Kriegshandwerk* (Munich, 1954), vol. I, p. 358.

[2] Roon, *Denkwürdigkeiten*, vol. II, p. 48 ff.

[3] Julius von der Osten-Sacken, *Preussens Heer von seinen Anfängen bis zür Gegenwart* (Berlin, 1914), vol. III, p. 1.

[4] *Militärische Schriften* I, p. 146–7.

service the man will be even more liable than hitherto to be looking forward to his demobilisation and so to consider the military life as something to be got over with, so that he hardly thinks it worth the bother and certainly never gets to the point of seeing it as an occupation in which he could remain for longer . . . The shorter the period of service, the more the soldierly spirit is bound to diminish in an army.

With two-year service, he feared therefore, they would never breed those N.C.O.s and long-serving regular soldiers who were the backbone of the Army. In fact they should give the highest priority to the building up of such a cadre, 'in whom the warrior spirit can flourish and through whom it can be transmitted to the nation's youth'. This would pay political as well as military dividends.

It is the tendency of the revolutionary or Liberal parties in Europe [the prince stated in the same document,] to gradually demolish all the supports which guard the sovereign power and authority and give it security in the moment of danger. It is natural that the Army should still be the foremost of these supports; and the more it is inspired by a true military spirit, the harder it is to subvert. But discipline and blind obedience are things which can be engendered and given permanence only by long practice, and it is to these that a longer period of service is relevant, so that in the moment of danger the Monarch can securely rely on his troops.[1]

A year later he was still arguing his case. 'Through the reduction in the period of service the infantry is reduced to the level of other small German armies and one will not be justified in asking any more of our men than of theirs.' The money, he argued urgently, must somehow be found. 'We are standing', he concluded, his imagery somewhat confused by passion, 'at the turning point of this question, which disturbs me to my inmost being, and with whose solution is bound up the destiny of the Fatherland and the Throne!'[2]

But nobody else felt so deeply about it as did Prince William. To his repeated complaints, the officials both of the Treasury and of the Ministry for War continued to reply that the money simply could not be found. Even when, in 1854 he gained the support of his royal brother Frederick William IV, bureaucratic opposition remained immovable. 'I know', wrote the King petulantly, 'that the Treasury, against my verbal and written orders, rejected three-year service for the infantry'; and he insisted that it must now be carried through.[3] But the matter was still being debated within the Ministry of War when William took over full powers as Regent in 1858; and this debate he was determined, after a quarter of a century, to bring to a summary end.

With the question of length of service was bound up the yet more contentious matter of the Landwehr, that independent territorial force which was

[1] Ibid., 153–5.

[2] Ibid., 177–8.

[3] E. von Frauenholz, *Entwicklungsgeschichte des Deutschen Heerwesens* (Munich, 1941), vol. V, p. 249.

regarded by the Prussian bourgeoisie, much as the English regarded their militia, as the true symbol of the liberties granted with such reluctance by the Hohenzollerns during the *Erhebungszeit*. The small size of the regular army meant that in any mobilisation it was heavily dependent on the Landwehr to make up its numbers; and since the efficiency and morale of the Landwehr, in William's view, depended on the training which such of them as had served with the regular army had received with the colours, that was another argument, he considered, for providing three years' service, whose imprint would really endure. But he was convinced that far more sweeping measures of reform would be necessary to make the Landwehr a truly effective military force. The destruction of the independence of the Landwehr and its subordination, both in training and command, to the regular army, was one of the principal points in Roon's Army Bill of 1860; but precisely these measures had been urged by William twenty years earlier in a notable exchange of correspondence with no less a figure than the father of the Landwehr, General Hermann von Boyen, whom Frederick William IV recalled from retirement in 1840 to become Minister for War.[1]

In this confrontation between the veteran general and the middle-aged Prince two generations met and entirely failed to understand one another. Boyen's arguments, based on the lessons of 1806, already had an archaic ring. The basic object of universal service, he recalled, was that 'no class of citizen could remain neutral when war broke out, and that the government could be assured of the general co-operation of the People'. ('Quite correct', minuted the Prince.) The object of the Landwehr, said Boyen, was to maintain units capable of taking the field; to preserve the idea of *Landesbewaffnung* by regular exercises in peacetime; to give its members the feel of arms without too much disturbance of their civil life; and to keep alive the knowledge acquired during military service. This was a task which demanded different techniques and different standards from those of the regular army, and few professional officers and N.C.O.s possessed them. The Landwehr, he insisted, neither could nor should try to ape the pattern of the Line. 'Those who lose sight of this fact, rooted as it is in human nature, in their treatment of the Landwehr', he concluded warningly, 'are undermining, perhaps unwittingly, the Landwehr spirit, without which it cannot survive for long and for which the rigid drill-book of the Line is poison.'[2]

William would have none of this. 'I know that argument very well', he commented, 'but I intend to remain deaf to it, for it is only put forward in order to give the idea that the Landwehr is something quite separate. It is in fact an Army on furlough, and as an Army it must be identical with the Line.' It must, he insisted, 'be able to drill, manoeuvre and shoot like the Line, from whom it has learned how to do so. Obedience, discipline, subordination are common to everyone; these cardinal points of the soldier must be strictly

[1] *Militärische Schriften* I, p. 333 ff.

[2] Ibid., I, p. 366.

maintained and every patriot must be imbued with them. To conceive of the Landwehr as behaving, under arms, in a way different from the troops of the Line is the first step to a revolutionary Army.'[1] Landwehr officers, he concluded, could be considered effective soldiers only in so far as they achieved an effective 'blending' (*Verschmelzung*) with the Line, and to this end regular officers should be detached to the Landwehr in the largest possible numbers. The enthusiasm of 1813 was not to be expected again; as for the experience of those years, as he rather unkindly reminded Boyen, it was something of a wasting asset.

Events were to bear out William's arguments. The showing of the Landwehr in the mobilisation of 1849–50 was, by all accounts, lamentable, especially so far as cavalry, artillery and supply was concerned; and Prussia's evident military incapacity on this occasion led to the traumatic humiliation of Olmütz. General von Bonin, who was later to champion the Landwehr against von Roon, was commanding a division at the time, and complained bitterly about the inadequacy of the officers and the indiscipline, the lack of 'good, blind military obedience' among the men. He concluded 'that the Landwehr in itself and in its present organisation is not to be considered an absolutely reliable and efficient body, that its disbandment and reorganisation is necessary, and together with this should be linked a fundamental reform, in many respects, of the standing Army'.[2]

Two months later William drafted a proposal which contained all the elements of the Roon reforms ten years later.[3] The rapid mobilisation which railways now made possible, he pointed out, made the *immediate* effectiveness of reservists a matter of fundamental importance. They must be organised and officered as if they were companies of the Line. Their cadres should be combined with the reserve companies of Line regiments to form fourth battalions of those regiments, which could on mobilisation expand into three Landwehr battalions. They should be put in peacetime, with their linked regular units, under the commander who would lead them in war; and to provide for this new reserve organisation, the number of regular officers and N.C.O.s should be considerably increased.

Six years before he assumed power, therefore, William already knew exactly what he wanted to do. Three-year service must be established; the cadres of regular troops must be expanded; and the Landwehr must be 'blended' with the regular army. Assuming, with some reason, that von Bonin shared his views, he made him Minister for War in the 'New Era' Ministry which he appointed on becoming Regent in the autumn of 1858, and he addressed to that Ministry a message emphasising the urgency of making the Army 'powerful and respected so that when the time comes, it can lay a heavy weight in the scales'.[4] The mobilisation of 1859 lent emphasis to his words. Though less of a shambles than that of 1850, it showed that the traditional weaknesses

[1] Loc. cit. [2] Ibid., II, p. 152–3. [3] Ibid., II, p. 135.
[4] Osten-Sacken, op. cit., II, p. 9.

were still unremedied. The regular army was too weak to do without the Landwehr, which took the field partially equipped and undertrained, leaving its families unprovided for and its jobs unfilled, while a substantial number of young bachelors, as we have seen, escaped all liability. William resolved that this should never happen again. On July 15, four days after the truce concluded between the Austrian and the French Emperors at Villafranca, he laid down principles for a reform of the Army to be accomplished within one year from August 1, 1859.[1] Landwehr cadres and reserve battalions were to be amalgamated; the size of cadres was to be doubled; and the cost, he suggested optimistically, should be swallowed up in the general expense of the mobilisation.

To Bonin and the officials in the Ministry of War, however, the reform did not appear quite so easy. They had been quietly working on the problem themselves, and in certain respects were in whole-hearted agreement with their new *Kriegsherr*. They were fully alive to the absurdity of an army so heavily dependent on the older age groups whose military efficiency was declining and whose death or incapacity in a bloody war would, in the words of one official, 'reduce their families to the Proletariat in the worst sense of the word'.[2] They therefore accepted the need for the extension of the call-up, as also for some degree of *Verschmelzung* between Army and Landwehr. But they still believed, as had their predecessors, that financial stringency must set rigid limits to any projected reform. Bonin had already committed himself to a weighty opinion on this question which has a thoroughly twentieth-century ring.

> To employ disproportionate quantities of men and resources on normal war preparations, to screw these up beyond the proper level, does not give real strength, but only the deceptive illusion of strength, and inevitably reduces it, if continued for a prolonged period, as the productive capacity of the nation becomes exhausted. But Prussia should not be a State of outward show alone, but a State of intensive internal strength. The real increase of our military capacity can only keep step with the growing productive capacity of our people. This alone, that is to say the industrial and moral resources of our population, constitutes the solid foundation for our military power, and thereby the lasting influence of the State.[3]

This was all very well, but what it really meant was that, if the call-up was to be extended (as everyone agreed that it must) three-year service was out of the question. Nor was Bonin 'sound' on the question of the Landwehr. In spite of his strictures on the Landwehr's performance in 1850, he was reluctant to contemplate any fundamental transformation of the pattern laid down in 1815, and even more reluctant to pilot any such proposal through a Chamber in which, since the election of 1858, the Liberals enjoyed a commanding majority. When, therefore, on August 9, 1859, he ordered his

[1] Ibid., p. 17.

[2] Memorandum of Lieut.-Col. von Clausewitz, July 1857, reprinted in *Militärische Schriften* II, p. 326. See also Osten-Sacken, op. cit., III, p. 4.

[3] *Militärische Schriften*, II, p. 378.

officials to draw up proposals based on the royal outline of July 15, he laid it down that there should be 'no essential alteration of the organisation of the Army in its fundamental principles, that is, any disestablishment of the mobile Landwehr'.[1] Moreover he insisted that 'increased recruiting and rejuvenation of the Army could be achieved by a reform on the basis of the existing Defence Law [Boyen's Law of 1814] without the Landtag being asked for its approval to an increase in appropriations'.[2]

A document based on such principles was unlikely to meet with the Regent's approval. In fact the War Ministry, with some ingenuity, succeeded in producing a scheme which preserved three-year service, but only at the cost of substantially reducing the size, both of peace-time cadres and war-time establishments; thereby transgressing another of the Regent's fundamental principles. It was at this stage, September 1859, that William invited the commander of the 18th Division at Düsseldorf, Albrecht von Roon, to join the discussions.

The previous year William had received from Roon a long memorandum on the Prussian armed forces,[3] and on this memorandum, as is generally known, the Roon reforms were eventually based. But it is hard to detect in this memorandum a single proposal which William had not already determined to carry out. Three-year service; increase of cadres and improvement of career opportunities for regular officers and N.C.O.s; the transformation of that 'politically false' institution, the Landwehr, into a first-line reserve for the army under the control of professional soldiers—none of this, as we have shown, was new. What mattered was that it mirrored exactly William's own intentions; and William detected in Roon a man who not only shared his own views, but who could be relied on to force them through over the objections first of his more moderate or timorous colleagues, and then of a Landtag in which all the forces of opposition, economic, social and sentimental, would be formidably assembled.

This role Roon joyfully accepted. He saw himself as the King's man, Kurwenaal to his Tristan, 'a sergeant in the great Company of which the King was captain'.[4] In the discussions which ensued with Bonin and his assistants, he loyally pressed the royal view that the larger establishments were necessary even though they increased the estimated cost of the reforms by a quarter, from seven million to nearly nine million thalers. On the Commission which the Regent set up to study the question, at the end of October 1859, he refused to debate the matter at all, simply taking the line that since the Regent had made up his mind, no further discussion was possible—a view which most

[1] i.e. the "Landwehr of the first call", which could be called out to take the field. The "Landwehr of the second call", older men reserved for garrison duties, did not come into question.

[2] Osten-Sacken, op. cit., III, p. 19.

[3] Reprinted in Roon, *Denkwürdigkeiten*, II, p. 521 ff.

[4] Ibid., II, p. 151.

of his military colleagues shared. Bonin, false to his *Kriegsherr*, tainted with liberalism, was marked out by Roon and Manteuffel for destruction. Bonin's subordinates indeed bitterly suggested that his adversaries had deliberately brought forward totally unacceptable proposals in order to force his resignation[1] —if not indeed to force a constitutional crisis to wreck the New Era for good and all.

In any case, William made it clear that he could no longer work with Bonin.

> You quite rightly point out [he wrote to him on November 24, 1859] that military, economic and financial interests must stand together in a certain harmony; but it is equally true that in a Monarchy like ours the military consideration must not be curtailed by the other two; for the European position of the State, on which so much else depends, rests upon that. Peace itself, without which the welfare neither of individuals nor of the community can be conceived, would be endangered by any restriction on the internal efficiency and readiness of the Army.[2]

Could Bonin honestly declare, asked the Regent, that he accepted these principles and would apply them in driving through the reforms which he now proclaimed as an 'iron necessity'? Naturally Bonin could not. He asked to be relieved of his post and slipped away to the obscurity of a provincial corps command. In his place, on December 5, William appointed Roon.

Was the government now set on a collision-course with the Landtag, as Manteuffel so devoutly hoped? Such a judgment would be premature. The bills which Roon introduced in the Landtag in February 1860 were not impossibly contentious. The need to improve the efficiency of the Army and to rejuvenate it was almost universally recognised. The expense was disagreeable but not intolerable: much could be found by an overhaul of the land tax, to ensure the passing of which William was prepared to swamp the Upper Chamber with newly created peers, and Roon was prepared to withdraw the most unpopular of the proposed levies on trade. The technical arguments for the abolition of the old-style Landwehr were overwhelming. Only on three-year service did no agreement seem possible—a measure justifiable principally by the political arguments so bluntly advanced by William in his younger days, which threw doubt (or, some might say, light) on the whole underlying purpose of the reforms. The object appeared, as a liberal senior officer complained, to turn the Prussian Army into a 'Partei-Armee'.[3] Torn between their suspicions of the government's intentions and their recognition of the necessity of the reforms, the liberal majority in the Chamber hit on the indescribably stupid expedient of voting a provisional grant for one year only. The Minister for Finance, von Patow, tortuously explained that the government saw the situation as provisional 'in the sense that within the specified period it would only do what it is able within the existing legal provisions and within the limits of the credits requested; what it is able without encroaching upon the

[1] Theodor von Bernhardi, *Aus meinem Leben* (Leipzig, 1893), vol. II, pp. 295–6, 309–10.
[2] Osten-Sacken, op. cit., III, p. 26.
[3] Bernhardi, op. cit., III, p. 325.

constitutional rights of the representative body'. None of this stopped William from immediately issuing a series of Orders in Council for the creation of new regiments, out of the old Landwehr cadres and line reserve battalions, which effectively provided the framework for the new enlarged and integrated force which was to bring Prussia the dominance, first of Germany and then of Europe; or Roon from carrying these through with a rapidity which enabled William to report on June 19, 1860, after a tour of inspection, 'Although the new structure of the Army was decreed by me only a few weeks ago, I recognise with satisfaction that its foundations are already complete.'[1]

This was not what the Prussian electorate had expected of the New Era. In February 1861 the discontented elements in the Landtag broke away from the Old Liberals, those Establishment moderates who had so cravenly sold the pass, to form the D.F.P., the *Deutsche Fortschritts Partei*, to press for the reforms in which the government appeared so uninterested. 'Can the salaries of civil servants be raised?' demanded one radical with bitter sarcasm. 'Oh no, the Army comes first. How about schools and universities? The Army must head the queue. Arts and crafts, business and shipping? No, the Army! Perhaps great land improvement measures, railways and canals? Barracks first of all!'[2] The provisional grant was renewed until the end of the year, but only by a majority of eleven votes; and in December the electorate made clear its own view of the matter by increasing the total liberal representation from 266 to 333, as against 15 conservatives. In such a house the government could make no headway. It gratefully resigned in January 1862, to be succeeded by a shadowy conservative caretaker régime in which the only outstanding figure was Roon; and Roon made no pretence at regretting the disappearance of colleagues whose political programme he described as 'the surrender of the historic Kingdom of Prussia and the enthronement of parliamentary sovereignty'. His own task he now saw simply in terms of conflict. 'I must seek out the struggle, to that I am compelled by my duty and my conscience . . . The young David had only pebbles and a brave heart—it is God that gives the victory' he concluded piously, 'not strength or cunning.'[3] Poor Roon, battling single-handed against the forces of darkness and destruction!

In spite of appearances however, Roon was no fool; nor was he, like Manteuffel, a conspirator deliberately driving tension higher to give an excuse for a royal *coup d'état*. The conservatives and the radicals he regarded as being equally 'impossible parties',[4] and the bellicose noises which he made in his letters did not prevent him from maintaining, during this session, an air of courteous reasonableness in the Chamber and, throughout the spring and

[1] Frauenholz, op. cit., V, p. 253.

[2] Adalbert Hess, *Das Parlament das Bismarck widerstrebte* (Köln, 1964), p. 20. See also Anderson, op. cit., pp. 88–95.

[3] Roon, *Denkwürdigkeiten*, II, p. 72.

[4] Bernhardi, op. cit., IV, p. 114.

summer of 1862, exploring with the moderates the possibility of compromise. For as usually happens in revolutions, the appearance of men with more extreme demands drove the moderates, with whom the conflict had started, to consider an accommodation with their original adversaries as the lesser of two evils. Elections in March 1862 strengthened the left still further at the expense not only of the conservatives but of the Old Liberals as well; and to the latter Roon's programme was very much more acceptable than some of the proposals which this group now brought forward, for slashing reductions in the standing army, for promotion of officers from the ranks and for the conversion of the Landwehr into a Swiss-type militia. The Old Liberals were prepared to accept virtually the whole of the government's measures if it would only make the one concession—the abandonment of three-year service.[1] They could face their electorates with nothing less.

Then an extraordinary thing happened. Roon gave in. On September 17 he announced that the government was prepared to consider a compromise proposal along the lines of that urged by the Old Liberal leaders; the passing of the military budgets in return for the acceptance of two-year service.[2] But hardly had the astonished Chamber digested the news than Roon had the disagreeable duty of telling them that it was all a mistake. The King, more convinced than ever that the Chamber was set on 'ruining the Army, in its state of readiness and in its military spirit and in its training'[3] refused to consider the idea for a moment. It is still difficult to see why Roon ever thought he could get away with such a flagrant transgression of his royal master's wishes, or how indeed he reconciled it with the 'conscience' to which in his letters he so proudly referred. It was the kind of blunder which ministries are liable to make in their death-throes. 'After this wondrous episode it will be very difficult for the Ministry to hold on much longer', observed Bernhardi; 'We are rapidly approaching a Bismarck-Schönhausen ministry, of that there can be no doubt.'[4] They were indeed. Roon's colleagues resigned; the Chamber, on September 23, finally rejected the military appropriations in the Budget; and the King, on Roon's advice, turned to Bismarck as the only man with the nerve to ride out the storm.

But that was still not the end of the story. Though Bismarck was prepared to govern without the Chamber if he had to, he was anxious to co-operate with it if he could; and his dispassionate eye saw the absurdity of making the break over a principle which, in the view of many military experts, was no principle at all. Almost his first act was to revive the bait of two-year service, in a form which he hoped would settle the matter for good.[5] The principle of three-year

[1] Waldemar Graf Roon, *Roon als Redner* (Breslau, 1895), vol. I, p. 191.

[2] Gordon A. Craig, *The Politics of the Prussian Army* (London, 1955), p. 158.

[3] Letter of August 30, 1862, reprinted in *Roon als Redner*, I, p. 320.

[4] Bernhardi, op. cit., IV, p. 325.

[5] See Ludwig Dehio, 'Bismarck und die Heeresvorlagen der Konflikzeit', in *Historische Zeitschrift* CXLIV (1931).

service was to remain, but at the end of the second year the conscript might be released on payment of 'substitution money' which could be used to swell the ranks of the regular soldiers; an open imitation of the system which applied since 1818 in the French Army and which in the Italian War of 1859 had apparently produced excellent results. The argument advanced so often, that two-year service would make it impossible to produce enough regulars and N.C.O.s, was thus to some extent met. Linked with this was a further proposal, of more far-reaching significance. Henceforth the size of the Army should be fixed at a constant percentage—1.2 per cent—of the population; and defence expenditure should be assessed simply on the basis of the number of troops thus raised. The right of the Landtag to vote the defence budget, which even Roon had never questioned, would thus be quietly abdicated, and this disagreeable conflict need never be repeated again.

This project of a *Pauschquantum*, which was to find its way in a modified form into the constitution of the North German Confederation in 1867, has since been condemned as an 'imposition of military absolutism'.[1] In fact, as Manteuffel was quick to perceive, it would have limited the authority of the Crown no less than that of the Landtag, and for that reason, he persuaded the King, it was entirely unacceptable.[2] But the King cannot have taken much persuading. The proposal involved the surrender of the basic principle for which he was fighting. The reduction of length of service, and with it of the size of infantry units, would lead, he considered, to 'the destruction of all military spirit'. And he sent back the document to Roon with, as we have seen, the blistering comment 'a death sentence on the Army!'[3]

So three-year service remained, and the Army was saved. It was to be on parliamentary government in Germany that the death sentence was pronounced—on that, and a great deal else besides. Is it too much to suggest that, had matters been settled rather differently, the Gedächtniskirche might not today be in ruins after all?

[1] Ibid., p. 35.

[2] Gordon A. Craig, 'Portrait of a Political General: Edwin von Manteuffel and the Constitutional Conflict in Prussia', in *Political Science Quarterly*, LXVI (1951).

[3] See n. 5 above.

ALFRED GOLLIN

Asquith: A New View

ALFRED GOLLIN

Asquith: A New View

NO political reputation has suffered more in recent times because of the activities of apologists and supporters than that of Herbert Henry Asquith. Those established authorities who decide our opinions about the men and events of recent political history have done Asquith's memory a genuine disservice in their efforts to impress upon contemporaries certain high and curious opinions about him.

In a newspaper interview Sir Harold Nicolson said of Asquith: 'He was a liberal . . . Good liberals aren't fighters. Asquith wasn't a fighter even on domestic questions . . . there was no aggression in him.'

The interviewer then remarked: 'It seems odd not so much that they got him out of No. 10 as they ever put him there.' To this Sir Harold replied: 'I agree. He was an intellectual and he believed in things like honesty and mercy. He would never prevaricate. To prevaricate was to lie, and to lie was to sin. And he simply couldn't trample on people. It *is* rather odd that he got where he did. . . .'[1]

Surely, these are singular reflections. They are the opinions of an admirer. But they are neither accurate nor valid. They perform no genuine service for Asquith's memory: and none for history.

Asquith rose to eminence in the Liberal Party without the support of a private income or the patronage of an influential family. His steady advance depended upon firmness of purpose, and upon the brilliance of a first-class brain. It may be observed in this connection that in his day a triumphant career at Balliol and at the Bar did not produce a personality distinguished by meekness or humility.

Asquith was a hearty fighter, on domestic and foreign questions alike. In 1903 he was recognised as a serious candidate for the highest office. In that year he followed Joseph Chamberlain round the country in order to oppose his programme of Tariff Reform and Imperial Preference. That contest was one of the most exciting in recent political history. In it, Asquith stood out as the most formidable of Chamberlain's opponents. Only a fighter would have dared to defy the most dangerous politician of the day at such close quarters.

After Sir Henry Campbell-Bannerman became Prime Minister in 1905

[1] These remarks were published in *The Observer* for November 12, 1961.

Asquith was looked upon as the most devastating debater upon the Liberal side of the House. Whenever a crisis in the Commons threatened Campbell-Bannerman would call for Asquith by saying—'send for the sledge-hammer'.[1] In time, Asquith won for himself the nickname of 'The Hammer'. This soubriquet was applied by contemporaries to a man who had demonstrated fighting qualities of the very first order.

*

After Asquith succeeded to the Premiership in 1908 some of his contemporaries believed that prevarication was his most obvious characteristic.

Most of his opponents, and some of his friends, were convinced that his ability to prevaricate, to act evasively, was the key to his mastery of affairs. His public utterances were on occasion so encumbered by qualifying phrases that contemporaries, Liberal and Tory alike, could never be certain of his meaning.

Sometimes he went too far in his devious courses. In a speech at the Albert Hall in December 1909 he was understood to have said that the King, if the situation required, would consent to the creation of a large number of peers so that Government legislation could be passed, despite the hostility of the House of Lords.

In the following February, however, the Liberal rank and file were astonished to learn from him that his remarks at the Albert Hall had been misunderstood. He explained in the House of Commons that he had no such 'guarantees' from the Sovereign, nor had he intended to suggest that the promise had been made.

John Redmond, the Irish leader and Asquith's parliamentary ally, was outraged by this attempt at prevarication. Even the radical *Daily News* of February 22 declared: 'In believing the guarantees were guarantees from the Crown, Mr Redmond was in company with every journalist, every politician, and every ordinary citizen.'

Liberal officials in the constituencies resigned in cohorts as a protest against Asquith's equivocal course. His prestige, in the words of his friend the Liberal Chief Whip, 'fell to so low an ebb . . . that I despaired of his ever recovering it'.[2]

In the same way Conservatives were often distressed by Asquith's capacity for evasive actions. Professor Albert Venn Dicey, a Unionist partisan, wrote in 1914: '. . . Asquith as a political leader is thoroughly untrustworthy . . . Asquith . . . will probably not tell a direct lie . . . His attitude is always that of a very wily advocate speaking from his brief, and not morally responsible for the statements contained therein. . . .'[3]

Sir Edward Carson's opinion was more blunt. Once, when he compared

[1] See J. A. Spender, *Life of Lord Oxford and Asquith* (London, 1932), vol. I, p. 181.

[2] See A. C. Murray, *Master and Brother* (London, 1945), p. 39. And for the justice of the Irish and Liberal interpretation of Asquith's remarks see the clear account in Sir Harold Nicolson, *King George The Fifth* (London, 1952), p. 128. It explains why Asquith adopted a course of prevarication at the time.

[3] Milner Papers, Dicey to Milner, May 9, 1914.

Lloyd George with Asquith, he remarked: '. . . that one is a plain man of the people and shows his hand, and though you mayn't trust him, his crookednesses are all plain to see. But the other is clever and polished and knows how to conceal his crookedness.' Bonar Law, another of Asquith's enemies, had begun this conversation by attacking Lloyd George. When Carson was finished Bonar Law said: 'Well, perhaps you are right!'[1]

These vicious opinions need not be endorsed. Equally, they should not be ignored.

*

Nor can it be correct to say that Asquith's accession to the Premiership was odd. The rise of any man to the 'top of the greasy pole' must be of interest to the curious. But Asquith's ascent was no more odd than that of many who preceded or came after him. In fact, Asquith took good care to make certain that he arrived in Downing Street as Campbell-Bannerman's successor. Accidents and oddities played no part in his upward flight.

In 1903 Lord Milner, High Commissioner for South Africa, prepared to introduce indentured Chinese labourers into the mines of the Transvaal. His purpose was to revive the mining industry after the ravages of the Boer War; and thus begin upon the rehabilitation of the entire area.

Milner realised the political dangers of this course. He understood that he would lie open to the attacks of Liberals, Radicals, Labour men and Nonconformists as soon as his plans became known to the British public. In order to avoid a campaign against 'Chinese Slavery on the Rand' Milner, in October 1903, approached his friends, Asquith, Grey and Haldane.

As leaders of the Liberal Imperialist wing of their party he hoped that they would appreciate the Imperial purpose behind his plan; and protect him from the criticism of their Liberal colleagues. The three men promised Milner their support: 'On that understanding, and that understanding alone, he decided to go on with . . . (the) . . . project.'[2]

When the testing hour came, however, Asquith failed to stand by his friend, despite the promise. Early in 1904 the Radicals savagely attacked Milner because of the Chinese labourers. At first Asquith remained silent. Then he condemned Milner's policy in the House of Commons. Leo Amery wrote to the High Commissioner: 'I did think you had got Asquith straight on the point, but I am afraid the temptation, with office looming so near and wall paper for 10 Downing Street already selected by Mrs A., was too much for him, and his performance was as bad as anybody else's, if not worse.'[3]

Asquith's political future would have been damaged irreparably had he spoken out in Milner's behalf in 1904. By abandoning Milner, Asquith's position as Campbell-Bannerman's heir-apparent was confirmed and reinforced. This development took place at a moment when the political tide

[1] See H. Montgomery Hyde, *Carson* (London, 1953), p. 407, n.
[2] Cecil Headlam ed., *The Milner Papers* (London, 1933), vol II, p. 477 and n. 1.
[3] Amery Papers, L. S. Amery to Milner, February 26, 1904.

was turning in favour of the Liberals; at a moment when, for the first time after years in the political wilderness, they could see the gleam of office before them.

*

In this general connection mention must also be made of the curious affair of the Relugas Compact. The incident is ignored in Spender's biography, and also in Asquith's political memoirs. It was, however, a matter of vital consequence on the eve of the Liberal accession to power.

In the summer of 1905 Arthur Balfour, the Conservative Prime Minister, told R. B. Haldane of his intention to relinquish office at a favourable opportunity. As a result of this information Asquith, Grey and Haldane came together in order to decide upon a plan of action.

In Haldane's phrase 'Grey had a fishing at Relugas', a lodge in the far north-east of Scotland. There, early in September 1905 the three Liberal Imperialist leaders met, and agreed upon a plan. They referred to it later as the Relugas Compact.

They resolved that when Campbell-Bannerman became Prime Minister he should at once take a peerage and surrender the leadership of the Liberal Party in the House of Commons to Asquith, who would also serve in the new Cabinet as Chancellor of the Exchequer. They further agreed that if Campbell-Bannerman refused to accept this condition none of the three would join any Government he might try to construct. They also felt that Grey should become the new Foreign Minister, and that Haldane should go to the Woolsack as Lord Chancellor. By the terms of the Relugas plan Campbell-Bannerman, after six trying years as the leader of a bickering party, was to be removed from his place in the very hour of victory.

The Liberal Imperialists proposed to dominate his Government from the start of its life. They proposed to master the Radical wing of their party by seizing the chief offices in the Ministry for themselves.

They were clear that care must be taken not to embarrass the King by their arrangements. With this object in mind Haldane told King Edward of the plan, and succeeded in winning his support for it.

However, it was now Sir Henry Campbell-Bannerman's turn to exercise his mind over the plums of political office. He acted with sure instinct and unobtrusive skill. He knew that Haldane was hostile to him. And he understood the nature of Asquith's ambition. On November 13, 1905, he arranged for Asquith to call upon him.

After a few preliminaries Sir Henry suddenly declared that the King might ask him to form a Government in the very near future. He then said to Asquith: 'What would you like? The Exchequer, I suppose?' He went on: 'I hear that it has been suggested by that ingenious person, Richard Burdon Haldane, that I should go to the House of Lords . . .' He emphasised that it would be extremely distasteful for him to follow that course.[1]

[1] For these details see Margot Asquith, *Autobiography* (London, 1922), vol II, pp. 66 ff.

When Asquith came away from this meeting he knew that he would be the next Liberal Chancellor of the Exchequer.[1]

It was also clear that the Relugas Compact had enjoyed only a month of vigorous life, and that it was no longer so vital an issue in politics. Campbell-Bannerman had succeeded in separating Asquith from his friends. Asquith had agreed to join the new Ministry without conditions, although he did argue that Grey should become Foreign Minister and Haldane Lord Chancellor. Asquith crippled, or at least seriously weakened, the Relugas Compact a few weeks after he had helped to construct it.[2]

Later, when Balfour resigned in December, Sir Henry proceeded to form his Ministry. For a time Grey and Haldane refused to join him. Asquith, however, explained to his friends that it was his duty to become a member of the Government for the sake of Free Trade and the future of their party. The conditions were fundamentally different, he said, from those contemplated at Relugas. The party had not yet won the election, and if he remained aloof the fate of Liberalism and all that it stood for would be placed in danger.[3]

The Liberals were required to form their Government before the election as a result of Balfour's tactics. It was for this reason that he resigned office instead of dissolving Parliament. Had he dissolved, the Liberals would not have been confronted by the problem until after their victory at the polls, and then with success already assured, all would have been easy for them. Balfour hoped that the Liberals might quarrel among themselves in their pre-election Cabinet making, and that the public might get a glimpse of their lack of unity and vote accordingly. The object of his resignation was to force the Liberals to form an Administration before the country went to the polls, and not after.

But Asquith's argument in this situation was not wholly accurate. His decision was largely made at his meeting with Campbell-Bannerman on November 13, more than a fortnight before Balfour resigned.

It had been arranged then that he should be Chancellor. He failed to press the point that Campbell-Bannerman should relinquish the leadership of the Commons to him. He abandoned the Relugas Compact before the problems created by Balfour's resignation arose. Of course he always desired to achieve the objects of Relugas, throughout the period September-December 1905.

[1] Spender, op. cit., vol. I, p. 172, baldly declares of this meeting of November 13 that: 'It was arranged . . . that he should be Chancellor of the Exchequer. . . .'

[2] The conclusion in a brilliant biography, S. McKenna, *Reginald McKenna* (London, 1948), p. 21, is to the point: '. . . the Relugas Compact had collapsed at a hint from Campbell-Bannerman. . . .'

[3] Asquith's explanation is well stated in Sir F. Maurice, *Haldane* (London, 1937), vol I, pp. 155 ff.; and repeated in Roy Jenkins, *Asquith* (London, 1964), pp. 151 ff. In his *History of the English People* (London, 1952), p. 6, Halevy refers to Grey and Haldane as being 'deserted' by Asquith. This was also Haldane's opinion. See Dudley Sommer, *Haldane of Cloan* (London, 1960), p. 149.

But he never, in all these weeks, presented an ultimatum to Campbell-Bannerman, despite the Relugas agreement. He urged his leader to accept the arguments of Grey and Haldane. He never insisted.

It seems reasonable to conclude that Asquith demonstrated a certain skill in these developments. By cleaving to Sir Henry Campbell-Bannerman he made sure of his own position as successor to the older man. Sir Henry's health at that time was not good. Everyone believed that his Premiership must be of short duration.

And that is how the affair turned out. Two years later from his sick-bed in Downing Street Sir Henry surrendered his high office; and was replaced by his Chancellor of the Exchequer, in April 1908.

*

Asquith acted even more decisively in the crisis of May 1915. At that time the war was going badly. Lloyd George upon the one hand, and the mass of the Tories upon the other, were critical of the conduct of affairs.

For his part Asquith pursued one cardinal object during his years as War Minister. This object was the preservation of national unity.

In order to control the grumblings of his critics Asquith decided to accept the proposal of Lloyd George and Bonar Law that a Coalition Government should be formed. By this device, the Prime Minister believed, he would be in a position to arbitrate or mediate between the different factions. Power would remain in his hands. Discord would be confined to his Coalitiion Ministry, where he could control it. And national unity in war, his chief goal as the King's First Minister, would be upheld in the hour of crisis and danger.

Unfortunately, for base and unworthy reasons, the Tories insisted that Haldane must not be a member of the Coalition Government. Bonar Law, harsh and unyielding, made it clear that his party would not join the new arrangement unless Haldane were excluded.

R. B. Haldane, in Asquith's own phrase, was the 'oldest personal and political friend I have in the world . . .' Haldane had served the Liberal Ministry with distinction for nearly a decade. But the Prime Minister required the co-operation of Bonar Law and the Tories, for a high national purpose. Haldane was instantly excluded from the new Ministry. He was banished.

There can be no doubt that Asquith was bitterly distressed. It is equally clear that his friend was thrown out in a brutal fashion. Asquith's biographer has written of this incident: 'It is a fact that can only be recorded that Asquith omitted to write to Lord Haldane . . . No doubt he had intended to see him, but the moment passed and Haldane went in silence . . . the omission inflicted a wound which was never quite healed.'[1]

If these words mean to imply that Haldane's case was forgotten in the press of more urgent business they are surely curious. It is impossible to forget the Lord Chancellor. It cannot be done; not even by a Prime Minister.

[1] Spender, *Asquith*, vol. II, p. 167.

Asquith's political course was dictated by cruel necessity. But his failure to communicate with Haldane cannot be defended. He trampled upon the feelings of his oldest friend despite the pain the episode undoubtedly caused him. Asquith's daughter, Lady Violet Bonham Carter, fittingly, an ardent partisan in her father's cause has written: 'My father's failure to see or write to Haldane I cannot defend though knowing him, I understand it. It was due not to lack of feeling but to its intensity. He . . . often . . . left the deepest things . . . unsaid.'[1]

*

Henry Asquith was a creature of flesh and blood who struggled with mighty issues: 'Against him were ranged all the stolid Conservative forces of England'. When the political occasion required it, he could, and did, act with ruthless harshness.

As Winston Churchill wrote of him in *Great Contemporaries*: 'In affairs he had that ruthless side without which great matters cannot be handled . . . a stern, ambitious, intellectually proud man fighting his way with all necessary ruthlessness . . . Not "all done by kindness"! Not all by rosewater! These were the convulsive struggles of a man of action and of ambition at death-grips with events . . .'

Judged by any reasonable standard, and measured against that of the other statesmen of his day, the record of his achievement can survive any test. It does not require the ridiculous eulogies of the panegyrists who came after him. Asquith was a great statesman. He made great sacrifices in the public service. He was not the plaster saint of a spurious legend that has been built up around his name.

[1] Lady Violet Bonham Carter in *The Times*, November 2, 1964. In this article Lady Violet also writes in connection with the crisis of 1915: 'To part with Winston Churchill who had given brilliant service . . . would be an act of gross injustice.' But there are many signs that Asquith, by that date, was annoyed by Churchill's vigorous actions. And by 1916 Asquith's wife, the famous Margot, could write to Arthur Balfour that: '. . . Winston . . . is a hound . . . a fool of the lowest judgement, & contemptible . . .' Of course, Asquith cannot be held responsible for his wife's effusions. But in this letter she reports Asquith's anger with Churchill; and the whole may be looked upon as indicative; as another sign. Margot's letter is preserved in B.M. Add. MSS. (Balfour Papers), and is dated March 8, 1916, 10 Downing Street, Whitehall.

JAMES JOLL

Rathenau and Harden: A Footnote to the History of Wilhelmine Germany

JAMES JOLL

Rathenau and Harden: A Footnote to the History of Wilhelmine Germany

ONE of the many paradoxes of Germany in the reign of William II is the contrast between the powerlessness of the imperial parliament and the vitality of the opposition to the Kaiser's régime expressed by publicists and satirists. It was as if the very irresponsibility of the Kaiser's personal rule gave rise to criticism which, though vigorous, pointed and radical, was yet in the last resort as irresponsible as the system it attacked. Throughout the decades before the First World War a number of eminent and sincere Germans were deeply worried about the nature and direction of German politics and society; the historian Theodor Mommsen, for example, talked of his inner estrangement from his people. Yet these men were powerless to influence the course of events or to check or even hold out against the prevailing trends; and, when the Empire finally collapsed in 1918, many of them were unable to give to the new Republic the loyalty and support it desperately needed if it was to survive. Their criticism of the Kaiser's Germany had either been wholly negative or else their remedies had little relation to the realities of German history and politics.

Two men are in some ways typical of many such critics—Walther Rathenau and Maximilian Harden. They were for a time close friends but ended as bitter enemies, and, while their personal feelings for each other are a subject for a psychologist as much as for a historian, their relationship throws some light on contemporary German society as well as on their own characters and perhaps also suggests some of the special problems confronting critics of a régime who have no direct political means at their disposal for actually changing the system they are attacking.

Harden and Rathenau could hardly be more different in origin or indeed in temperament. Harden[1] had a sad childhood and grew up in poverty in a home

[1] On Harden's life see: Harry F. Young, *Maximilian Harden—Censor Germaniae* (The Hague, 1959); Erich Gottgetreu, *Maximilian Harden: Ways and Errors of a Publicist*, in Year Book VII of the Leo Baeck Institute (1962). There is also much interesting, though tendentious material in the book of the Nazi historian Walther Frank: '*Apostata*'. *Maximilian Harden und das Wilhelminische Deutschland* in Forschungen zur Judenfrage Band III (Hamburg, 1943).

which his mother had been obliged to leave because of the father's growing mental instability, and, at the age of fourteen, he ran away and joined a travelling theatrical company. Shortly afterwards he abandoned his own name, Felix Witkowski, and took that of Maximilian Harden. He seems to have had some success as an actor and in fact never lost his histrionic gifts; he was a noted lecturer later in his life and he always had the actor's gift of assuming a new role, even if it was inconsistent with a previous one, and of simulating passion in such a way that it is impossible to say where sincerity ends and hypocrisy begins. His devotion to the theatre however, was genuine; and his theatrical criticism, his essays on Ibsen or on the actress Réjane, for example, remain among his best work, while Rathenau was to single out for special praise an article on Hofmannsthal's *Electra* published in 1904, in which, incidentally, Harden showed that he was already familiar with the work of Freud.

However, by the time Harden was thirty, it was as a journalist that he was making his reputation and, from 1892 on, he had his own weekly paper, *Die Zukunft*, which rapidly became famous for its ruthless attacks on public abuses and its exposure of political scandal as well as for the high quality of its literary and scientific contributions. Harden's talents as a polemical journalist attracted Bismarck's attention, and in his embittered retirement, the old man used Harden on a number of occasions as a mouthpiece for his attacks on the Kaiser. Harden was from time to time a guest in Bismarck's house and became and remained a close friend of Dr Schweninger, Bismarck's personal physician. Bismarck's patronage undoubtedly laid the foundations of Harden's public career and Bismarck's encouragement set the pattern for his attacks on the Kaiser and his friends, as well as providing him with information which he was later able to use with good effect when he began to mount his all-out attack on Philipp Fürst zu Eulenburg and the other members of the 'camarilla' which he believed, probably rightly, to be dominating the Kaiser. However, although Harden's association with Bismarck, like many others of his friendships, furthered his career, his admiration for the old Prince may well have been genuine, as when he writes of the Wotan-like figure in Lenbach's famous portrait:

> With a mastery worthy of Rembrandt, [Lenbach] has painted the Bismarck of history and myth; the iron seer and herald of new ideals brooding over great things and unscrupulously forging ahead on paths opened up by himself.[1]

In so far as Harden had any consistent aim in his political polemics, it was perhaps to recall Germany to the Bismarckian paths from which it had strayed.

By the Nineties, then, when Walther Rathenau first made his acquaintance, Harden was already established, and *Die Zukunft* a success (at its peak it was to have a circulation of 22,000). Its editor was a touchy, vain man of considerable political courage—in 1898 and in 1900 he served terms of imprisonment

[1] Quoted from an article in *Die Gegenwart*, 1892, by Gottgetreu: *Maximilian Harden*, p. 222

for his outspoken attacks on the Kaiser—widely respected and also widely feared. Harden was not without human affections; his devotion to his young daughter and later to his friend Frau E.S. were genuine enough. But he had made his own way in the world independently of his family—two of his brothers made successful careers in business and the law, but it was characteristic of the family that they had taken a different name from either their father or Harden—and his friendships were nearly always uneasy, strained and at the mercy of his neurotic and suspicious temperament.

Walther Rathenau[1] first began to contribute to *Die Zukunft* in 1895, and made Harden's personal acquaintance soon afterwards. He was then about thirty years old, and the heir to the vast electrical business which his father, Emil Rathenau, had founded. Walther was by this time independently successful as an industrialist and financier, but was longing even more for a literary reputation and intellectual recognition. Although, unlike Harden, he had close family ties—a mother to whom he was devoted, a father of whom he wrote: 'We discovered each other late. First came respect, then friendship and finally love,'[2]—he was nevertheless a lonely man, constantly seeking ideal friendships, especially after the death of his much-loved younger brother in 1903, and as constantly being disappointed in them. All his life he was deeply aware of the contrasts and contradictions in his own nature, financier and intellectual, millionaire and ascetic and, above all, Prussian patriot and Jew. His early contributions to *Die Zukunft*, which were his first bid for recognition as a thinker, illustrate some of his preoccupations. In 1895 he published an expert factual article on the German electrical industry, while in 1897 he published one of his most notorious essays, *Höre, Israel*. This was in fact a contorted piece of Jewish anti-semitism and an attack on those characteristics of his fellow Jews on which anti-semitic propagandists always seized: 'They live in a half-voluntary invisible ghetto and are not a living limb of the people but a foreign organism in its body,' a typical passage runs.[3]

These were views which Harden largely shared. Although he had dissociated himself from Judaism to an extent which Rathenau never did, and had been formally baptised into the Lutheran Church, he never denied his Jewish origins. On the other hand, he was always ready to denounce the same aspects of the Jewish character as Rathenau attacked in his essay, and he has been called an example of 'Jewish self-hatred'.[4] It was typical that, like some other radical figures in Germany, including the Social Democrat

[1] Harry Kessler, *Walther Rathenau: His Life and Work* (English translation, London, 1929), remains the best study of Rathenau. A more recent biography is Hellmuth M. Böttcher, *Walther Rathenau* (Bonn, 1958). See also, for an analysis of his character and thought, James Joll, *Walther Rathenau: Prophet without a Cause*, in *Intellectuals in Politics* (London, 1960).

[2] Letter to Wilhelm Schwaner June 30, 1915. *Walther Rathenau: ein Preussischer Europäer. Briefe*, ed. M. von Eynern (Berlin, 1955), p. 137.

[3] *Die Zukunft*, March 6, 1897.

[4] Theodor Lessing, *Judische Selbsthass* (Berlin, 1930), includes an essay on Harden.

leader Wilhelm Liebknecht, he was anti-Dreyfusard. Harden in his paper alleged that the Affair would never have assumed the proportions it did, if Dreyfus had not been a Jew and if the Jews had not banded together to make a great issue of it. It is true, however, that he could not deny his admiration for Zola's stand; he was an admirer of his writing and wrote an excellent essay on it, and Zola's appearance in court after the publication of *J'Accuse* must have reminded him of his own recurrent defiance of the libel laws.

From 1897 Rathenau was a frequent contributor to *Die Zukunft*, anonymously or under the pseudonyms Renatus, W. Hartenau, Ernst Reinhart or Ernst Rainer. How close politically he stood to Harden at this period is shown by the fact that one of his anonymous articles in 1898 was believed to be by Harden and was cited as evidence against Harden when he was accused of *Majestätsbeleidigung*. Rathenau appeared in the witness-box, protested that he was a Monarchist and National-Liberal, admitted authorship of the article, and that particular item in the charge was withdrawn. The article in question was in a form which Rathenau used several times during this period—an allegory in the form of a legend set in biblical Palestine, based on his knowledge of traditional Jewish writing. In this case, while it clearly did have a reference to contemporary Germany, it was the mildest of parables about the results of bad government, and in fact very different in style and tone from Harden's much more direct attacks.

However, Rathenau's contributions to *Die Zukunft* were not at this point primarily political. What his association with Harden offered him was an opportunity to think of himself as a serious writer and philosopher. His articles ranged from travel sketches and allegorical parables and fables to portentous essays on morals and aesthetics. They included a satirical piece about American burial customs, foreshadowing Evelyn Waugh and Jessica Mitford, but their main purpose was to outline the ideas which were to recur in Rathenau's later writings, in which a mystical belief in vague spiritual values is contrasted with the materialism of the twentieth century, although this did not prevent Rathenau from writing some rather more hard-headed articles on economic problems and questions of business administration. It is hard to think that these contributions to *Die Zukunft* aroused much enthusiasm. Its readers were used to something more original; in addition to Harden's own pungent political commentary, the magazine included stories by many prominent contemporary writers—Maupassant, Kipling, Gorky, Maeterlinck and Chekov, for example: Rilke was a regular reviewer, and there were occasional articles by A. J. Balfour and Beatrice Webb. The reader could expect each week serious and expert criticism of art and music, as well as frequent articles on scientific and medical subjects, which devoted much space to the new ideas about sex which the work of Krafft-Ebbing and Magnus Hirschfeld were beginning to make familiar to advanced circles. When, in 1906, Harden launched the most notorious of his political campaigns and suggested that Prince Eulenburg and other members of the Kaiser's intimate circle were homosexual, the topic was one with which his readers had had plenty of opportunities of becoming familiar.

However, Harden offered Rathenau more than an opportunity of publishing his work and establishing himself as a literary figure. He seemed to Rathenau to promise the friendship of another outsider, a man who rejected the social and political values of Wilhelmine Germany as completely as he was beginning to do himself. Rathenau and Harden had become friends. In Rathenau's letters, of which Harden kept copies[1], the tone changes from the formal discussion of economic problems, arising out of articles in *Die Zukunft* on Germany's food imports, to that of a growing intimacy: 'I will not send you my portrait but will bring it around on the first fine evening.'[2] In the summer of 1900 they were having discussions about a possible holiday together in Brighton. They met regularly, although this was not always easy. Rathenau was often away on business trips, and Harden worked unbelievably hard; there were many occasions when he wrote a large part of each issue of *Die Zukunft* himself, and it was a paper which appeared weekly—unlike *Die Fackel* in Vienna, a comparable one-man undertaking, the editor of which, Karl Kraus, passed through the stages of being a friend of Harden and then a bitter enemy.

Harden himself seems to have been pleased and flattered by Rathenau's warmth and growing affection; but he was never a man to give his friendship for nothing, and there seems little doubt from the correspondence that Rathenau was useful to him in giving him inside information about the world of industry and finance of which Rathenau was an increasingly prominent member, and thus providing material for the excellent financial and business column which 'Pluto' published in *Die Zukunft* week by week. It seems also that Rathenau helped Harden through some of the paper's financial difficulties. In August 1904 he made a donation of 4,000 marks, and towards the end of the year, when *Die Zukunft*'s difficulties were made worse by the fact that the printers whom Harden used had gone bankrupt, Rathenau was advising on a reorganisation of the paper's financial arrangements.

Thus both Rathenau and Harden got something out of their relationship; and for both of them their friendship offered an intellectual companionship which each could accept. Certainly Harden's friendship helped to console

[1] This correspondence is in the Harden *Nachlass* in the Federal German Archives at Koblenz. I am most grateful to Mr Hartmut Pogge von Strandmann for drawing my attention to it and for much help, criticism, and advice in the preparation of this essay. Harden's letters to Rathenau seem mostly to have disappeared. The copies of Rathenau's letters in the Harden *Nachlass* are in typescript and were made after Harden's death. Their accuracy is attested by a notary's certificate, but it is not always possible to date them accurately in cases where Rathenau used the day of the week or month without specifying the year. Letters quoted here are from this collection unless otherwise stated. According to Helmuth Rogge, the *Nachlass* was edited by Harden's widow after his death. See his general account of the papers in the introduction to his *Holstein und Harden* (Munich, 1959).

[2] Rathenau to Harden, April 28, 1900.

Rathenau for the death of his brother Erich in 1903; and it was doubtless to please him that Harden published an appreciative obituary by the well-known social scientist Professor Georg Adler, which Erich, whatever his personal qualities, would not otherwise have earned on the strength of one modest contribution to *Die Zukunft* on advances in electrical technology. Afterwards, Harden was scrupulous in sending his condolences to Rathenau each year on the anniversary of Erich's death. But Rathenau constantly wanted more out of all his friendships.

> You write to me in the most friendly terms, [he says in a letter to Harden in the summer of 1905] and I have to answer that I am furious with you. In three hours you did not say one word that you had something on your mind. I would have come today, if it were not Monday, *pour vous confesser*. Is this friendship? Your punishment will be to see your money go down the drain (*Ihr ganzen Mammon flöten gehen*) bloody jobber you are.[1] Differdingen up, Hofmann down, Japan broke. Please tell me what is depressing you! Otherwise I shall come in the middle of your work.

However, Rathenau was too sensitive and touchy a man to work for long with any editor, however great a friend he might be, without there being trouble. In October 1905, for instance, he published an article 'On Modern Painting', in which, characterically enough, he neither mentioned a single specific painting nor a single artist by name, but used the opportunity to reject what was happening in contemporary society. The article was not a success; Julius Meier-Graefe, a leading authority on contemporary art and a regular contributor to *Die Zukunft*, wrote to Harden disagreeing and apparently taking personal exception to part of Rathenau's article. 'I do not want to hurt anyone, God knows,' Rathenau wrote to Harden. 'But what are a few obscure lines to an experienced publicist?' And a few days later he continued:

> I am deeply depressed by the failure of my essay . . . You will think me mad if I tell you that people will in good time unearth every sentence I have written and turn it over and over. For the two basic laws which have never yet been expressed, are in it. And living men, to whom I should like to speak from time to time, allow me to rot. . . . If I humiliate myself enough to send this letter, you must excuse it on our friendship.

Harden on this occasion succeeded in pacifying and reassuring Rathenau, but this was not always the case, and at the end of 1906 there was a bitter quarrel which neither of them ever forgot. It started with the usual trouble all editors expect: Harden rejected an article by Rathenau.

> You have spared me the decisions [Rathenau wrote on December 20]. 24 hours before the *Zukunft* went to press and two hours before the departure of my train for Mülheim I found the returned article. I must be grateful to you, for you have preserved my political virginity and acted in a far-sighted and providential way . . .

[1] English in the original.

Harden was clearly upset at the idea that he had not informed Rathenau of his decision until the last minute—he had expected him to receive his letter a day earlier—and apparently tried to suggest that, as they did not agree on certain political questions and methods, they should agree not to discuss certain subjects. For Rathenau, with his all-or-nothing view of friendship, this was quite unacceptable.

> How can we 'strictly' exclude whole areas of life from our relationship? What strange situations that is bound to produce! If we hold different views about objective topics what has that to do with our human relations? And how does this wish relate to the events of the last few days? I cannot understand. . . . You say that my political judgment is inadequate. I accept this gladly and without ill-humour, for I regard any criticism of and reservation about my personality as justified as long as it is not an end in itself. But I do contest your premise that continuous preoccupation with personalities is a basic condition for judging a situation. For when you say that for a year on end I do not bother about such things, you are thinking of personalities. That I do not lack a certain insight into situations I consider one of the few justifications for my activity. . . . I can also not agree with you that you would be able 'sentence for sentence' to oppose my errors with objective truth or *conductio ad absurdum*; not because I doubt your authority, but because I cannot believe in an apodeictic doctrine in matters of ethical, social or political opinion.

Rathenau ended his letter with affectionate Christmas greetings, and sent Harden as a present an 'old tea-kettle as a warming, never-rusting symbol'.

Harden was not satisfied; and Rathenau wrote again on Christmas Day:

> I thought you had found in me a lack of understanding of personalities; you now say it is more: lack of understanding of the constitution, of contemporary history, of legislation. Whether you are right or wrong, you are my friend and cannot hurt me. You cannot want to, and you cannot do so; do not read between the lines; there is and was nothing between them. But there is one strange thing: you feel that I underestimate your importance. My dear friend, I am too proud to flatter anyone, and yet I have told you a hundred times in plain words what I think and expect of you. Do you think that was just a passing mood or a half-hearted opinion? And do you think I want to see your own particular field encroached on, a field in which, if I recognise any authority, it is yours?
>
> If I deny the Absolute in questions of opinion—and thus can, at a pinch consider 'proved' mechanical and material things, police-court facts, but never the picture, the connection, the contact—is that a rejection? Is that to doubt your value? What is more, objective topics, even when illuminated with the inmost light radiating from soul and intellect, can neither now nor ever confuse my inner relationship to another person. . . . On the contrary. If you were more like me, you would never have become of such value in my life. To hell with it (*Und zum Teufel*): I like you and tell you so and you can do what you like, in your heart you are not serious with your coldness.
>
> So this is the last note I exchange with you: I cannot bear this tone and I shall come and see you today or tomorrow. I cannot put up with being a friend of

someone for years and then starting from the beginning again. Dear friend, humanity is the highest thing in life. We are both too old to learn afresh.

It is an episode which needs to be set against the background of Harden's public activities at this period. It was in the summer of 1906 that Harden found a new friend and ally, Friedrich von Holstein. This strange relationship has been analysed by Mr Hellmuth Rogge and Professor Norman Rich,[1] and only two points need be noted here. First, as in the case of Rathenau, Harden seems to have been drawn to a lonely difficult character, but one who could also be of considerable political and journalistic use to him; and Holstein, solitary, ageing and ailing in his retirement after being the most influential man in the German Foreign Ministry, seems to have felt a genuine affection and warmth for Harden and his family. Secondly, it was with Holstein as his confidant and ally, though not, as was once supposed, as his direct inspirer, that Harden embarked on the most notorious of all his campaigns, that against the Kaiser's intimate friend and adviser, Philipp Eulenburg. In this campaign, Rathenau could not be of much help, and it seems almost certain that this is what underlies Harden's accusations that Rathenau did not understand the importance of personalities in politics. Indeed, as Rathenau wrote in July 1906, a few months before the campaign against Eulenburg got under way (though it is not clear what he is referring to): 'I can't be of any use to you, and all this goes against the grain with me—lawyers in action, lawsuits, personal attacks, consultations'.

Thus the period of coldness between the two men which followed the episode of Christmas 1906 came at a time when Harden needed Rathenau's help less than on earlier occasions, and when his friendship with Holstein—which gave him, among other things, a channel of communication with Bülow, the Imperial Chancellor—was more important than that with Rathenau. However, after a few months, something like the old intimacy, if not the old professional collaboration was re-established. In June 1907, for example, Harden was the first person, after his father and his immediate business colleagues, whom Rathenau told about his forthcoming official trip to Africa with Dernburg, the Colonial Secretary. (He sailed from Naples on July 15 and was away until the end of October.) But by now the limitations of their friendship were clearer, and Rathenau expressed them well, as well as revealing some of his own basic political attitudes, in a letter written at the height of Harden's involvement in the lawsuits arising out of his attacks on Eulenburg:[2]

Our friendship has lasted for more than twelve years. I am well and gratefully aware what it has meant to me, and believe that it has been fruitful for us both. We are no longer of an age when one can form new friendships; and it is rare enough if one can find a man whom one can love. Therefore, Maxim, we must

---

[1] Hellmuth Rogge, *Holstein und Harden* (Munich, 1959); Norman Rich, *Friedrich von Holstein* (2 vols., Cambridge, 1965).

[2] Rathenau to Harden, April 11, 1908.

stick together all our lives. You will have to accept my many weak points, but I believe they will be softened by loyalty and affection, and when you remember your worst moments, then you will feel that I supported you morally (*herzlich*) and, as far as I could, physically (*leiblich*). Only two things are impossible for me; I mention them although I know that in a calm mood you have never asked them of me and will never ask them: I can be nobody's partisan, and I shall not be afraid of any man, even of you. Independence has imposed great sacrifices on me. Fearlessness can lay claim to a life which, though full of mistakes like anything human, yet only wanted what was good, wanted it with honourable means and wished harm to nobody . . .

It was just this refusal wholly to commit himself which kept Rathenau somewhat aloof from the Eulenburg affair; and the fact that he was away in Africa for several months in 1907 and again in 1908 may well have saved the friendship, for a few years longer at least. It was typical of the limitations of Rathenau's support for Harden and of his reluctance to be a partisan that, when in December 1907 there was some question of a public statement in support of Harden in his polemical attacks against Eulenburg, Rathenau refused to sign and wrote to Harden:

I do not know whether you have been told about this plan, which is doubtless well-intentioned. If not, you have all the same the right to test it and see whether you think the move is a sympathetic and useful one. Apart from the selection of signatories and recipients (thoroughly honourable, some of them well-known names, but notably unpolitical and including some foreigners), I wonder whether such a defence will do justice to your position and whether it can do you credit. That there are a large number of people, among whom I count myself, who love and value you, the world knows already, and rightly. Whether it is right to proclaim this in print with a political emphasis, you will be able to judge.

Harden's campaign was in fact a triumphant one. After he had alleged that Eulenburg and Count Kuno Moltke, the general commanding the Berlin garrison and an A.D.C. to the Kaiser, were homosexual, the Crown Prince at length brought these accusations to the notice of the Kaiser in May 1907. There was immediate panic at court; Eulenburg resigned his official posts and retired to his estates; Moltke was removed from his command; and several other high officers, even though they had not been directly named by Harden, lost their jobs. Moltke, after trying unsuccessfully to provoke Harden to a duel, took legal proceedings against him. This led to a complicated series of lawsuits between the two men, and also to the trial of Eulenburg on a charge of perjury. Harden was at the height of his notoriety and the most controversial figure in Germany, a man who stopped at nothing to obtain the evidence he needed (one need only read the cross-examination which he instigated of a fisherman from the Starnberger See, who eventually broke down and incriminated Eulenburg, to see how far Harden and his lawyers would go—a cross-examination proudly published in full in *Die*

Zukunft).[1] One cannot help feeling that it was a good thing that anyone as fastidious as Rathenau was not more closely involved. In the early stages Bülow was anxious to hush up the scandal as much as possible and Rathenau seems to have been asked to persuade Harden to reach some agreement with Moltke without going to court—an attempt which was also made by other friends of Harden, including Baron Berger, the director of the Hamburg theatre, and Count Ernst Reventlow, a frequent contributor to *Die Zukunft* on international affairs and an extreme Pan-German nationalist who was to end as a Nazi supporter. These attempts were quite unsuccessful, and Rathenau did not play any further part, limiting himself to expressions of sympathy for Harden and to a warm, even if double-edged message of congratulation—

> I read the report of the trial yesterday morning between 7 and 8 in one go. Since the glorious time of Lassalle, nothing like it has been seen in a German law-court. Bravo Maxim![2]

But one cannot help feeling that after his return from the second trip to Africa—a trip which had, it seems, considerably strained his relationship with Dernburg—he was speaking for himself as much as for Harden when he wrote on Christmas Eve 1908—

> My Christmas greetings today find you, thank God, in a much better situation than a year ago and in a more cheerful mood. May the coming year hold nothing but good for you and bring you what you wish for!

The year did in fact bring an end to the Eulenburg affair, even if an inconclusive one, with Eulenburg spared further humiliation in the courts because of his ill health, and Harden finally persuaded to accept a contribution to his legal expenses from the Hamburg shipping magnate, Albert Ballin, at the suggestion of Bülow, in return for not taking his lawsuit with Moltke to a higher court. In the meantime, too, Holstein had died, and during 1910 relations between Harden and Rathenau seemed to be on something like the old footing. Rathenau continued to give Harden confidential information about his financial activities. In May 1910, for instance, he was in Paris involved in the complicated negotiations by which the Mannesmann brothers, in the interests of their own economic ambitions in Morocco, were trying to break up the co-operation between France and Germany resulting from the Agreement of 1909 and from the collaboration of Krupp and Thyssen with the French in the Union des Mines Marocaines. Rathenau was acting as confidential representative for the Mannesmann brothers in an attempt to reach an agreement with their rivals, but he had to abandon the attempt as the Mannesmanns apparently would not accept the compromise he had arranged.[3]

[1] May 9 and 16, 1908.

[2] The letter is dated May 1, but no year is given. It would seem to be 1908.

[3] Ernst Jäckh (ed.), *Kiderlen-Wächter, der Staatsmann und Mensch* (Berlin-Leipzig, 1925), p. 120.

A letter to Harden on May 31, 1910, gives the atmosphere of the conversations in Paris, the failure of which was to contribute to the Moroccan crisis of the following year:

> Briefly, hurriedly and in strict confidence you shall have the first report I have written about the affair. The complication is incredible, the prospects still poor. You are right in your judgment about the Ambassador [Prince Radolin]; however, yesterday he left for Kissingen which I hope will do both him and us good. The government is not unfriendly, Pichon [French Foreign Minister], with whom I finally came to deal as the matter falls under his department, a stout, sensible bourgeois, not at all unreliable. In the Embassy there are two good friends, Lancken and Mutius who do what I advise them. Matters are harder with the *Union des Mines* headed by a first-class industrialist (Darcy of Chatillon-Commentrie); they know what they want and have as little opinion of German 'rights' as of the mineral deposits with which they are concerned. Perhaps they are wrong about the latter. But the most complicated thing of all is the behaviour of the crazy brothers who madden each other, never let the telephone and telegraph out of their hands and throw themselves body and soul into back-stairs politics, half Sherlock Holmes, half Monte Cristo. Fortunately my work here is not yet known, otherwise in addition to the internal difficulties the technical external ones would be extremely fatal—rendez-vous at limited times and only possible after considerable preparation. I have seen nothing of Paris except a quadrilateral of grey or blue sky above my gable. The heir to the Turkish throne and d'Annunzio are living in the same hotel—both invisible.

However, although the friendship between Harden and Rathenau now seemed to be on a firmer and less neurotic basis than it had been before, appearances were deceptive, and in 1912 a new crisis shattered the relationship almost beyond repair. This time the quarrel seems to have been a purely personal one and to have been the result of an indiscretion by a mutual friend who showed Harden a letter Rathenau had written in 1908 in which he sharply criticised Harden. The incident seems to have led to such intense bitterness, because it revived the complicated and resentful feelings which the previous quarrel had left behind. In Rathenau's diary[1] for April 1912, he noted 'I wrote a long, very conciliatory and warm letter to H.' The letter itself starts:

> I am deeply shocked and upset (*Ich bin aufs tiefste erschüttert*). I am terribly alarmed that I could be seized by such passionate anger, and I feel that we poor men can become helpless missiles in the hands of demonic powers. But I am not less disgusted by the fact that a woman of whom I have been deeply fond, produces documents from a time of violent feelings, coldly tests their cutting edge and drops them as a dagger to strike and poison two hearts.

For the moment the breach was averted, and during the next months, Harden was complaining that Rathenau had not contributed to *Die Zukunft* for a

[1] Walther Rathenau, *Tagebuch*, 1907–1922. Privately printed 1930. This contains some notes on his trips to Africa, a comparatively full diary for 1911–13 and a number of important political notes from the war and post-war periods.

long time. The contribution that he did eventually receive and publish in October, signed 'Herwart Raventhal', was perhaps unexpected—a series of sombre and rhetorical poems to commemorate the centenary of the German 'war of liberation' of 1813. Moreover, Rathenau was preoccupied during these months with his father's health, as Emil Rathenau had been seriously ill and had to have a leg amputated. However, the reconciliation only masked growing suspicion, which Rathenau's women friends seem to have encouraged. At the end of the year, Rathenau was complaining that Harden had repeated to the same lady who had caused the trouble earlier some critical remarks Rathenau had made about his fellow-directors of the AEG, and this seems to have involved Frau Lili Deutsch, the wife of one of them, and herself someone with whom Rathenau had an intimate, but not untroubled, friendship for many years, in the intrigues and gossip. On December 15, 1912, Rathenau noted in his diary: 'I have put in writing a categorical question to H.' His letter was brief: 'Is it true that you have repeated by telephone to the other party concerned the details of our confidential conversation of the day before yesterday?'

He was not wholly satisfied with Harden's reply and demanded a stronger denial. The tone of the correspondence becomes increasingly bitter and unfriendly. 'An unpleasant correspondence with H.' Rathenau wrote 'which I finally closed on 29 December, calmly and firmly, after a very angry and unfair letter.' Rathenau's letter was a dignified one:

> After an anxious night and repeated re-reading of your letter, I can promise myself nothing further from a fresh appeal to you. The wounding harshness of your words can mean nothing else than the wish to end our friendship. With a heavy heart I submit. We were linked for eighteen years and I am glad to think of this period with gratitude and warmth. Farewell, Maxim. The year 1913—and may it bring you all good fortune—will find us separated . . .

It was not however, as easy to end the relationship on a dignified note as Rathenau had hoped. Harden was full of resentment and seems to have tried to enlist the support of Frau Deutsch, saying—or so Rathenau alleged—that Rathenau did not deserve to have 'a beautiful and noble woman to serve as an ornament for his life'. The exchange of notes continued, cold and formal: 'Lieber Maxim' has become 'Sehr geehrter Herr Harden.' Finally, after a last attempt at reconciliation, Rathenau took the melodramatic step of challenging Harden to a duel. His second duly called on Harden and suggested pistols as the weapon; Harden refused the challenge; and there the matter ended.

It was a sad end to a friendship, which, for Rathenau at least, had seemed to hold so much—literary fame, political influence and the sense that he was not alone in his growing revulsion from many of the prevailing trends in contemporary Germany. In fact, from 1913, the year of the breach, Rathenau's influence and importance grew, while that of Harden declined. For all the violence with which *Die Zukunft* had attacked the Kaiser, the effect on the system had been negligible. True, Eulenburg, ill and disgraced, had withdrawn to his country-house, his trial adjourned indefinitely, but the advisers who had succeeded him were not much more responsible. In general, the system of personal rule seemed to be intact and, with the outbreak of war in 1914, it was even strengthened. *Die Zukunft* continued to criticise throughout the war, and was suspended on a number of occasions. But Harden, although he was celebrated and enjoyed in the war years a great reputation as a lecturer, remained an outsider, powerless to influence events. Rathenau, on the other hand, was becoming more and more a member of the German establishment, however much he may have denied it. He was entrusted by the government at the outbreak of the war with the task of organising supplies of vital war materials; and, although he held no official position after 1915, his opinions were increasingly listened to. He was a friend and neighbour of Bethmann-Hollweg; he saw the Kaiser frequently and was on excellent terms with Ludendorff and other leading figures.

Relations between Harden and Rathenau were to some extent resumed in spite of the quarrel, through the intermediacy of Rathenau's brother-in-law, Fritz Andreae. Telegrams were exchanged on birthdays and at Christmas, and, under the stress of war, they began to see each other and to write letters about political subjects,[1] though Harden remained suspicious and Rathenau complained he was misunderstood. Harden was jealous of Rathenau's growing importance, and Rathenau protested in vain that he had enemies everywhere and was just as much on every black list as Harden himself—hated by the industrialists, hated by the Social Democrats for the views expressed in his books such as *Zur Kritik der Zeit*. By the end of the war, although they shared a dislike of the revolution and the republic, they were agreed on little else.

In October 1918 Rathenau was one of the main proponents of *guerre à l'outrance* rather than of armistice, and of arming the people for a last desperate fight rather than accepting the defeat of the regular armies at the front. Harden at least had the sense to see how disastrous this would be, and he attacked Rathenau's views, so that Rathenau felt obliged to reply on October 8, 1918:

> We have fought together for the *Volkstaat*. It exists and cannot be overthrown except by a civil war, and then not permanently. I have not fought for Social Democracy, Progressives or Centre Party. Nor I think have you. We do not belong to any of these parties; these ruling parties do not govern today by means of competent delegates but rather through anonymous inter-party soviets . . . We both wanted the fall of the autocracy, not the destruction of the country. I am convinced (although I do not usually think in terms of catastrophe) that we are heading for civil war, military revolt and food strikes, sealed by the uncontrolled collapse of the front. We can only save ourselves if we win time. Whether we want it or not we shall be compelled to continue the war.

---

[1] Some of these have been published in Walther Rathenau, *Politische Briefe* (Dresden, 1927).

After the armistice had been signed and the Republic declared, both men disapproved of the way things were going. While Harden was struggling to keep *Die Zukunft* alive through all the economic and political difficulties of the post-war years (he was finally forced to cease publication late in 1922), his attacks on the previous régime were soon forgotten, or at least went unrewarded. He had long before broken with the Social Democrats. The new Democratic Party which had represented a genuine attempt to create a true liberal movement in Germany, merely seemed to him to embody the flabbiness of pre-war progressive Jewish circles. Occasionally defending an eccentric cause—the right of the Crown Prince to return to Germany, for example—he was even more of an outsider than he had ever been, and was bitterly disappointed that he had not been given a job by the republican government. (He had offered his services to Prince Max of Baden in October 1918 and had been refused.)

Rathenau, on the other hand, in spite of his previous reluctance to enter public life, and, after a brief flirtation with the Democratic Party in November 1918, his ostentatious refusal to commit himself politically, was a man of influence and importance, whose economic advice was sought by the government and who finally, in 1921, was to accept an invitation to join the government, first as Minister of Reconstruction and then as Foreign Minister. During 1919, indeed, in spite of many political disagreements with Harden, he had contributed, under his own name, several times to *Die Zukunft*—which had marked the change of régime with a change from Gothic to Roman type. And no doubt his articles were particularly welcome at a time when, more than ever before, Harden was writing whole issues himself. Rathenau continued to regret that Germany had surrendered before starting to negotiate instead of negotiating while still under arms, 'not defenceless, under enemy occupation, hungry and awaiting the enemy's orders',[1] and, once it was clear that the Treaty of Versailles would have to be signed, he urged the complete abdication of the German Government and administration so as to leave the responsibility for governing Germany wholly to the allies: 'a unique situation, the unheard of collapse of a state; but the preservation of honour and of a clear conscience.'[2] But these and a chapter from his general theoretical book *The New Society* were Rathenau's last contributions to *Die Zukunft*.

This final period of collaboration, as might have been expected from the previous pattern of the relationship, left behind renewed suspicions between Rathenau and Harden. Harden became convinced that Rathenau's acceptance of the republic was simply the result of his desire for recognition and office. He was bitterly scornful when Rathenau published an article in the *Vossische Zeitung* in April 1920, acknowledging President Ebert's qualities, soon after the Kapp putsch, during which Rathenau had called on Kapp and, according to Harden, addressed him as 'Herr Reichskanzler'. Rathenau felt obliged to answer Harden's criticisms:

[1] *Die Zukunft*, January 11, 1919. [2] *Die Zukunft*, May 31, 1919.

> You take my remark about Ebert, he wrote, 'clever, good-natured and conciliatory' and contrast it with my phrase 'I am not striving for recognition' and add 'This is unparalleled' (*Das ist ohne Beispiel*). The rebuke is wounding and unjustified. The judgment on Ebert corresponds to my conviction and was not written to obtain advantages and amenities . . . I do not feel rancour for the insult, for I know it does not come from your heart . . . You will ever find me in the state of friendship and affection in which you left me.

This time it was really the last break.

When Rathenau became Foreign Minister in 1922, all Harden's pent-up envy and resentment came out, and the attacks on Rathenau in *Die Zukunft* were almost as virulent, even if not quite as scurrilous, as any that had been launched against the Kaiser's advisers fifteen years before. He attacked, not unreasonably, the vagueness and inconsistency of Rathenau's thought. He made the obvious point that the man who wrote at the end of his book *Von kommenden Dingen* 'We do not exist for the sake of riches, we do not exist for power or even for happiness; but we exist for the glorification of the divine in human spirit', was the chairman of fourteen companies and a director of twenty-seven others. He had known Rathenau intimately at the time of his mission to Africa with Dernburg, when Rathenau felt that Bülow had not recognised his services sufficiently and let it be known that he had hoped for a high order, " 'a decoration for his evening dress', as Herr Rathenau said.[1]" Harden used his knowledge to accuse Rathenau of vanity and worldly ambition. He was able to quote from Rathenau's writings passages which showed Rathenau's contempt for the principle of collective responsibility of the Cabinet and his belief in the necessity of a strong man.[2] He mocked the rich man who professed to despise social life and yet was to be seen in the smart salons of Berlin. He wrote of Rathenau—and liked the passage so much that he quoted it word for word two months later at the time of the Treaty of Rapallo:

> Herr Rathenau is very useful in economic negotiations within limits which he cannot pass; thoroughly incompetent in the cool sizing up of what is politically possible and necessary. In history, public administration, private and public diplomacy, national and international law he has no training; he has, because he only thinks of himself, not the smallest psychological vein, not one drop of the blood which must flow in a statesman's veins; politics is one of the few things for which he lacks all talent. A schoolmaster from a provincial town or a trade union secretary would not be as dangerous as a director of the Reich's destinies as this multi-millionaire with all the abundance of his intellectual and industrial riches and technical knowledge of banking.[3]

One hears indeed all the old criticisms which had led to that first serious quarrel at the end of 1906. But Harden's last word on Rathenau was the cruellest. Rathenau was murdered by young nationalist fanatics on June 24, 1922.

[1] Wahnschaffe to Loebell, December 28, 1908 (Bundesarchiv, Koblenz. RK 927).
[2] *Die Zukunft*, January 28, 1922; February 11, 1922; February 18, 1922.
[3] *Die Zukunft*, January 28, 1922; April 22, 1922.

On July 1, a week after Rathenau's assassination, *Die Zukunft* published an article about the dead man which repeated all the charges against him with a violence of language which was under the circumstances an almost pathological example of bad taste. A short quotation is enough to give the disagreeable flavour of the whole:

> This man was at heart never a republican or even a democrat. The bitterest blow of his life was that he was never allowed to take the officer's examination in spite of eagerly serving in the *Gardekurassier* regiment; and this wound only healed after he had laboured to obtain high Prussian decorations such as only ministers, generals and court favourites hold, which he proudly and ecstatically wore . . . His sharp practical sense and his constant fear of being on the 'wrong' side, of getting onto a sinking ship, led him belatedly to recognise that democracy was necessary and a republic for the moment unavoidable; and it then became the goal of his efforts to place his exceptional gifts, which, in spite of all his attempts, had been despised by the monarchy, at the service of the republic, so that, happy at giving orders, he forgot his complaints against this nation . . .

The phrases are all the more painful because of the grain of truth they contain. Harden drew attention to Rathenau's similarity of outlook to that of his murderers and quoted long extracts from *Höre, Israel*, Rathenau's critique of the German Jews which had been published in *Die Zukunft* a quarter of a century earlier.

A week later, however, Harden revealed the ambivalence of his feelings for Rathenau, which he had already shown in a warm letter of sympathy to Rathenau's mother, and published a long account of their early association, of a trip to Italy when Rathenau had talked of leaving business and retiring to live an artistic life in Paris. But Harden had by now a new reason to ask 'Were our paths inseparable?' Nine days after Rathenau's murder, he himself was attacked and badly wounded by men of the same kind as Rathenau's assassins. For all their differences in career, outlook and temperament, they were linked by two things; both were Jews and both had tried to find a basis from which to criticise German society. Their tragedy was common to them both. It was that nobody of Jewish origins in Germany could avoid the attacks of the nationalist right, however much they may have, like Rathenau, tried to identify themselves with the Prussian tradition and German national feeling, or however much, like Harden, they proclaimed their assimilation and ridiculed, as Harden had done at the time of the Dreyfus case, Jewish solidarity and self-consciousness. Each was critical of German society, but neither was ready to identify himself with any of the political forces which might conceivably have changed that society. Each accused the other of inconsistency, and they were both right. Yet at certain moments both saw clearly what was wrong with German politics. Their involved, edgy friendship and the bitterness of their quarrels are perhaps symbolic of the difficulties of finding in Wilhelmine Germany any common ground, political, intellectual or psychological from which an assault on the whole system might have been launched.

SIR BASIL LIDDELL HART

French Military Ideas before the First World War

SIR BASIL LIDDELL HART

French Military Ideas before the First World War

A STUDY of military history brings ample confirmation of Rebecca West's mot: 'Before a war military science seems a real science, like astronomy, but after a war it seems more like astrology.'

Those who have progressed furthest in exploration of war realise that its scientific study has barely begun. They will also be the least inclined to venture upon detailed predictions. Confident prophecy is best left to generals, who as a class have a traditional fondness for it, and as prophets have no reputation to lose. We have only to recall some of their prophecies that stand on record.

It is a popular comment that each war is different from the last. Actually, a survey of the whole course of military history brings out, as a dominant fact, the remarkably gradual evolution of military methods and the slight difference of technique between one war and the next. Rarely do we find that even the contemporary experience of one war has been applied to the structure and tactics of armies when the next war overtakes them, sweeping them up like driftwood in a flood. Still more rarely has anyone taken time by the forelock and ensured victory by anticipating the trend of warfare.

The utilisation of new weapons in war has followed far behind the period at which they were technically possible or actually produced. Even Napoleon, who wrought such great changes in military methods, was curiously indifferent to the opportunity of introducing new weapons, and his era of warfare was notably unproductive, though it coincided with the spring tide of the Industrial Revolution.

So also in the American Civil War, armament lagged well behind the pace of invention. Both North and South went to war with muzzle-loading muskets, and even in the last year of the conflict breech-loading magazine rifles had only been adopted by a small proportion of the troops, who thereby had a decisive influence, out of all proportion to their numbers, in the critical battles near Atlanta and at Franklin. It was the acute verdict of the Confederate, General Alexander, that 'had the Federal infantry been armed from the first with even the breech-loaders available in 1861, the war would have been terminated within a year'.

The evolution of methods is still slower, because any step forward is usually followed by a slip backward. In *All Our Yesterdays*, H. M. Tomlinson remarked, 'The war the Generals always get ready for is the previous one.' He was wrong. The war for which they prepare is often the one before last.

If the French Army in 1914 had gone to war with the methods learnt in 1870 it would have fared much better, and the manhood of France would have suffered much less. The first post-war doctrine after 1870 was as practical as its last pre-war doctrine of 1914 was fantastic. Between the methods of 1918 and the French textbooks issued immediately after 1870 one finds only a difference of degree. But the textbooks of 1914 were far removed from 1918—as far as the Crimea.

Marshal Foch was making an appropriate confession rather than a scientific statement when he declared in 1926: 'The military mind always imagines that the next war will be on the same lines as the last. That has never been the case and never will be.'

One can well understand that in retrospect the 1914–18 war looked different to him from anything he had ever conceived, or prophesied of it, beforehand. But the conditions that dumbfounded him and his fellows were only the climax of an evolutionary process which they could have detected, but did not. Every war for half a century, since 1861, had made it plainer. Other minds did perceive it.

M. Bloch, a civilian banker of Warsaw, gave a remarkably accurate diagnosis of their essential elements in his *War of the Future*, published on the eve of the twentieth century, before he had even the data of South Africa and Manchuria to confirm his deductions. There were also military minds, if these belonged to bodies not in the seats of authority, that foresaw the coming stalemate and pointed out its chain of causation.

Captain Mayer, the French military critic, was provoked by Foch's fiery advocacy of the offensive to predict, only too well, the siege war that would engulf generals who were dreaming of mobile war without the means of mobility. He was boycotted for his audacity. So was the eminent military historian, Lt.-Colonel Grouard, when he turned from the past to the future, and forecast in 1911 exactly what would happen if the French Command adopted such a plan as they did, in 1914.

In the generation that followed the disaster of 1870, the generation of French military renaissance, the dominant figure was General Miribel, three times chief of the General Staff. Under him the General Staff was reorganised and the Army rebuilt on a new framework into which the reserve units were neatly fitted. Lastly a new plan of campaign was evolved, which took final shape in 1896 as Plan XIII. It was defensive-offensive.

The Germans were to be encouraged to commit themselves to an invasion, and when entangled they would be struck by a counter-offensive. Two wide gaps had been left in the fortified frontiers to tempt the Germans to enter and to 'canalise' their invasion. One was the 'Gap of Charmes' between Epinal and Toul, on the right centre. The other was on the extreme left, between Verdun and the Belgian frontier.

We now know that the elder—and abler—Moltke considered an attempt to work round this flank as being so dangerously exposed to a 'pinching' counterstroke from Verdun that he preferred to advance against the hardly less menacing Gap of Charmes. But both he and his successor, Waldersee, felt that the French dispositions made an attack too unfavourable to be risked. In other words, the work that was crowned by Plan XIII had ensured the security of France better than any problematical victory in battle. For the prospect of tackling such a defence, shrewdly framed and well balanced, was a strong deterrent to a German attack.

Miribel's plan posted four armies in three 'masses of manoeuvre', each to be backed up by a reserve army, and the whole assembling behind a frontier covering force. The reserve armies, placed in rear of the gaps by which the enemy might try to penetrate, had thus a role of resistance suited to their qualities. Meanwhile, the active armies, based on the fortified zones, could manoeuvre from a secure pivot to strike the invader in flank. The dislocation of the German offensive would then be followed by a thrust into Germany.

But all such ideas of defence, even as a prelude to counterstroke, were repugnant to a growing body of opinion in the Army. Its early leader was a Captain Gilbert, who ascribed the 1870 disasters chiefly to the French adoption of the defensive in tactics. It was a too simple explanation, but by its simplicity it carried conviction.

Discounting the growth of fire power, and the demonstration of its effect in such battles as Gravelotte, Gilbert appealed to the wounded vanity of his countrymen by a ringing call to revive the *furia franchese*, and by his implicit assurance that it would prove irresistible no matter what bullets might say.

By the power of his writings he stamped his impress on the rising generation of French soldiers. His views became those of the French Staff College, and of the Historical Section of the General Staff, which was described by a contemporary as 'only an emanation of him'.

One of those whom he influenced was the future Marshal Foch, who became the next link in the chain. Gilbert's influence can be seen in the historical illustrations that Foch used as well as in the way his teachings converged towards 'organising a shock both supreme and final'. That influence is also apparent in the way Foch interpreted what he read in Clausewitz, his other chief source of inspiration.

Foch's opportunity to influence French military doctrine started when, on October 31, 1895, he was appointed assistant to Colonel Bonnal, the Professor of Military History, Strategy and Applied Tactics at the *Ecole Superiëure de Guerre*. A year later he stepped into Bonnal's shoes. Bonnal had sought by study to extract the secret of Napoleon's method, and tended to ascribe it primarily to the use of a strategic advanced guard—employed to feel for and seize hold of the enemy, paralysing his freedom of action. When Foch was told that he would be Bonnal's successor, he is said to have offered a momentary objection on the score that he was not yet sufficiently sure of his principles. If the diffidence did him credit, it was based on a justified doubt.

For it becomes clear that the incompleteness of his own study was a real handicap. 'What forced me to work at my profession was having to teach it. . . . I asked myself: "What are the elements of war?" I read Clausewitz.' But only a mind already developed by years of study and reflection can dissolve Clausewitz into digestible particles.

An analysis of his books shows only too clearly that he took the philosophical basis of his theory of War direct from Clausewitz without discrimination. Thus he became an amplifier for Clausewitz's more extreme notes. In his mouth the destruction of the enemy's main army became the *only* means to the end.

This ultra-narrow view led him to disregard all other forms of pressure, naval and economic. Further, instead of seeing tactics as one of the tools of strategy, he made strategy merely a conduit pipe to tactics. 'No strategy can henceforth prevail over that which aims at tactical results, victory by fighting. Modern war knows but one argument: the tactical fact, battle.'

It is apparent that when he took over the professorial chair of 'Military History, Strategy and Applied Tactics', he tended to make the first two subjects subordinate to the third—which lay within the field of his professional experience. In other words, he was content to teach what he knew, grafting it on a general theory of war that he accepted from authority without critical examination. It is true that he told his pupils that they must learn to reason, that they must have 'freedom of mind, no prepossessions'; but he immediately qualified this by saying that they would be taught a theory which, in his words, 'would not be open to discussion'.

To this attitude of mind he was predisposed by his military training, if perhaps also by his religious faith. And he was the less likely to question the Clausewitzian foundations of his military faith because they accorded so completely with his own character, with his unquestionable strength of will and passionate conviction of the power of faith to overcome obstacles.

He was fond of quoting an aphorism of Joseph de Maistre: 'A lost battle is a battle which one believes lost; in a material sense no battle can be lost.' From this he argued: 'If defeat comes from moral causes, victory may come from moral causes also, and one may say, "A battle won is a battle we will not acknowledge to be lost."' Here he unveiled one aspect of the most fundamental truth in war. But his logic was illogical in order, and so incomplete. For the logical corollary to the argument that victory comes from moral causes is surely—'A battle won is a battle that we can persuade the enemy he has lost.'

Hence he gave too little attention to the active use of surprise, the most vital element in war, and the primary means by which one can persuade—or delude—the opponent that he has lost. Foch's teaching did not entirely ignore the use of surprise, but he narrowed it down to a mere accentuation of the physical act of concentrating superior force at one point. He dismissed the psychological subtleties practised by the pre-Napoleonic Great Captains as part of the 'old fencing' and of the despised 'small war' which had been superseded when the nation in arms came into vogue.

His teaching gave little heed to the possibilities of the defensive-offensive, to the idea, most fruitful in history, of inducing the enemy to exhaust himself in a fruitless assault and then launching a counter-stroke. It was significant that while proclaiming Napoleon as the supreme master, Foch omitted any analysis of his supreme battlepiece—Austerlitz. It was significant, too, that he completely ignored Wellington and the methods that had brought him success.

Foch followed Clausewitz also in underestimating the material factors, such as armament. He was, apparently, too engrossed in strengthening the morale of the leader to consider how the possession of superior or inferior weapons might affect the morale of the led, and react on the leader. Thus, when war came he himself was taken by surprise.

Is there a specific explanation of his disproportionate concern to strengthen the mind of the leader? Can we perhaps trace it to the disasters of 1870 and the impression they made on Foch's mind? He was determined to correct the sense of inferiority which those disasters had produced in the French Army. But in Foch's own concern, which led to a one-sided form of teaching, a psycho-analyst would probably detect a deep-seated 'inferiority complex'.

To make matters worse, he arrived, on purely mathematical grounds, at the astonishingly wrong conclusion that 'any improvement in firearms is bound to strengthen the offensive'. If he had but examined history critically, especially the American Civil War, he would have found ample evidence of the growing power of defence over attack.

His teaching on the moral side was admirably calculated to fortify the powers of resistance and endurance. But, he was encouraged by his disregard of the material side to become, paradoxically, the advocate of the offensive. And the generation of his pupils, running to extremes as is the way of disciples, exalted the will to conquer into a catch-phrase specific of victory.

Foch's influence became paramount when in 1908 he was made commandant of the French *Ecole de Guerre*. Indoctrinated with the theory of mass and obsessed with the virtues of the offensive, Foch's disciples came to believe that they had only to attack with sufficient ardour to be certain of conquering.

Most powerful of all, for France, was the influence of Colonel de Grandmaison, Foch's prize pupil, who became the leader of the younger school, staged a *coup d'état* within the army, and unseated its reigning chief. Joffre was enthroned in his place, as a chief conveniently devoid of original ideas.

Then, using Joffre as a Delphic oracle, Grandmaison proclaimed the new doctrine and the excommunication of all who dared to question it.

> The French Army, returning to its traditions, no longer knows any other law than the offensive . . . All attacks are to be pushed to the extreme . . . to charge the enemy with the bayonet in order to destroy him . . . This result can only be obtained at the price of bloody sacrifice. Any other conception ought to be rejected as contrary to the very nature of war.

After recasting the official doctrine in an imitation that was a travesty of Napoleon's, Grandmaison's next step was to make ready the human sacrifice. To this end he went beyond Napoleon to the Prussian model of Frederick, and aimed at a discipline of the muscles, not of the mind, sacrificing initiative in order, by an incessant repetition, to develop in the soldier the reflexes of obedience.

This crazy structure was crowned by a new war plan, blindly offensive, in which all the available forces were to hurl themselves on the enemy, sacrificing the immense defensive advantages provided by their own fortified frontier, and its value as a means to a truly economic distribution of force.

The weak point of 'the will to conquer' was shown in August 1914, when bullets—the hardest of facts—proved that they could overcome the will of the stoutest commander by their effect on the bodies of his men. It was proved again at ever-rising cost in countless abortive attacks, too many of them directed by Foch himself—until at last commanders took to heart the lesson that the will to conquer is powerless without a preparatory advantage, moral or material. That its point will only be blunted if its path is not prepared by surprise or by superior weapon-power.

The theory of mass suffered as rude a shock. Calculated to achieve success by a process of concentrating superior numbers at a so-called decisive spot, the formula was nullified by the mechanical progress which made one man sitting behind a machine the superior of a hundred, sometimes a thousand, who were advancing upon him with a bayonet. The more ranks of attackers, the more swathes of dead—that was all. The problem could only be solved by recourse to art—by developing new weapons, by creating surprise, or by taking advantage of obscurity, whether darkness or fog.

If the armies were so long in trying that solution, and had not fully achieved it even when exhaustion brought the war to a ruinous end, the cause may be traced to the failure of military thought to concern itself with tactical mobility—the means of advancing on the battlefield in face of fire.

In France, particularly, the fallacy of the 1914 doctrine started from a misinterpretation of history, or a wilful distortion of it—under an emotional reaction to the disasters of 1870. For it is not true that French doctrine then was defensive. In dispassionate analysis that would have been evident. It was realised by some of the more objective analysts of the campaign, such as General Colin—one of the best military thinkers and military historians in the French Army during the period before the First World War.

It is worth quoting his conclusion:

> In later years, under the impression created by the events of 1870, it was asserted that the opinions held in France, and above all the official instructions

issued from 1866 to 1870, had defensive tendencies which contributed materially to our disasters. This was not so. . . . On the contrary, they seem inspired by the purest offensive spirit.

But when it came to action the French attacks 'collapsed under the fire of the Prussian batteries'. More barren still was the result on such occasions as one side or the other had the sense to prepare a position. Colin, himself partial to the offensive, recognised that. 'The Germans never succeeded in taking a position by a direct attack, and the French still less so. . . . Well-chosen and well-arranged defensive positions, even when very weakly held, could not be carried.'

In case any question remains as to the French in 1870 being offensively minded, and more so than the Germans, it is worth citing the respective instructions. Moltke's laid down that

> It is absolutely beyond all doubt that the man who shoots without moving has the advantage of him who fires while advancing . . . and that if to the most spirited dash one opposes a quiet steadiness, it is fire effect, nowadays so powerful, which will determine the issue . . . We must desire the enemy to attack.

By contrast, the French official doctrine declared: 'Direct attack, ending in a bayonet fight, accords with the impetuous character and courage of our men. Let us persist in encouraging its use. . . . No fire, but a determined advance to close on the enemy with the bayonet and at the charge.' When this mentions the defensive, it is only to say: 'the best way of defending a position is oneself to attack.'

It was this nonsensical method of 'defence' which the French repeatedly attempted in 1870, with disastrous results.

The notion that the French came to disaster by relying on the tactical defensive is merely a myth which gained currency by constant repetition, on the part of the French advocates of the *offensive á outrance*, during the generation which preceded the 1914 war. The myth does not stand examination. While the German successes were mainly due to strategic manoeuvre, helped by their great superiority of numbers, the French vied with them in attempting attacks—which were crushed by the superior German artillery.

The actual policy which the French adopted was the tactical offensive combined with the strategic defensive—if what was really strategic paralysis, caused by epidemic incompetence, can be thus described. Only on rare occasions did the French take up a defensive position proper; and then, repulsed attacks with striking success. The disregard of these lessons by the 'offensive' zealots of the next generation showed how often military theory is built on faith instead of a dispassionate analysis of facts.

Colin's last pre-war book, *Les Transformations de la Guerre* (1911), was a much sounder appreciation than Foch's writings, and its good sense was in striking contrast to the nonsense of the official doctrine adopted at that time.

Still more farsighted were the writings, forecasts and warnings of two 'outsiders'—Captains Mayer and Grouard, to give them the rank they held on retirement from the Army. As military critics they were widely read, and became leaders of the unofficial and contra-official school of military thought. But neither of them had passed through the *Ecole de Guerre*—and their lack of such a qualification was often emphasised by the official claque as a ground for discounting their arguments.

Emile Mayer was a pupil at the Ecole Polytechnique at the same time as Joffre and Foch, and like the latter entered the artillery. After only a few years' commissioned service he produced a little handbook for N.C.O.s which explained the elements of gunnery in simple terms. It filled such a need that it quickly ran through three editions. Its success awoke the Ministry of War to the need, and led them in 1880 to produce a similar official handbook. Characteristically, they appointed another officer to write it—Mayer's friend, Foch.

A few years later, another friend asked Mayer to take on the editorship of the military side of the *Revue Scientifique*. He accepted with diffidence because he suddenly realised how narrow had been the bounds of his own military education. His new studies opened his eyes to the potential effect of new inventions on tactics. It also made him dubious of the restricted form of military history that was taught at the Staff College, and of the deductions drawn therefrom.

Much impressed by the development of smokeless powder he came to believe that it would have a rar-reaching effect on tactics, and came to doubt the realism of the school, beginning to be dominant, that was crying for a return to 'our national traditions of the offensive'.

From 1888 onwards he published successive articles, criticising this tendency. In one, of 1890, he significantly asserted: 'The artillery will become the principal arm, the axis of manoeuvre . . . The new powder will make all movement a danger. Immobility becomes a force. Does that not mean that the advantage henceforth goes over to the defensive?' In consequence he became convinced that the physiognomy of battle would be completely transformed and that it was dangerous to build up theories based on the German successes of 1866 and 1870.

His criticisms were upsetting to the stomach of the military public. Thus, after the first articles, they were refused by the French reviews, whose editors feared that such heresy would shock their readers. The offensive was now the mode and only its trimmings could be touched. In consequence Mayer was forced to seek literary sanctuary beyond the frontier, and to use Swiss military journals for the publication of his more fundamental, and hence more outrageous, opinions.

As they had to be submitted to the Ministry of War for authorisation to publish, his 'dangerous' unorthodoxy was known to his superiors. Thus it is not surprising that in 1895 he was still only a captain, while his former comrades, Joffre and Foch, were lieutenant-colonels.

Soon afterwards, his professional career abruptly finished. Authority, after regarding his articles for some time with contemptuous tolerance, suddenly found them irritating, and parted with the source of the irritation. He turned to make a living in military journalism, becoming a regular contributor to various journals and commenting on the annual manoeuvres for the *Temps*.

In 1902 Mayer returned to the charge. He was emboldened to deliver it by the experience of the South African War, which, unlike serving French soldiers, he had studied carefully. He was provoked to it by the publication of Foch's lectures on the principles of war, which proclaimed the sovereign virtues of the offensive and entirely ignored the South African War.

He now prophesied that a future war would develop into a situation which

> Put face to face two human walls almost in contact, separated only by a strip of death, and this double wall will remain almost inert in spite of the will to advance on one side or the other, in spite of the attempts that will be made to push on.
>
> One of these lines, baffled frontally, will try to outflank the other. That, in its turn, will extend its front; there will be a competition as to which can extend the most, so far as its resources allow. Or, at least, this would happen if it were possible to extend indefinitely. But nature presents obstacles. The line will come to a halt at the sea, at the mountains, at the frontier of a neutral country.

This remarkably fits and forecasts the course of the opening campaign in 1914. It would develop, he declared, into a siege war, 'dragging out its weary length with alternate local successes and limited resources' until one side had too few troops to hold its far-stretched line or until the war was brought to an end by external circumstances.

> For example, one will be compelled by the financial or political state of affairs to ask for peace or to accept it, even without having achieved the decisive objects, without having suffered decisive defeats. . . . The credit of the countries will be quickly exhausted, the treasuries will grow empty. In addition, every family will be in mourning and distressed; more than ever their heart-strings will be torn. They will grow tired of seeing the armies mark time, without advancing but not without suffering grievous losses. And it is that which will put an end to the campaign rather than the great victories of other times.

This forecast, of course, made no impression in France, where the offensive gospel was winning ever more adherents, and where even the defensive-offensive war plan of 1896 was undergoing the first of the successive modifications which would culminate in the extreme offensive plan attempted in 1914.

In that fateful hour Mayer was recalled to the service, coming back on mobilisation as a lieutenant-colonel among his juniors, as a junior among his contemporaries, now generals. While awaiting the fulfilment of the fatally foolish war plan, Plan XVII, he wrote a letter—not intended for publication.

> Everybody is acclaiming General Joffre, beginning with Clemenceau . . . It is not logical, however, because the table is well laid, and looks nice, to praise

the cooking. . . . Let's wait until the dishes are brought to the table, and we've tasted them, before passing judgment.

History adds a postscript to Mayer's letter. It says that the fare tasted ill. Because it had not been seasoned by realism.

The name of Grouard is better known than that of Mayer, for his books were widely read abroad, particularly his analysis of Napoleon's strategy—of which he was one of the best interpreters.

Grouard was not merely a military critic, but a military historian. Herein lay his strength, the broad foundation on which his criticism was firmly based. Herein also lay the cause why his historical no less than his contemporary works were boycotted by those who were responsible for the military education of officers.

His historian's instinct for truth was stronger than his soldierly instinct for unquestioning acceptance of what he was told. Necessary though the latter quality might be in practice, he felt that in theory everything must be tested by criticism, and rejected if it could not stand examination. True thought seemed to him more important than uniformity of thought. In war a bad plan might be better than no plan, but in theory of war an untruth might be worse than uncertainty.

Grouard's early writings made a strong impression on General Miribel, and had a considerable influence on the formulation of Plan XIII. As far back as 1882 Miribel read and was much impressed by a study written by Captain Grouard entitled *Le Plan de campagne contre l'Allemagne*. Miribel kept in touch with him and some years later wished to appoint him to the General Staff, only to be told that this was impossible as Grouard had not been through the Staff College! As the next best thing he arranged that Grouard should join General Headquarters on mobilisation.

But there was a worse obstacle to Grouard's advancement. His historical works on the war of 1870, with their frank exposure of faults, had raised up enemies, among them a powerful politician, de Freycinet. Thus in 1900, Grouard retired from the Army.

Once out of the Army, freedom from routine duties allowed him to devote his whole thought to the study of war and to historical research. He followed up his work on Napoleon's Maxims of War with critical studies of the 1813 and 1815 campaigns. They were utterly different from the prevailing military mode of books of Napoleon.

They questioned Clausewitz's interpretation of Napoleon. They examined Napoleon's use of the defensive and did not merely dwell on his offensive moves. They went back to Napoleon's forerunners and showed the evolution of his theory of war. They corrected the tendency to become absorbed in tactics to the neglect of strategic study.

These corrections of the conventional military outlook of the period were not popular. But perhaps Grouard's worst offence was that he damaged the Napoleonic legend, by dispelling the immaculate conception of Napoleon. Instead of confining his study to Napoleon's successes, Grouard examined his failures, showing how his faulty execution marred his conception, and where it diverged from his own teachings.

There is far more to be learnt from Grouard's analysis of 1813 and 1815 than from the historic but unhistoric panegyrics which were produced for the edification of the military schools. These obtained circulation the more easily because they were dictated from official 'chairs' of military history and tactics. And the occupants of these seats naturally did not encourage study of an author who challenged their more superficial deductions, who brought out ugly facts which would kill their beautiful theory.

Here lay the essential cleavage. Grouard was convinced that honesty was the necessary attribute of history; they were persuaded that beauty came first.

Grouard's isolation became even more marked when, three years before the war, he turned from the past to the future—or, rather, projected the truths drawn from the past onto the screen of the future. Hitherto he had been tacitly ostracised as a blasphemer; now he was excommunicated as a heretic.

His *Guerre Eventuelle* was published serially in 1911 and in book form in 1913. At the beginning he recognised the theoretical advantages of the offensive but made the practical comment that for it 'to have any chance of success, certain conditions must be fulfilled'. An army which launches an offensive at the outset of a war must be ready before its opponent, it must believe itself the stronger, that belief should be fortified by previous success, and it must be able to choose a feasible line of operations.

'The least reflection on the conditions of a war between France and Germany shows that they are contrary to those that we have enumerated.' 'It is certain that at the outset our army will have neither a numerical nor a moral superiority over that of the Germans.' 'Finally, even in the almost unrealisable case where we were ready first, we could only invade enemy territory along routes full of obstacles.'

Whilst these reasons against an initial offensive seemed to him conclusive, Grouard argued also that a decisive engagement should be postponed as long as possible in view of the intervention of England and Russia. Politically it was important to avoid any appearance of aggression. Militarily, it was necessary to give these countries time to place their strength in the scales.

'These observations bring me to the conclusion that, however desirable may be the offensive, it is absolutely impracticable for us at the outset . . . We must base our preparations solely on repulsing the invasion of our territory.' The governing idea he briefly summed up as 'to leave the enemy the initiative of making the first moves and, when we discover them, to reply with an energetic counterstroke on a well-chosen point'.

Grouard then discussed the enemy's probable plan. He pointed out the difficulties which the Germans would suffer, likewise, in attacking the eastern frontier, and how they could avoid them by coming through Belgium. 'All this region is open and easily practicable for armies; besides, Belgium is a rich country where the Germans would find abundant resources.'

Such a route would give the Germans a longer and more exposed line of supply, but 'believing themselves certain of victory they may care less about the security of their communications than the chance of giving battle in advantageous conditions, in seeking, above all, sufficient room to deploy their force and to achieve the envelopment of the French left wing'.

Grouard emphasised that if the French tried to reply by a counter-offensive in Lorraine, such a thrust would not only be easy for the Germans to block but would have no timely effect in dislocating the German move. For, as he pointed out, an enemy advance through Belgium would be based on Cologne and Coblentz, not on the upper Rhine, and so a counterstroke towards Strasbourg would not have an immediate effect on the masses wheeling through the Ardennes and Belgium, nor avail to ease the pressure on the French left wing.

The choice for the counterstroke would thus lie between the line through the Ardennes or that west of the Meuse. A counterstroke through the Ardennes could be the more dislocating, and throw the enemy's whole advance out of gear. But its success was 'improbable'. For the Germans had the initiative and it was almost certain that the French could not forestall them at Namur. In that case it would be too late to beat one army while this was separated from the other by the Meuse and entangled in the Ardennes.

Joffre and his staff in 1914 thought otherwise. After the failure of their thrust in Lorraine, they launched the next in the Ardennes. Unlike Grouard they did not take account of the time factor. Thus their troops blundered head-on into the German forces at the portals of the Ardennes, and were summarily thrown back, while the German right wing, well out of reach, was tranquilly pursuing its enveloping march past Charleroi.

Foreseeing such a result, Grouard's preference was for a counterstroke on the western flank. He would have awaited the Germans in the angle between the Sambre and the Meuse, and have been ready to switch his main reserves thither as soon as it was clear that the Germans were coming that way.

He went on to say:

> Yet to be certain of carrying out this concentration successfully, several conditions must be fulfilled; first of all that of being ready to make a manoeuvre in retreat, if the enemy attacks in strength before the concentration has been completed . . . in the zone of decisive operations. Everywhere also the manoeuvre in retreat ought to be the rule, so as to be able to accumulate the greatest possible force in the principal zone.
>
> There is need to insist on this point, because there is in France a whole school which does not like talking of it, on the pretext that in 1870 the Germans did not use this method, a fact which proves absolutely nothing, for circumstances were such that they were always able to take the offensive.
>
> The reply can be made that, in 1796, Bonaparte's strategy in Italy was based entirely on the strategic retreat for the simple reason that his movements were subordinated to those of the Austrians as ours will be against the Germans. It was because Napoleon did not follow this method in 1813 that he came to grief in

all his enterprises. One can also note that if the Germans in 1870 did not use this method, Blucher, despite his nickname of Marshal *Vorwaerts*, profited by it greatly during this very campaign of 1813.

Those who dislike talking about the strategic retreat pretend also that the morale of the soldier will be affected! We shall only remark that this depends on his military education.

If the reservists, without whom France cannot be victorious, are animated by a true patriotism, and if they have not been imbued with false ideas through the use of phrases that are highsounding but hollow, there is no reason why they should not show the same staunchness as Blucher's *landwehr* in 1813.

To the new school of bombast, here was a double heresy. It is hard to say which must have sounded worse—the idea of a purposeful retreat or the suggestion that reservists could and would play a vital part. The latter hypothesis was to be proved true in 1914, but only after the active forces had suffered defeats that were as dangerous as they were needless.

And the danger was to be averted, the tide of war changed, by the method that Grouard had proposed in the first place—that of switching the strategic reserve by rail to the western flank, for a decisive counterstroke as soon as the Germans were unmistakably committed to that line of advance. He would have made the railway system, and not a fixed forward area, the strategic basis of the general reserve, thereby giving to the French dispositions an essential flexibility.

Finally he summed up, in words of remarkable foresight—

The war ought to be, on the French side, defensive politically and militarily: politically, because it is only on this condition that we can count on the intervention of our allies; militarily, because we are forced to it by the relative rate of mobilisation of the respective armies, and also *by the nature of the ground on the frontier*. . . . Formerly . . . there was reason to think that the first great battle would take place in the Vosges; today, it is above all the offensive through Belgium on which we ought to fix our attention.

With this idea, the centre of gravity of our strategic deployment can be shifted somewhat to the left without forfeiting the means of concentrating on the right if circumstances demand it.

But the idea which ought absolutely to dominate the conduct of operations on the part of the French Army is that of renouncing the initial offensive and of acting only by a counterstroke. As far as one can foresee the logical consequences of the opening of our campaign, we can say without hesitation that with the initial offensive we shall be beaten, while in preparing ourselves for a riposte and executing it energetically all the chances are in our favour.

The generals thought differently—and were beaten. They then reverted to Grouard's teaching, and gained victory. But they had dissipated the energy which might have made it decisive.

The most dangerous delusions are those that arise from the sentimental misinterpretation of history, or its deliberate distortion for the supposed benefit of military morale. Such a treatment of war history hinders necessary changes to meet changing conditions. It conceals faults that might otherwise be remedied. Worse still, it creates false confidence—and false confidence has underlain most of the disasters in history.

The course of official military ideas in France is a warning that ought to be engraved on the walls of all War Colleges.

MAX BELOFF

The Special Relationship: an Anglo-American Myth

MAX BELOFF

The Special Relationship: an Anglo-American Myth

THE history of the early 1960s was much influenced by the belief (of which General de Gaulle was the most eloquent exponent) that the countries of continental Europe stood in danger of the development at their expense of an Anglo-Saxon world hegemony. The French veto upon Britain's entry into the European Common Market was based upon the assumption that Britain, once inside, would act as an agent of the essentially non-European policies of the United States.[1] French suspicions of Britain and America working together had of course a long pre-history.[2] And they were given particular point by the wartime experiences of General de Gaulle when he found Winston Churchill apparently acquiescing in the strongly anti-French policies of President Roosevelt and his Secretary of State.[3] But that there exists a natural harmony between Britain and the United States based upon a common linguistic and cultural heritage has long been an article of faith in continental Europe. Only the Marxists with their concentration on economic rivalries have tended to take the opposite view.

It is not difficult to challenge the belief in the closeness of the alignment between British and American policies where particular episodes are concerned. Washington did, of course, welcome the proposed British accession to the Treaty of Rome. But its reasons had little to do with the possibility of using Britain as a Trojan horse for entering the European citadel.[4] The real nature of the two countries' political relationship demands a more critical approach than it usually received.[5] In what sense is there a 'special relationship' between Britain and the United States from which all other countries are perforce excluded, and what is its nature?

[1] See, e.g. Nora Beloff, *The General Says No* (London, 1963).

[2] Writing to the Foreign Secretary from Geneva about American attempts to bring France and Germany together Viscount Cecil of Chelwood referred to the French 'Anglo-Saxon' complex as a serious obstacle. Cecil of Chelwood Papers. B.M. Add. 51082. Cecil to Reading, September 13, 1931.

[3] Lord Avon's volume of memoirs, *The Reckoning* (London, 1965), provides an illuminating treatment of this theme.

[4] See Max Beloff, *The United States and the Unity of Europe* (Washington and London, 1963).

[5] For an admirable treatment of the relations of the two countries since the end of the Second World War see Coral Bell, *The Debatable Alliance*, (London, 1964). It is not the intention of this essay to traverse the same ground.

The belief that there is such a relationship underlies two schools of historical thought upon the subject. On the one hand there are the American historians who account for the entry of the United States into two world wars by pointing to British intrigues designed to force upon the United States the burden of defending the British Empire.[1] On the other hand there are British historians who appear to justify de Gaulle's suspicions by recounting the history of Anglo-American relations in terms that suggest that a growing intimacy of action between Britain and the United States has been the great continuing theme of world history for the past sixty years.[2]

Both versions are too simple; yet both enshrine part of the truth. One must be careful not to overlook important factors in the situation simply because they are so obvious. It is for instance true that the existence of a common language has meant that ideas and myths have been able to circulate more freely between Britain and America than between most other countries.[3] Each has been prone to react rather sharply to a change of tone on the part of the other. Yet this very fact when translated into political terms, makes the record harder rather than easier to follow. British statesmen have often been very guarded in their public utterances about the United States, concealing both their hopes and their fears just because they were worried about the reaction in the United States. And where they have wished for public declarations of unity of purpose they have found their American friends warning them against such a course, either because of domestic considerations or for fear of arousing elsewhere the kind of suspicions voiced by General de Gaulle.[4]

For this reason the public record is not a safe guide and perhaps especially not where British policies are concerned.[5] What we are concerned with here is the reflection in British governing circles of major historical developments that are themselves adequately known. For the American reaction to these developments is no great mystery.

The most important development has, of course, been the diminution of Britain's status in the world, which has been a more or less continuous process since the 1890s, even if sometimes masked by apparent accretions of territory,

[1] 'The main objective in American foreign policy since 1900 has been the preservation of the British Empire.' C. C. Tansill, *Back Door to War* (Chicago, 1952), p. 3.

[2] See, e.g. H. C. Allen, *The Anglo-American Relationship since* 1783 (London, 1959).

[3] Some students would however argue that there was a relative weakening in the 1960s of the density of the contacts between the two communities as compared with earlier periods. See B. Russett, *Community and Contention; Britain and America in the Twentieth Century* (Cambridge, Mass., 1963).

[4] See, e.g. Eisenhower's warnings to Winston Churchill in 1952 where the accent was particularly on the danger of the United States being identified with the policies of a colonialist or ex-colonialist power. Dwight D. Eisenhower, *Mandate for Change* (London, 1963), pp. 97, 249–50.

[5] The present essay relies primarily on papers not part of the public record. Public speeches, magazine articles, etc., would no doubt produce a very different impression.

and the contemporaneous ascent of the United States, which at least until after the Second World War was a much more uneven process. Naturally enough, as American power has increased, so has the importance of relations with Britain decreased in American eyes. In 1940 at the time of the fall of France, the fate of the British fleet was a matter of vital concern to the United States.[1] Even in the 1940s and 1950s, Britain's geographical role as a stationary aircraft carrier was still of the first importance. With the development of intercontinental missiles this has ceased to be the case. Today the transfer of the entire war-making potential of Britain to the side of America's enemies would not greatly add to the dangers that face the United States. For this reason by the 1960s, the whole idea of 'special relationship' was something of an irritant to Americans in official positions, in whose world outlook the British played a fairly subordinate part.

The British response to these changes has always been a more complicated one. On the other hand there were those who were reluctant to believe the process was an inevitable one and who held that all that was needed was a proper firmness in the defence of British rights. Such arguments were at their most powerful in the period of American isolation between the wars.[2] And they coloured British reactions to tentative American moves towards greater participation in world affairs in the 1930s.[3] Some sought to strengthen Britain's hand by exploiting her imperial or, later, her European, position. But it has been pointed out that the most remarkable thing in the whole story is that Britain never responded to the growth in American power by the classical method of organising a counter-coalition.

It has been strongly argued that the reason was an intuitive British assumption 'that British and American interests would in the end prove complementary in the central issues of international politics'.[4] But one could put this in more modest terms by saying that as Britain's consciousness of her growing weakness increased, so did her leaders' feeling that the only way to meet the situation was to make certain of American support against her other challengers, and

[1] See Max Beloff, 'The Anglo-French Union Project of 1940' in *Mélanges Renouvin* (Paris, 1966).

[2] 'Time after time we have been told that, if we made this concession, or that concession, we should secure goodwill in America. We gave up the Anglo-Japanese Alliance. We agreed to pay our debts and we have again and again made concessions on this ground. I have never seen any permanent results follow from a policy of concession. I believe we are less popular and more abused in America than ever before, because they think us weak. The only thing that has really done any good has been the Balfour note on international debts, where we stood up to them firmly. I would refuse either to be blackmailed or browbeaten and stand absolutely to our preconcerted plan of action.' Sir Maurice Hankey to Lord Balfour, June 29, 1927. Balfour Papers. B.M. Add. 49704.

[3] By early 1933 there was a party 'with its representatives in the Cabinet' that believed that the record of the United States since 1920 in refusing 'all decent co-operation with the rest of the world' made any negotiations with the Americans doomed to failure. Lord Lothian to Colonel House, February 13, 1933. Lothian Papers. (Scottish National Archives). Box 221.

[4] Bell, op. cit., p. 116.

that it was here that the particular nature of the relations between the two societies made itself felt.

If one were to put it in the most brutal fashion possible, one would have to say that ever since the 1890s the dominant element in the British 'establishment' has known in its heart that the world order dependent on British sea-power which was the key to the unparalleled growth of the western economy in the nineteenth century could no longer be sustained by British power alone. It was therefore the intended lot of the United States, perhaps its moral duty, to take over an increasing share of this burden and to use its new strength to further Britain's original purposes.[1] In this modified form, shorn of its demonological element, the theory of the American isolationist writers was nearer the truth than the *bien-pensants* on either side of the Atlantic like to admit.[2]

It could thus be maintained that the 'special relationship' was something in which many British public figures felt the need to believe, so as to be able to argue that the displacement of power from Britain to the United States need not directly damage British interests. It was for them the test of their own ability to exercise sufficient influence at Washington, to make this interpretation of world politics plausible to themselves and others. To trace the vicissitudes of this idea would be to recount the whole story of the relations between the two countries in the present century; it is enough here to point out some of its origins and some of its consequences.

The Venezuela crisis may be taken as the moment at which Britain, alerted to the consequences of permanently alienating the United States, virtually ruled out the use of armed force as a method of settling Anglo-American disputes and appealed to the idea of belonging to a common community as the fundamental reason for so doing.[3] But this did not, of course, rule out competition in armaments nor contingency planning for their use.[4]

[1] 'There have only been two long periods of world peace in history. One was created by the Roman Empire. The other was the great Pax of the nineteenth century which was created by the British navy. That is why I have always believed that the only foundation for world peace was close co-operation between the British Commonwealth and the United States for the restoration of the nineteenth-century British system operated not by Britain alone but by the whole English-speaking world.' Lord Lothian to General Smuts, June 6, 1939. Lothian Papers. Box 208.

[2] This is not to say, of course, that either Woodrow Wilson or Franklin Roosevelt were willing accomplices in a 'British plot'.

[3] Balfour declared in a speech at the height of the Venezuelan crisis that the idea of war with the United States carried with it 'something of the unnatural horror of a civil war'.

[4] See J. C. Grenville, *Lord Salisbury and Foreign Policy* (London, 1964), p. 422. There was much discussion of the problems of defending Canada in British Government circles in 1903–5. Balfour Papers. B.M. Add. 49707. Asquith Papers, Bodleian Library, Oxford. Dep. Asquith. 132. But some people felt from very early on that there should be no competition with the United States in armaments. Lord Selborne, the First Lord of the Admiralty, wrote to Lord Curzon on April 19, 1901, that he would never quarrel with the United States if it could be avoided. If the Americans chose they could easily afford to build a navy larger than Britain's and would probably do so. G. W. Monger, *The End of Isolation* (London, 1963), p. 72.

What is interesting is the speed with which British statesmen passed from the position of merely making certain of American neutrality to that of looking for positive support.[1] But even so, in the crisis of the First World War it seemed as if the former objective might prove difficult enough of attainment.

For it is clear that in 1915 there were real fears as to how far the United States might go in defending its neutral rights against the British measures aimed against the economies of the Central Powers; and in 1916 there was very great anxiety about the possible consequences should the Germans offer, in response to American moves for mediation, to accept proposals falling far short of the Allies minimum demands.[2] It is true that the eventual American entry into the war put an end to these particular nightmares and gave comfort to those who had placed their faith in the ultimate coming together of the two countries.[3] But it did not in fact mean any such thing when seen from Washington. The British remained baffled and saddened. For them it was axiomatic that the maintenance of Britain's world position conduced to the general welfare and they felt that all Americans should be able to perceive this obvious fact unless blinded by prejudice. It was from the contrast between the perceptions of British needs, so clear in London, so cloudy in Washington, that there were to arise all the subsequent misunderstandings and disappointments.

For the differences in perception many reasons could be adduced, particularly on the American side. Some of these were not as visible as they should have been to British leaders who found their natural American interlocutors among the educated elite of the eastern seaboard with their many personal and cultural ties with England, rather than among the preponderantly non-British elements in the country's population whose gradual ascent to political power was a principal feature of the American scene in the decades in question. It was because of the restricted social sympathies of British statesmen and diplomats that they failed to grasp the extent to which American anglophilia was part of the ideology of a class struggling to maintain its ascendency at home in the face of a series of urgent challenges from below.[4]

[1] We must, of course, note the point recently made by an historian that the changes subsequent to 1941 must not make us forget how remote the United States felt, generally speaking, from questions of the European balance of power before 1917. G. Barraclough, *Introduction to Contemporary History* (London, 1964), pp. 106–7.

[2] In the course of Anglo-French conversations at Downing Street on December 26, 1916, Balfour pointed out the dangers inherent in President Wilson's attitude to possible peace terms, in view of the fact that 'the United States had it in their power to compel peace'. Austen Chamberlain Papers (University of Birmingham Library) AC20/76. Cf. Arthur Link, *Wilson* (vol. 5, Princeton, 1965).

[3] When the news reached London of the United States breaking off relations with Germany, Austen Chamberlain wrote in his diary (February 4, 1917): 'It is not the material support we should receive but the memory of having once at least co-operated in a great struggle that has made me long for the intervention of the United States in the war—long for it without expecting it.' Diary (University of Birmingham Library).

[4] For this interpretation of the changing climate of American opinion in the 1890s see

Indeed, the degree to which British statesmen and diplomats expected a natural sympathy for British policy to exist in the United States and equated any hostility to or criticism of Britain with treason to America and not merely to Britain can be abundantly illustrated. In the cold light of reason there was little cause for Irish-Americans, or German-Americans or refugees from Tsarism to favour American intervention on the Allied side in the First World War[1]; but it was assumed by Cecil Spring-Rice, the British Ambassador, and by other Englishmen that some especial turpitude attached to the 'hyphenated Americans',[2] while it was perfectly natural that the sympathies of New Englanders should be with old England. And while some excuse might easily be found for their spleen in the fact that Britain was fighting for her life against a militarist aggressor—after all the Germans had invaded Belgium and not vice versa—the same could not be said of all such episodes.

Disputes such as those over Indian policy during the Second World War and Palestine later on made the ideas of an Anglo-Saxon partnership as adumbrated in the 1890s very remote indeed when viewed from the perspective of less than fifty years later. But some of the frustrations engendered by the subsequent divergences of view are perhaps only fully understandable in the light of the hopes originally aroused: 'The danger is that we should hope too much and we should be angry because we are disappointed from too much hoping.'[3]

The notion of 'Anglo-Saxondom' has been more fully explored on the

---

C. Strout, *The American Image of the Old World* (New York, 1963): Chapter 8, 'The Old Sweet Anglo-Saxon Spell'. The course of American opinion during the Venezuela crisis should have shown where the strength of pro-English feeling lay: 'The opponents of Jingoism and of Cleveland's performance are the businessmen, clergy, professors and the like of the eastern coast. The hatred of England in the west and south-west is rabid, bitter and ferocious, and would welcome war tomorrow . . . The children have been taught in all the schools for twenty-five years to hate England and to believe that we can thrash her and that we did so in 1812.' E. L. Godkin to James Bryce, January 9, 1896. Bryce Papers, Bodleian Library, Oxford. U.S.A. Papers, vol. 5.

[1] The dangers to British interests arising from the importance of these voting blocs had been foreseen by some British students of affairs. Writing to Balfour's secretary, Sanders, on January 27, 1910 to suggest a compromise on Home Rule, J. L. Garvin wrote: '. . . what we most need is better relations with America. The new alliance between the Irish and the German vote is a more important thing than almost anybody here seems to realise. It is one of the greatest dangers that ever threatened the Empire.' Writing to Balfour himself on October 17, Garvin added that through alienating the United States, Britain also ran the risk of forfeiting the sympathies of Canada. Balfour Papers. B.M. Add. 49745.

[2] 'If we regard ourselves as fighting for a cause bound up with the existence of America and as a people of the same blood and language and principles as the people of the United States we might be filled with rage at the thought of their attitude.' Spring-Rice to Grey, December 5, 1916. Balfour Papers. B.M. Add. 49731. The passage is one of those omitted from the printed version of the letter in S. Gwynn, *The Letters and Friendships of Sir Cecil Spring-Rice* (London, 1929), vol. 2, pp. 357–9.

[3] Spring-Rice to Balfour, January 11, 1917 (*not* January 12), Gwynn, op. cit., vol. 2, p. 369.

American side than on the British one and perhaps rightly so. From the time when James Russell Lowell concluded as a result of his experiences as American Minister that 'the differences between Yankees and Englishmen were "mostly superficial" ',[1] a whole school of American writers had dilated on the superiority of the Anglo-Saxon race and its destiny to dominate the world.[2] But there were British parallels; and the musings of Cecil Rhodes as adumbrated in the successive drafts of his will suggest a climate of opinion in which policies of Anglo-American partnership could be made acceptable.[3] It has been pointed out, for instance, that while, in general, the European press took Spain's side in the Spanish-American war, the British press supported the United States, which seemed to be fighting the kind of struggle that it had elsewhere fallen to Britain's lot to wage.[4] The words of Ambassador John Hay claiming that there was as between the United States and Britain 'a sanction like that of religion' which bound them 'in a sort of partnership in the beneficent work of mankind' were answered by Joseph Chamberlain in a number of celebrated utterances.[5]

The vogue of such ideas was relatively short-lived, since overt racialism was compatible neither with the essential nature of American society nor with the general British outlook on world problems. Only some of its inherent ambiguities were fully explored at the time; but two of them were decisive for the failure of any fully fashioned policy of partnership to emerge. The more obvious was the ambiguity in the position of the Germans who from the point of view of an American racialist like John W. Burgess formed part of a Teutonic master-race.[6] Chamberlain in his speech at Leicester on November 30, 1899, spoke of the need for a triple alliance between 'the Teutonic race and the two branches of the Anglo-Saxon race', and attempted to bring about a British alignment with Germany. But such views, which reflected Chamberlain's concentration upon the purely commercial aspects of foreign policy, could not long survive their absence of echo at Berlin, and the clear determination of Germany to seek a position of naval strength which would inevitably threaten the established position of Britain upon which American security had also been permitted to rest. Nor were they in accordance with most British sentiment.[7] In a memorandum of November 1901 Lansdowne listed

[1] Strout, op. cit., p. 138.

[2] R. W. Leopold, *The Growth of American Foreign Policy* (New York, 1962), pp. 125–7.

[3] See generally, A. P. Thornton, *The Imperial Idea and Its Enemies* (London, 1959), and B. Semmel, *Imperialism and Social Reform* (London, 1960). For Rhodes see F. Aydelotte, *The American Rhodes Scholarships* (Princeton, 1946).

[4] Grenville, op. cit., pp. 214–15.

[5] Leopold, op. cit., pp. 206–7; J. L. Garvin, *Life of Joseph Chamberlain*, vol. 3 (London, 1934), pp. 296–306. For this period generally see also A. E. Campbell, *Great Britain and the United States*, 1895–1903 (London, 1960), and C. S. Campbell, *Anglo-American Understanding*, 1898–1903 (Baltimore, 1957).

[6] Strout, op. cit., p. 141.

[7] Grenville, op. cit., pp. 128, 156, 281–3.

among the objections to a German alliance the risk of becoming entangled in an anti-American policy.[1]

In the long run the more important ambiguity lay in the fact that Britain's overseas dominions included not only peoples of overwhelmingly or at least predominantly British stock but also millions of Asian and African subjects of the Crown to whom the ideas of Anglo-Saxondom were clearly irrelevant. British exponents of the idea of an Anglo-Saxon brotherhood such as Dilke saw no future for the race in the possession of alien dependencies.[2] And Kipling's Indian sympathies did not prevent his imperial ideology from being dominated by the same reliance upon the tie of blood.[3] For Americans this aspect of Britain's imperial heritage presented even greater problems. Despite their acquisition of Hawaii, Porto Rico and the Philippines, they never seriously contemplated the idea of a long-term dependent empire for themselves, and regarded Britain's imperial possessions as an obsolete incubus. Once Britain was set on the path of developing non-white dominions which would, however slowly, come to take their place permanently beside the older members of the Commonwealth, there could be no fusion between the Commonwealth ideal and the notion of an Anglo-Saxon confederation. Different Englishmen were to face the consequences of this fact in different ways, but that they would have to face it should have been apparent from very early on.

If they chose to follow to its logical conclusion the argument that an Anglo-Saxon confederation was the safest object for Britain to aim at they might argue as Philip Kerr (later Lord Lothian) did in a paper in 1909 that this policy involved a relinquishment of British political control over India and Egypt. Its guiding concept would be the world-wide maritime supremacy of the British and American fleets able to protect territories like Australia and South Africa which though fit for white settlement were too thinly populated for their own defence.[4]

[1] Monger, op. cit., p. 66.

[2] Thornton, op. cit., p. 39.

[3] See J. I. M. Stewart, *Eight Modern Writers* (Oxford, 1963), p. 286.

[4] Balfour Papers. B.M. Add. 49797. In his life of Balfour, Mr Kenneth Young attributes this paper to him. *Arthur James Balfour* (London, 1963), pp. 281–2. This is clearly an error. It appears that Kerr, who was then in South Africa, also sent it to Theodore Roosevelt, then about to visit Europe. An introductory note marked 'not sent to Roosevelt' points out that one of Germany's objectives in building up her fleet is to be able to oppose imperial preference, and she might make this impossible if she could get the United States on her side. The advantages of the 'Anglo-Saxon Confederation' must be impressed upon Roosevelt so that he will not be tempted towards an American-German alliance. On Roosevelt's own rather ambivalent attitude to the British Empire, see 'Theodore Roosevelt and the British Empire' in Max Beloff, *The Great Powers* (London, 1959). Fears lest the United States and Germany might come together were not confined to Kerr and his friends. Admiral Fisher expressed the same anxiety in a letter to King Edward VII on October 4, 1907. Marder, *Fear God and Dread Nought*, vol. 2 (London, 1956), pp. 142–3. It was this in part, no doubt, that made Fisher, earlier rather anti-American in sentiment, a protagonist from at least 1907 of 'that great and impending bulwark against both the Yellow man *and the Slav*—"the Federation of all who speak the English tongue" '. Marder, op. cit., pp. 191, 298, 343, 346, 348, 361–2.

Americans of the more conservative school who might be attracted for internal political reasons to a policy of alignment with Britain were in an ambivalent position, since they tended to be protagonists of a policy of expansion by the United States itself and so to look upon Britain as a rival and competitor especially in the field of trade. In this way the hostility towards all forms of imperialism on ideological grounds which was the mainstay of American thinking on world affairs was fortified by a particular degree of distrust in reference to the British Empire. And such sentiments were aroused in particular whenever it seemed likely that the Empire (or later the Commonwealth) might fortify its ties by a system of preferential tariffs, common currency arrangements or other forms of commercial discrimination.[1]

In this respect the achievement by the Dominions of independence in the field of foreign and defence policy after 1919 placed the Americans in something of a dilemma. They put up some resistance to accepting the fact of the change, for instance in their strong opposition to separate representation for the Dominions in the League of Nations.

Another example was in relation to the limitation of naval armaments. The American invitations to the Washington Conference of 1921 ignored the existence of the Empire and it was Lloyd George who had to insist upon Dominion representation. 'It is amusing,' wrote one of his secretaries, 'to think that one of our underlying objects in this great Conference must be to make the United States recognise the British Empire. Their present attitude seems to be that the Dominions are nondescript appendages whose natural instincts would be to link up with the stronger English-speaking power. They have never yet even begun to grasp what the underlying sentiment of the Empire is.'[2]

But in the final treaty and in subsequent discussions, the Americans insisted on reckoning the Dominion navies in with the British. Since their ships were not under Admiralty control it could be argued that any increase in the Dominions' navies left Britain itself weaker in regard to the United States.[3] Similar problems about air forces arose at the Disarmament Conference.[4]

For his earlier view: 'The Yankees are dead against us', see his letter to Rosebery, May 10, 1901, ibid., vol. I (London, 1952), pp. 188–9.

[1] Note the remark by Sumner Welles in 1943: 'The whole history of British Imperial Preference is a history of economic aggression', quoted by L. S. Amery, *My Political Life*, vol. III (London, 1955), p. 385.

[2] Edward Grigg to Lord Cromer, November 15, 1921. Grigg Papers (property of Mr John Grigg), General and Political. 1922. A-K. It would seem that Lloyd George was himself acting under Canadian pressure. See Roger Graham, *Arthur Meighen*, vol. II (Toronto, 1963), pp. 103–4.

[3] John Dove to Philip Kerr, July 18, 1927. Lothian Papers. Box 189.

[4] 'We can of course say that the Dominions are self-governing, that we have no control over their forces, that we are bound to them by no military treaties or understandings. But can we say that their aeroplanes would not be available to us in case of war? I hardly think so, and if we did, with the record of the Dominions during the last war fresh in the memory of other nations, no one would believe us. This is likely to cause grave difficulty, especially

What was true of armaments was equally true of finance. Even in the Second World War, British financial emissaries to Washington found most Americans unable to distinguish between the resources of the United Kingdom, which the Government could mobilise, and those of the Empire, which it could not.

Britain's relations with the United States had, of course, always been affected by the special position of Canada. As early as the beginning of the century British statesmen were facing a new worry—the 'great influx' into Canada of Americans and American capital, and were connecting with it the fact that while some Canadian statesmen were looking to ultimate independence none were seriously advocating closer ties with Britain.[1] For this reason the internal Canadian battle over 'reciprocity' was one of the neuralgic points in the whole Anglo-American complex of the pre-1914 period, though one where the United States often seemed peculiarly insensitive to British susceptibilities.[2]

It is the imperial angle which provides one persistent theme in the relations between Britain and the United States. It began with Joseph Chamberlain's campaign for tariff reform in the early years of the century and concluded with the rearguard action fought against the American loan of 1946 by such spiritual heirs of Chamberlain as Leo Amery and Walter Elliot. The genuine imperialist school in British twentieth-century politics with its programme of economic unity based on trade and migration, combined with common defence and foreign policies for all the self-governing members of the British family of nations, never, it is true, attained a fully commanding position in British politics. When its minority strength was sufficient for one or other aspect of its policies to get a run—as imperial preference did at Ottawa in 1932—

with the United States.' Anthony Eden to Sir John Simon, May 1, 1933. Simon Papers (property of Viscount Simon).

[1] See, e.g. the letter from the Governor-General, Lord Minto, to Sir Edward Hutton, July 16, 1901. Hutton Papers. B.M. Add. 50081. In a letter to Balfour of January 25, 1907, W. A. S. Hewins, who was looking over the prospects for imperial preference in Canada, pointed out that a substantial part of the brains and capital behind Canadian expansion was American. Balfour Papers. B.M. Add. 49779.

[2] On July 23, 1905, Andrew Carnegie airily wrote to Balfour pointing out that the absorption of Canada by the United States was natural and that Canadian demonstrations of loyalty to Britain merely provoked unfavourable reactions in America. For the same reasons he condemned imperial preference proposals and looked forward instead to the ultimate unity of the English-speaking world. Replying on the 28th, Balfour wrote that while he was very well disposed towards the Americans 'whom he did not in any sense regard as a foreign community', he thought them unreasonable about Canada and about preferences generally. Balfour Papers. B.M. Add. 49742. Balfour as Prime Minister was primarily concerned to secure American support for British policies, notably in the Far East, ibid., 49729. But he regarded himself then and later as 'a Pan-Anglican'. 'I have always held', he wrote in 1911, 'that the English-speaking peoples have traditions, interests and ideals that should unite them in common sentiments and in not inconceivable eventualities in common action.' To Philip Kerr, March 18, 1911, ibid., 49797. And indeed as early as 1898 we find him writing of himself as cherishing a 'pan-Anglo-Saxon ideal'. Letter to J. St Loe Strachey, July 22, 1898, ibid.

this aspect did so in isolation from what made up a coherent if not convincing master-plan for Britain's future. For the most part the imperialists were actually in impotent opposition.[1] But the movement lacked neither leaders nor mouthpieces, and its influence cannot altogether be set aside in discussing Anglo-American relations.[2]

In their scepticism as to the desirability and feasibility of a close Anglo-American combination the true imperialists were in line with the views of the intellectual father of the school, Lord Milner. While expressing in 1909 and 1912 his desire to keep on the best possible terms with the United States he regarded ties with that country as of quite a different order to those which could develop within Britain's 'own family' which should be of a constitutional kind.[3] Indeed, with particular reference to Canada, Milner realised that any confusion between the Empire and Anglo-Saxondom would be positively dangerous.[4]

It might have been expected that this suspicion of the United States on the part of the British 'right' would have been compensated for by the traditional sympathy of the British 'left'. And there were moments when such an alignment seemed to be taking place, most strikingly perhaps in relation to the question of 'war aims' during the First World War when Woodrow Wilson was influenced by, and in turn influenced some radical elements in British politics.[5] But such episodes were on the whole exceptional. For as the British left became increasingly identified with dogmatic socialism, so the United States

[1] The so-called 'Suez group' of the 1950s may be regarded as the final remnant of the old imperialist school.

[2] Even more difficult was the position of 'The Round Table Group', who combined their ideal of greater Commonwealth unity with a generally 'English-speaking' orientation. For a recent assessment of Anglo-American relations from this point of view see the first Ditchley Foundation Lecture, H. V. Hodson, *The Anatomy of Anglo-American Relations*, delivered April 27, 1962. Kerr, who was one of those most preoccupied with American issues, wrote in relation to the 1927 Naval Conference: 'The English-speaking nations have either got to bring themselves under one sovereignty or they will drift into antagonism.' Kerr to Lionel Curtis, September 2, 1927. Lothian Papers. Box 189.

[3] Milner to Colonel Denison, November 3, 1909. Milner Papers, Bodleian Library, Oxford. C. LXXIV. Milner to Haslam, May 24, 1912. Ibid. Imperial Union Box.

[4] Milner to H. Bourassa, October 9, 1912. Milner Papers C. LXXIV. For Milner's not altogether consistent views on the relations between his racial and his imperial ideas, see A. M. Gollin, *Proconsul in Politics* (London, 1964), pp. 128–32, 401.

[5] See L. W. Martin, *Peace Without Victory* (New Haven, 1958). In addition to Colonel House's information derived from the United States Embassy in London, there were also close contacts between the *New Republic* circle in New York and the British 'Union of Democratic Control' and other Liberal and Labour elements. A. J. Mayer, *Political Origins of the New Diplomacy* 1917–18 (New Haven, 1959), pp. 335–7. Wilson's biographer, Professor Arthur Link, has argued that the breakdown of the first Anglo-American alliance was due to the failure of British statesmen to understand Wilson's purposes or accept his leadership. A. Link, *President Wilson and his English Critics* (Oxford, 1959). On Anglo-American relations after the Armistice see S. Tillman, *Anglo-American Relations at the Paris Peace Conference of* 1919 (Princeton and London, 1962).

as the great bulwark of capitalism increasingly appeared to be the principal obstacle to the spread of its ideals.[1]

The actual Labour governments of the period in respect of their broad attitude to Anglo-American relations showed no significant departure from their predecessors. Indeed, if anything, they attached even greater importance to attempts to secure agreement with the United States. It was Ramsay MacDonald during his second term as Prime Minister who became the first British holder of the office to visit the United States. It was under the post-war Attlee administration that the American loan, the Marshall Plan and the Atlantic Alliance together made the fortunes of Britain much more closely dependent upon the United States than in any preceding peace-time period.

Even therefore if due allowance be made for the opposition of extreme factions on both wings of British politics, it remains possible to discuss standard British attitudes towards the United States as a continuing expression of a clear majority viewpoint, first formulated by Balfour and Grey. And basically, as has been suggested, this viewpoint involved a continuous search on the British side for a 'special relationship', first, so that no British resources should be tied up in actually opposing the United States, and second so that America's power should be brought to bear wherever possible in support of British interests.

The former of these ambitions could be fulfilled without too much difficulty because it depended fundamentally on what the British were willing to surrender—their claims on the isthmus,[2] any significant naval strength in Caribbean waters,[3] the contested Canadian frontier claims. The process was virtually complete by the time of the (unratified) Arbitration Treaty of 1911, but there were still echoes of it in the celebrated destroyer-bases deal of 1940.[4]

It was more difficult to apply the notion to the general problem of sea-power and of imperial communications so long as Britain continued to regard herself as a world power. It is true that as early as 1908–9 when the Asquith Government reviewed the problem of the two-power naval standard the advice it received was to exclude the strength of the United States in assessing Britain's naval needs. The former First Lord of the Admiralty, Lord Cawdor, put the case at its simplest: 'it is incredible that we should go to war with an Anglo-Saxon power'.[5]

[1] See Henry Pelling, *America and the British Left* (London, 1956).

[2] On the significance of the Hay-Pauncefote treaty in Anglo-American relations generally see especially Grenville, op. cit., pp. 376–389.

[3] There was, of course, an element of discretion in deciding how far this retreat should be admitted. Writing to Balfour's secretary, Sandars, on March 31, 1905, Colonel Clarke (later Lord Sydenham), the secretary of the Committee of Imperial Defence, made a caveat about a proposed answer to a Parliamentary question: 'What it is best not to say is that we believe that the idea of opposing the navy of the U.S. in the Caribbean and the North Atlantic close to its bases must be abandoned.' Balfour Papers. B.M. Add. 49701.

[4] See Philip Goodhart, *Fifty Ships that Saved the World* (London, 1965).

[5] Asquith Papers. Dep. Asquith. 21.

But the experience of the 1914–18 war itself made a difference. It was clear that the United States had not abandoned for good those doctrines of the freedom of the seas that had caused so serious an Anglo-American crisis before America herself entered the war.[1] The war ended in a wave of 'big navy' sentiment in the United States which had serious repercussions on British thinking.[2] The disputes that ensued and the American reluctance to admit the close connection between naval armaments and the general armaments position in Europe caused intermittent and sometimes considerable friction between Britain and the United States until the London Conference of 1930, which may be taken as the point at which Britain finally acquiesced in effective American preponderance.

This naval controversy is also illuminating for a different reason. The British case for more light cruisers rested, as is well known, upon an assessment of the requirements arising from the responsibilities of patrolling the routes connecting the scattered portions of what was now an Empire *and* Commonwealth. The United States had no similar problem and tended to minimise the importance of such considerations on the British side.[3] The two countries had different geographical visions. The United States saw itself as a compact land-mass with certain outlying island bastions. The British saw their world in the form of a network of maritime communications threatened with possible strangulation by predatory powers on their flanks. The Mediterranean, the Suez Canal and its approaches, the Cape and Singapore—these were still a

[1] For an attempt to explain to a well-wishing American friend the dangers to Britain of an, indiscriminate use of the phrase 'freedom of the seas', see James Bryce's letters to Charles Eliot, May 11, July 1, August 8, 1915, January 29, 1916. Bryce Papers. U.S.A. 2. For Eliot's attempt to show that international guarantees would suit Britain better see his letter of August 26, 1916, ibid. U.S.A. 1.—partly printed in Henry James, *Charles Eliot* (London, 1930), vol. II, pp. 263–5.

[2] Wilson himself seems to have entertained the idea for a brief time that only the United States and Britain should be allowed to have navies at all and that together they should police the world. Letters from Lord Derby to Balfour, December 20 and 22, 1918. Balfour Papers. B. M. Add. 49744. Later, however, he appeared to British ministers to be advocating two incompatible policies, the League of Nations and a big navy for the United States. It was thought of the greatest consequence that Britain should not be forced into naval competition with the United States, both because of the latter's greater financial strength and because the British were unwilling to assume that the United States might ever be hostile. See Walter Long to Lloyd George, February 16, 1919. Austen Chamberlain Papers. A.C. 25. The American repudiation of the League Covenant and the triumph of isolation naturally played into the hands of those who believed that Britain must be able to rely on herself. The idea of making Britain's future security dependent on an international organisation had indeed been opposed during the war in some quarters largely on the ground that the Americans could not be relied upon. See, e.g. a minute from Hankey to Balfour of May 25, 1916, opposing the idea of a compulsory International Tribunal of Arbitration. Balfour Papers. B.M. Add. 49704.

[3] In a letter to General Smuts, referring to a paper by him on peace conversations, Kerr wrote that it was 'fatal to suggest that the German colonies must be retained because they are essential to British communications'. The United States would not look at that for a moment. Kerr to Smuts, December 14, 1917. Lothian Papers. Box 187.

focus of British attention and concern whose importance Americans were slow to appreciate. Not until the great debates over strategy in the Second World War was the full importance of these differences in perspective made altogether apparent.

But they had their effect even earlier. Those who during the First World War and the Peace Conference looked hopefully to Anglo-American co-operation as the basis of a future world order were dismayed at finding the Americans not merely ignorant of the problems of 'backward peoples' but convinced that the assumption of any kind of responsibility for them was 'iniquitous imperialism'.[1] In general the British were very anxious to encourage American participation in world affairs to the full extent America's revealed power justified. When it became likely that the United States would not ratify the Covenant some of those most attached to the American connection felt that Britain should also seek release from the obligations she had assumed.[2] Similarly it was felt that if Britain surrendered the Japanese alliance to Dominion and American pressure, the United States must in some form provide an alternative.[3] Only with this background in mind can one appreciate the nature of the important divergences over Far Eastern policy between Britain and the United States in the early 1930s.[4]

But the differences in outlook were not confined to naval and imperial questions. Roosevelt's indifference to Britain's need to see France restored to the position of a Great Power after the Second World War was in a line with the continuous refusal of the Americans in the inter-war period to understand European attitudes to the central problem of security. The British might disagree (at times violently) with the French over methods but they did not dissent from their objective. And after the failure of the Anglo-American guarantee treaty itself it was the American unwillingness to under-write any

[1] See, e.g. Philip Kerr to Lionel Curtis, October 15, 1918, quoted in J. R. M. Butler, *Lord Lothian* (London, 1960), p. 69.

[2] See the memorandum by Philip Kerr of November 14, 1919. Lothian Papers. Box 139. The blow was greatest for those whose American friends had assured them that ratification was certain. See, e.g. Charles Eliot's letters to Bryce, April 10, and May 12, 1919. Bryce Papers. U.S.A. 1.

[3] See Philip Kerr to John Dove, July 13, 1920. Lothian Papers. Box 186.

[4] Writing to Simon on September 1, 1934, Neville Chamberlain urged on him the danger of drifting into unfriendly relations with Japan. We should not allow ourselves to be brow-beaten by the United States who would not repay us for sacrificing our interests to conciliate her. Simon Papers. 'The discussions in London are getting into difficulties', wrote Lothian, 'not because there is any fundamental difference of view but because Great Britain before she knows where she is with the United States, is doing her best to avoid taking up an attitude of hostility to Japan. The United States, on the other hand, being in a much securer position, is trying to press us to take an attitude of opposition to Japan before she has really thought out what she is going to put into the pool if Japan forces the pace.' Lothian to Colonel House, November 30, 1934. Lothian Papers. Box 221. It is significant that Canadian sympathies were with the United States on this issue. Letter from Vincent Massey to Sir Alfred Zimmern, May 4, 1934, quoted in Massey, *What's Past is Prologue; Memoirs* (London, 1963), p. 207.

other British guarantees of French and European security that conditioned the whole of Britain's European policy from 1919 to 1939.

After the Somme and Passchendaele, after the submarine warfare crisis of 1917, Britain, it was clear, could never again contemplate a full-scale battle for existence without some assurance of American support. For this support she was prepared to bid high, as the Baldwin debt settlement indicated. Britain felt obliged to surrender other guarantees of her position which were incompatible with American friendship. The Anglo-Japanese alliance was in fact terminated.[1] But caution about the 'sanctions' clauses of the Covenant and a general predisposition to limit continental commitments were also products of the priority accorded to America.[2] Unless the negative influence of American policy is properly assessed—whether exerted directly or through Canada—one cannot understand the whole complex of policy that goes under the name of 'appeasement'.[3]

It is true that the United States' attitude played rather a minor part in the final stages of this policy except in its impact upon the Dominions. The reason may be that of all the British statesmen of the period, Neville Chamberlain was perhaps the least disposed to give major weight to the American factor. His position in this respect may have been affected by his deep mistrust of Cordell Hull, arising from the latter's persistent campaign against the Ottawa system of preferences. In February 1937, when Chamberlain was still at the Exchequer, he received a message from the American Secretary of the Treasury asking whether the United States could do anything to help bring about an agreement on disarmament. Chamberlain's reply (after consulting Baldwin and Eden) was that the main source of danger and fear in Europe arose from Germany's intensive military preparations, propaganda

[1] Walter Long, the First Lord of the Admiralty, told his colleagues on May 30, 1921, that political relations with the United States were of such transcendent importance to Britain as to outweigh all other considerations of policy. He had been assured by Admiral Sims that the American people were vehemently opposed to the alliance and that while it lasted it would be impossible to curb the American cry for increased Armaments. Austen Chamberlain Papers. A.C. 26. Americans were prone to argue even after their repudiation of the League that the Anglo-Japanese alliance belonged to the 'old order' and could not be squared with the new theories of international relations being advocated by the British and American Governments. See Paul Cravath to Edward Grigg, October 4, 1921. Grigg Papers.

[2] The American Secretary of State Hughes worked hard to prevent ratification of the Geneva Protocol. According to the leading French historian of the period, Britain was forced to choose between the United States and the Protocol and chose the former. J. B. Duroselle, *From Wilson to Roosevelt: Foreign Policy of the United States*, 1913–45 (London, 1964), pp. 164–5.

[3] As early as 1924 Mackenzie King was pointing out to the Governor General, Lord Byng, the importance of Canada keeping aloof from European affairs. 'If the people got the idea we were to be drawn into the European arena there would certainly be a movement to the United States which had kept out of the League of Nations on that account and political union with the U.S. might become a subject of discussion.' Mackenzie King's Diary, December 1, 1924, quoted by H. Blair Neatby, *William Lyon Mackenzie King*, vol. II. *The Lonely Heights*, 1924–32 (Toronto, 1963), p. 44.

against other countries and violation of treaty obligations. Only a superiority of force could contain her.[1] Another approach from Hull made through Lord Tweedsmuir, the Governor-General of Canada, that autumn after Chamberlain became Prime Minister again, met with the answer that economic appeasement was insufficient and that Germany would have to be brought to co-operate on political issues as well.[2]

It is important to understand this background to the much-debated negative that Chamberlain returned to Roosevelt's initiative in January 1938.[3] The American offer did not alter the political and strategic facts of the situation, which was not susceptible to handling in purely economic terms. Perhaps this belief that the United States could not materially assist in 'appeasement' helps to explain the surprising decision to abandon the policy without any assurances of American support for the alternative—resistance.

For 'appeasement' was abandoned in the end without any positive guarantees of American aid, although of course in the knowledge that the nature of the enemy this time made it certain that there would be no repetition of the equivocations of the American policy of the 1914–17 period. The United States could not be genuinely neutral in a Hitler war. Whether British statesmen felt in their hearts that sooner or later the United States would be drawn in to it is something we are not entitled to say. Only after June 1940 was Britain's resistance obviously predicated on the expectation of ultimate American involvement. Anything else would have been quixotic in the extreme.

But although Churchill might play upon the sentiment of the 'special relationship' in public utterances, once it became safe to do so without causing embarrassment to Britain's friends in America, he did not rely upon it. He was fully aware of the seniority of the Americans in the partnership and in spite of some gestures of defiance, in the main acted upon this awareness.[4]

In the post-war world, America's growing determination to 'contain'

[1] See John Blum, *Years of Crisis* (From the Morgenthau Diaries, vol. I, Boston, 1959), pp. 458 ff. Cf. Lord Avon, *Facing the Dictators* (London, 1962), pp. 526–7; Ian Colvin, *Vansittart in Office* (London, 1965), pp. 140–3.

[2] Lord Tweedsmuir to Neville Chamberlain, October 25, 1937; Lord Simon to Lord Tweedsmuir, November 24, 1937—both in the Simon Papers.

[3] It should not be thought that the answer to Roosevelt was solely the work of Chamberlain. Roosevelt's message kept the Foreign Policy Committee of the Cabinet 'busy all week.' Sir John Simon's diary in the Simon Papers.

[4] Churchill's inevitable concessions to the Americans contrast with the ability of Asquith in the First World War to resist suggestions that Irish policy might.be modified, or the blockade, 'black list' and censorship measures seriously weakened in order to conciliate American opinion. See the Foreign Office memorandum of October 30, 1916. Asquith Papers. Dep. Asquith 130. and other documents in this collection. Some concessions were of course made: 'on 22 July 1915, the Cabinet decided that in view of the situation between the United States and Great Britain, no American ships outward bound from Europe, although presumably carrying German goods, should be stopped by our cordon.' Cecil to Balfour, April 12, 1916. Balfour Papers. B.M. Add. 49738.

communism coincided with the British desire to perpetuate American involvement in the defence of areas considered vital from the British point of view. Few incidents in the transfer of responsibility were as clear-cut as that involving the enunciation of the 'Truman doctrine' when Britain confessed herself unable any longer to uphold the independence of Greece and Turkey. And this perhaps prevented a full understanding on the British side of the sacrifices that had to be made in return for this aid.

The new nature of the 'special relationship' was most fully illustrated in relation to the 'Suez' affair of 1956: and this not so much in John Foster Dulles' cavalier disregard for his allies' interests, and the deception practised upon them in leading them to expect that the Americans would give an active support to their claims which they clearly had no intention of providing, but rather in the nature of the opposition to, and subsequent criticism of the British Prime Minister. If one discounts the hysteria of the Left, the real charge brought against Sir Anthony Eden (now Lord Avon) was precisely the fact that he had kept America in the dark about his plans, and undertaken military measures without making certain of American backing should the country run into difficulties. The Americans were not blamed for frustrating a British action so much as the British Prime Minister was blamed for embarking upon an action which the Americans would wish to frustrate. And it is significant that criticism of this kind was most strongly echoed in Whitehall itself, the repository, as it were, of the central traditions of British external policy.[1]

It is therefore likely that when the records of Mr Harold Macmillan's premiership come to be revealed we shall find the re-establishment of confidential relations with the United States as having been his prime objective. The 'Nassau Agreement' of December 1962 may fittingly illustrate the nature and limitations of his success. It could be represented, as it was by its British negotiators, as a perpetuation and recognition of Britain's survival as a Great Power, based upon the availability to it of an independent nuclear deterrent; it could be represented by their critics, and notably by General de Gaulle, as the acceptance by Britain of a degree of dependence upon the United States amounting virtually to satellite status.

What is not clear is the extent to which earlier British statesmen and the exponents of their policies perceived the rate at which the process of the substitution of American for British power and influence was in fact taking place. One is inclined to think that for the most part they were largely unconscious of it.[2] The equilibrium had been shaken but sooner or later it would

[1] Here time had made a difference; in 1911 the Foreign Office was described as so anti-American as to make it always difficult to discuss American affairs with its senior officials. George Young to James Bryce, July 13, 1911. Bryce Papers. U.S.A. 32.

[2] There were exceptions. In reference to the Kellogg Pact negotiations Gilbert Murray wrote to an American friend: 'The world is now engaged on an exceedingly delicate process, inevitable whether we regret it or rejoice in it, viz. the transference of wealth, power and

be re-established. The concessions that had to be made did not detract from Britain's essential requirements, or were paradoxically justified by the need to hold the Commonwealth together.[1] For one must not forget that after 1930 at any rate the relationship did not any longer concern London and Washington alone. First, and inevitably, Canada, and later Australia and New Zealand sought their own national security in relations with the United States of a kind that did not necessarily strengthen the Commonwealth tie, although for Britain to have opposed their intentions would certainly have weakened it. We have still to estimate the role of Mr Mackenzie King either as an honest broker between the British and the Americans, or as a grave-digger of Empire, according to one's point of view.[2]

The degree to which Britain had no choice was something which many either failed to understand, or if they understood it, kept to themselves. The faith in the 'special relationship' that seemed to remove Anglo-American relations from the ordinary sordid calculations of power politics may have prevented proper assessments of the situation from being made, or from being made known to the public when they were. The difficulty was that the 'special relationship' was not all illusion—if it had been there would have been no problem. On the personal level, whether between government servants or between the armed services—truer here of army than navy, one must add—a very high degree of intimate contact between individuals was possible in wartime;[3] and from its existence both nations, but especially the British, reaped handsome dividends.

Nevertheless, as we have noted, such personal contacts, including the numerous Anglo-American marriages, as might have fitted British statesmen or diplomats for working closely with the United States were limited by their narrow social range.[4] Business ties were largely those with the financial world

leadership from Great Britain to America. It wants a very high standard of public duty and intelligence on your part and on ours to conduct that proceeding of the dethronement of Great Britain and the enthronement of the United States without war.' Gilbert Murray to S. Levinson, December 3, 1928. Gilbert Murray Papers. Bodleian Library.

[1] It was argued by some that the Locarno Pact would have the effect of destroying the diplomatic unity of the British Empire and so would drive the Dominions into the arms of the United States. Kerr to Lloyd George, November 13, 1925. Lothian Papers. Box 188.

[2] This brokerage began before Mackenzie King's premiership. Theodore Roosevelt tried to use him as a channel to the British Government in 1908 over the question of reaching a joint policy on Japanese immigration on the Pacific Coast in respect of which the Anglo-Japanese alliance put difficulties in the way of a direct approach to London. R. MacGregor Dawson, *William Lyon Mackenzie King: a Political Biography*, vol. I (London and Toronto, 1958), pp. 152–61.

[3] On sentiment towards Britain in the American navy see Goodhart, op. cit., pp. 64–5.

[4] Before the First World War the contacts at the highest level were few indeed. In 1917, the American Ambassador, W. H. Page, pointed out to Balfour that neither he himself since 1875 (when he was only twenty-seven years old), nor Grey, Lloyd George, Asquith, nor any other important British statesman had visited the United States. Kenneth Young, op. cit., p. 379.

of New York, which was itself a very suspect factor in American life.[1] The two trade-union movements were separated from each other by profound differences in structure and spirit.[2]

Much has been made of the alleged failure of the British at large to give serious attention to American history or the American polity. Such criticism was in part exaggerated; at no time was the British reader at a loss for serious studies of important aspects of the American scene. No other European country was served so well. Indeed, the real damage may have been done when conscious efforts were made to improve things. For the introduction of American history and politics into school and university courses was inevitably the work of enthusiasts who, being animated by laudable desire to improve the two countries' relations, were prone to underestimate the importance of the real differences between them. Similarly the visiting American professors who after the First World War, and even more during and after the Second, found their way to British shores were unlikely to represent those elements in the American population which it was very important for the British to get to know, just because they repudiated so many aspects of the British view of the world.

Even in peacetime, such personal relationships played an important part as those who took part in the transactions of the Marshall plan era are always willing to testify. It was a rare Frenchman who, like Jean Monnet, could acquire a similar place for himself in the counsels of official Washington. But great democracies are not deflected from their national policies by personal friendships. Individuals might help to dissipate genuine ignorance or genuine misunderstandings—a Lothian, a Halifax might make relations easier, a Brand or a Purvis break through jungles of red-tape that might have strangled lesser men. On the other side, it was no doubt helpful when a John Winant and a Harry Hopkins replaced Joseph Kennedy as the authorised interpreters of the British scene to Roosevelt. But the great issues were decided as a result of factors outside their control.

The very understanding which some Americans showed for the British predicament in war-time may have contributed to difficulties later on, when the essential national interests of the two sides came into play. For it may have been hard for people to believe that this cordial intimacy in the common task did not preclude an ultimate divergence in aims. The abrupt termination of lend-lease, the exclusion of Britain from further co-operation in the exploitation of what were largely British discoveries in the field of nuclear energy are two examples of the way in which reliance upon assumptions of a common purpose was falsified in the event.[3]

[1] The utility and limitations of such contacts are well brought out in Sir Harold Nicolson *Dwight Morrow* (London, 1935).

[2] When Ramsay MacDonald visited the United States in 1927 he felt no strong bond of sympathy with the American trade-union hierarchy: 'he was amazed at their conservatism and affluence.' Massey, op. cit., p. 150.

[3] To adduce the latter example does not mean to exculpate the British from all blame for

Even if one discounts the personal factor there remains the need to study in much greater detail than has been done the changing scope and nature of the official representation of each country in the other during the whole of the period. Apart from the special case of Bryce, it was the First World War which saw the first serious attention paid to the question of who should be British Ambassador in Washington, and what additional representation was required. And for some time afterwards, it was still felt that the post could not be treated on ordinary lines. If, following Lord Reading's successful mission, a diplomatist were appointed, it was felt that Britain would lose the exceptional position she had acquired at Washington.[1] Almost everyone of note in British political life was canvassed for the post—Speaker Lowther, Lord Finley, Lord Devonshire, Lord Salisbury, Lord Crewe, Balfour, Austen Chamberlain and the Canadian, Sir Robert Borden—before the choice fell on Sir Auckland Geddes.[2] Subsequently, the view that a public figure was required was abandoned,[3] and until Lord Lothian's appointment in 1939 the Washington Embassy was again filled by the normal operation of the diplomatic *cursus honorum*.[4]

Under Lothian and Halifax the Washington Embassy became, as it has remained, and for obvious reasons, rather a microcosm of Whitehall overseas than an ordinary diplomatic post.[5] But the issue as between a 'political' and a 'career' ambassador remains interestingly unsettled.[6]

To sum up: the 'special relationship' is a fact, but a fact of a rather peculiar kind; for myths are also facts. It would be interesting, however, to inquire further into why it has been found psychologically so necessary to dress up in this way a perfectly honourable relationship as though national self-interest were something which should play no part in this branch of international politics. One possible reason is to be found in a remark by A. V. Dicey, whose own legal and constitutional interests may explain his advocacy of an Anglo-

developments that were to be costly for both countries. While they had a comfortable lead in the field the British were slow to enter into full partnership with the Americans; had they done so it is possible, though not certain, that they might have got arrangements for co-operation which would have stood them in good stead later on. See M. M. Gowing, *Britain and Atomic Energy*, 1939–1945, (London 1965). Cf. Sir John Wheeler-Bennett, *John Anderson, Viscount Waverley* (London, 1962), pp. 332 ff.

[1] Drummond to Balfour, January 23, 1919. Lothian Papers. Box 141.

[2] Balfour Papers. B.M. Add. 49734.

[3] In 1929, MacDonald thought of sending Gilbert Murray, but it was felt that his own visit to the United States had so changed the situation that a diplomat would serve Britain's purposes better. Murray to Miss I. Munro, October 25, 1929. Gilbert Murray Papers.

[4] No ex-Ambassador to the United States had until 1961 filled the post of Permanent Secretary at the Foreign Office.

[5] On the background to this see Max Beloff, *New Dimensions in Foreign Policy* (London, 1961).

[6] One also needs a study of the effectiveness of the representation of the British Press in the United States. A beginning has been made in *The History of the Times*, vol. IV (London, 1952), chapter 9.

American *entente cordiale* and his tendency to talk of the Americans as though they were just another branch of the English people.

> Both branches of the English people [he wrote in 1911] seem to me to act somewhat better in foreign affairs than do Continental States. But to make up for this both branches of the English people persuade themselves that they pursue in international affairs far more disinterested principles than they in reality act up to.[1]

In this respect the lapse of over half a century has brought about little change.[2]

[1] A. V. Dicey to James Bryce, March 23, 1911. Bryce Papers. English Papers. Vol. 3.

[2] The present essay sketches out some broad themes which the writer hopes to develop further and document more fully as part of a general study of the development of Britain's world outlook in the twentieth century which he is writing under the auspices of the international affairs programme of the Rockefeller Foundation. He would wish to acknowledge the assistance of the Foundation (and also its hospitality at the Villa Serbelloni where the essay was written). He would also wish to thank his research assistant, Mrs M. Croft (née Heeley), B.A.

H. N. FIELDHOUSE

Noel Buxton and A. J. P. Taylor's 'The Trouble Makers'

H. N. FIELDHOUSE

Noel Buxton and A. J. P. Taylor's 'The Trouble Makers'

IT is no denigration of A. J. P. Taylor's more substantial works to say that the most captivating thing which he has written is his *The Trouble Makers: Dissent over Foreign Policy*. He, himself, wrote that 'the Dissenters existed: therefore they deserve to be put on record' but he added 'they have been deeply English in blood and in temperament'. The addition is important because while the study of foreign policy conducted according to the rules of *realpolitik* has its own fascination (particularly if one can set aside one's moral judgment and agree to regard the virtuosi among the practitioners of *realpolitik* in the spirit of art for art's sake), the trick (at least, since the eighteenth century) does not come easily to Englishmen. Taylor saw that 'dissent is a quality peculiar to English-speaking peoples' and, if we broaden 'dissent' to include those humanitarian impulses at which Professor Brogan poked legitimate, if exaggerated, fun,[1] then it can be said that a history of British policy which omits it is limping history.

It was Sir Edward Grey, not, as Taylor has more than once remarked, the least sympathetic, among Foreign Secretaries, to the Dissenters, who wrote:

> In other countries, whatever the humane sentiments of individuals may have been about their own affairs, they did not take the form of pressure for philanthropic action abroad that might involve their own Government in complications with continental neighbours. It was only an island such as Britain that could safely afford to embark on diplomatic crusades. To continental countries, these British efforts were often inconvenient, . . . and they were often resented, because they were not understood. They sometimes ran counter to obvious British interests, but this did not predispose foreign Governments to think them sincere. On the contrary, it stimulated them to search deeply for some concealed motive, though the true one lay on the surface before their eyes.

The purpose of this essay is to consider one trouble maker, Noel Buxton, in Taylorian terms.[2] Taylor understands the difficulty of defining 'Dissent'

[1] *Is Innocence Enough?* (London, 1941).

[2] The Buxton Papers are in the Redpath Library of McGill University. Save where otherwise specified, all references in this essay are to Letters and Memoranda in the Papers.

in foreign policy. 'A man can disagree', he wrote, 'with a particular line of British foreign policy, while still accepting its general assumptions. The Dissenter repudiates its aims, its methods, its principles. What is more, he claims to know better and to promote higher causes; he asserts a superiority, moral or intellectual.'

But Taylor realises that the lines are not easily drawn. In particular, he saw that though the Dissenters were 'not good party men', they were 'usually linked with the Liberal or later with the Labour Party' and that 'this produces confusion'. This distinction, between Dissent and the parties, he, on the whole, sustained, but it is less easy to adhere to his distinction between Dissent and 'the high-minded'. Both the outcry against the Bulgarian Horrors and that against Mussolini's attack on Abyssinia were not, Taylor thinks, the work of Dissent but of the high-minded: the first inheriting 'rather the moral passion of the abolitionists against slavery, by no means a Dissenting affair'; the second, the work of 'the League of Nations Union . . . heirs of Gladstone maybe, but certainly not of Bright. . . .'

In these terms, Noel Buxton belonged not to Dissent but to the high-minded. The key is in the phrases about 'moral passion' and 'the heirs of Gladstone'. Buxton's father had been a Gladstonian Liberal and Buxton's own early concern was 'to connect philanthropy and business activity with Christian ideals',[1] i.e. to promote that social reform in which, in Taylor's view, Gladstone had so largely submerged Dissent in foreign policy. His early mentors had been the latitudinarian Canon Barnett, the High Church Bishop Gore and Bryce ('my political father'[2]); and, from 1905 to 1910, he was watched over and exhorted by G. W. E. Russell in terms of the purest Gladstonianism.[3]

Most lyrical in this cause was Charles Masterman, of the Christian Social Union and 'the most brilliant contemporary who gave me his friendship in my youth'.[4] Masterman had enlisted Buxton in the cause of Temperance Reform and, writing to his 'Beloved Cadet', pointed out that 'where our opportunity lies is in the hopeless disorganisation of the Liberal party and their *real need* for some social policy. They don't know where they are or what they want. We might help to supply this and so get notoriety—poor and ignorant though we be. The Tories know their own minds and don't want *our* teaching,'[5] Fifteen months later, he cried 'Would that we could get you in the "slums".

[1] Buxton's typed draft of an *Autobiography*, chapter VIII.

[2] *Idem.*

[3] When Buxton entered the Commons, in 1905, Russell wrote (June 2): 'In all earnestness, I pray God to help your parliamentary career and to make you His faithful and successful soldier in the difficult battlefield of public life.' Later (n.d.) he was to write: 'I never should have entered Parliament if it had not been for Mr. Gladstone's lead in the matter. But, since his day, no one seems to realize the truth about the anti-Christian spirit, in its bearing on the E(astern) Q(uestion).'

[4] Draft of an *Autobiography*, chapter VIII.

[5] Masterman to Buxton, March 16, 1901.

What hope is there in the "froth" of English Society—the Asquiths etc. who are cheerfully dancing us to destruction. Really the condition of this nation gets ever more and more pitiable. "If thou hadst known, even thou in this thy day, the things that belong unto thy peace,—but *now* they are hid from thine eyes." That is the New Testament and I believe utterly applicable to London in the year of our Lord 1901."[1] And, at the time of Buxton's election to represent Whitby: 'Have not we planned together on the slopes of the Juras, in the English Channel, at many diversified times and places, the building of the temple of the Lord and the smiting of the heathen? And shall not we continue together to engage in such work until our life's end? If only you knew how much I longed for you to get in at Whitby! If we can still keep health and hope we will yet do some damage to the forces of hell and all uncleanness.'[2] In this atmosphere, it is not, perhaps, surprising that Lord Beauchamp should have written to Buxton 'that Churchmen dislike our politics and politicians dislike our churchmanship.'[3]

Taylor emphasised the decisive effect of the Boer War in creating the New Radicalism which triumphed in 1906 and flourished for the next decade, and Buxton's development exemplifies his point. 'It required the Boer War to give me much contact with the Liberal Party view', he wrote, 'and even so it was only with the Campbell Bannerman section of the Liberals.'[4] It was always to the Campbell-Bannerman tradition that he adhered. Even in the letter of 1902, quoted above, Masterman had begun to marry social reform with Dissent in foreign policy: 'Read Peabody—pray for light—smite all "Liberal Imperialists" when they are evidently shown, hypocrites, self-seekers and "souls"—and think of schemes to draw Christians together in the midst of a pagan world.': and, when Buxton returned to Parliament, in 1910, he was soon joined with Phillip Morrell in what he called 'a crusade against the Russian Government' for imprisoning a Polish girl Socialist and against the Government for its lethargy in the matter. 'I remember raising the question on the adjournment,' he wrote, 'and using the expression, "Oh for an hour of Palmerston!" '[5]

The Liberal Party was now under Liberal Imperialist chiefs in Asquith, Haldane and Grey, and Buxton recorded: 'We were all sympathetic with Ramsay Macdonald, who had just become Labour leader, and we were naturally disapproved of by the mass of Liberal members, many of whom appeared to us little distinguishable from the Tories.'[6]

Given his conception of Liberalism, his later passage over to the Labour

[1] *Idem*, June 4, 1902.

[2] *Idem*, 1905.

[3] To Buxton, March 24, 1904. There was question of Buxton joining Beauchamp in giving financial help to the weekly review 'of politics, literature & learning', *The Pilot*.

[4] Draft of an *Autobiography*, chapter IX.

[5] *Idem*.

[6] *Idem*.

Party, in 1919, was natural enough. To a supporter in his constituency of North Norfolk, on November 6, he wrote:

> You will agree with me that those who belong to the school of Campbell Bannerman are indebted to the Labour Party for urging views, both about the Peace Settlement and about Social Reform, which he would have expressed but which the Liberal leaders of to-day have left to the Radical section of the Liberal Party. At the same time I realise that we shall best defeat the reactionary forces in the country if Radicalism and Labour work together . . . Radicalism and Labour have the same views on Free Trade, Conscription, the campaign against Public Waste and Profiteering, Ireland and Russia. The supposed antagonism between the Parties is a fiction engineered by Toryism for its own advantage.

In retrospect, in his draft for an *Autiobiography*, he elaborated these views:[1]

> Until the Great War it never crossed my mind that I might join the Labour Party . . . During the war two aspects changed my mind. On the one hand the Liberals who, under Asquith's leadership, tended to pursue respectability and drop the Radical idealism of Campbell Bannerman, seemed to conform more and more to the Conservative outlook. The activities of wartime brought Parties together. For the first time Liberals found themselves free from hostility, and on war questions they displayed no difference of view. There were admirable exceptions. Buckmaster in particular, who had been a Law Officer, held views like those of Lansdowne on the settlement which should be pursued. I urged him to give a lead in that direction, and he felt strongly drawn to this but said he could not break loose from Asquith to whom he owed so much. Indeed Asquith himself would have made a better peace than Lloyd George, but until his overthrow he showed no public sign of disapproving the purely 'knock out' policy which L.G. definitely pursued, thereby winning public favour, and justifying his expulsion of Asquith. The result of this attitude of the Liberals was to make us who took a special interest in war and peace questions feel keen to support candidates of our view, even if they were Labour. . . . I was convinced that the Labour Party represented a far greater interest in the question of peace and war than did the Liberal Party. The question was so little spoken of by Liberal politicians that one could be attacked as I was for talking of foreign politics and denounced to the electors as the friend of every country but one's own. It was the Labour Party which changed that, and it is essentially committed to international order because it is an international movement and organization. More than that, it was recognized by the best Christian leaders, e.g., Gore and Temple, as embodying Christian ideals.

His old friend of the Balkan Committee, Sir Edward Boyle, declared himself 'so glad I have . . . maintained my standpoint that historic Liberalism has nothing to do either with Imperialism or Socialism. Asquith let us down over the one and L.G. over the other. We must get back to C.B. and Morley.'[2] Another former ally, however, was looking to older mentors than C.B. and Morley. F. W. Hirst, who had been warm in his congratulations on Buxton's

[1] *Idem.*
[2] To Buxton, January 22, 1919.

first entry into the Commons,[1] now warned him: 'If you want a philosopy of human freedom you will have to return to Cobden and Bright. Tyranny and oppression of minorities are alas part of the socialist doctrine of over-government . . . The socialist who denies freedom to the individual at home cannot defend conscription big battleships and nineteen shilling income tax in order to secure the freedom of individuals in Turkey, Russia, Texas and Korea.'[2] Alan Taylor would have appreciated the omission of Gladstone between C.B. and Cobden and Bright.

Nevertheless, both the historic background of, and the inspiration for, Buxton's first incursion into foreign affairs (the creation of the Balkan Committee) was thoroughly Gladstonian. He always saw the liberation of Macedonia as being the particular responsibility of Britain because of Disraeli's action in having substituted the terms of the Treaty of Berlin for those of San Stefano.[3] This argument was common form among the supporters of the Balkan Committee and would seem to have originated with Bryce who wrote to Buxton, as early as August 31, 1903: '. . . it would be a good thing for the Commitee to prepare and issue a statement of the facts beginning with the Treaty of San Stefano and dwelling upon our *responsibilities* . . . it will be better to direct attention to the vital *facts* and the *responsibility* of Britain and the need to clear out the Turk once for all rather than to "justifying" the insurrection.'

The story of the intervention of Buxton and his friends in Balkan affairs is a supreme example of Taylor's remark that 'sometimes the Dissenters have accused the Foreign Secretary and his advisers of ignorance, sometimes of corruption' and that 'sometimes the critics transcended Dissent and tried to run a rival foreign policy of their own'.

In the years between the Macedonian Insurrection of 1903 and the Young Turk Revolution, the fact was that, first, Lansdowne and, then, Grey, had pushed British initiative in the matter of Macedonian reform as far as it was possible to go in step with the limitrophe Powers, Austria-Hungary and Russia, and that to go further would be to risk a rift in the Concert and to reopen, not the Macedonian, but the Turkish Question. As Grey warned the Commons:

> . . . In discussing the Macedonian question you are never far from the Turkish question. The Turkish question has more than once led to a European war. As

[1] 'Your glorious victory, which is especially appetising to Yorkshiremen who live in the neighbourhood' (June 6, 1905). Buxton's victory in a bye-election in 1905 and his defeat in the General Election of 1906 had been hailed and deplored, respectively, by those who, like a correspondent in Suffolk, saw him as 'joining the forces working for righteousness at St. Stephens'. Of his defeat, the Bishop of Birmingham (Charles Gore) wrote: 'It is pitiable. You are exactly the man we wanted in.'

[2] To Buxton, January 6, 1922.

[3] In his draft *Autobiography*, he wrote: 'When I first became acquainted with the pitiable condition of the Macedonian peoples I was intensely moved by their sufferings and by the fact that they were due to the action of our own country. In 1878 Disraeli preserved the Turkish Empire in Europe from being liberated by Russia.'

> long as the Concert exists you have a certain guarantee that that question will not lead to war at the present time; but if the Concert disappears you can no longer feel the certainty you have to-day, that the different Powers interested in the Near East will long continue to keep in touch with each other. Once they lose touch with each other you cannot tell what misunderstandings may creep in between them nor to what extent those misunderstandings may go on.[1]

The Balkan Committee was loath to accept this situation. Not all of Buxton's group shared the cheerful levity of Scott Holland who assured him (1903) that 'I am delighted to join you in your conspiracy against the Turk', but even Bryce (while suggesting caution in disclosing the full aims of the Committee, in public) wrote privately of 'the need of getting rid of the Turks'[2] and, nine days later, affirmed that 'I personally want to see Turkish rule removed out of existence altogether, in Asia as well as in Europe, and the sooner the better.'[3] It was a portent of disappointment to come that Campbell-Bannerman declined to be drawn into the Committee's orbit[4]; and it was a portent, too, that criticism of the Committee's activities came not only from the Foreign Office but also from Dissenters with other preoccupations.

From the Government side, Lord Eustace Percy doubted the need for the Committee's promptings. In a temperate letter of April 11, 1905, he wrote: 'I do not perhaps attach the value which you do to "agitation" in this country. It is not I think required by a British government and owing to its past history it excites the maximum of suspicion and resentment on the part of the Turks.'[5]

[1] Parliamentary Debates. Fourth Series. CXXXIV. 1701. See P. R. Jennings: 'British Foreign Policy with regard to the Macedonian Question, 1903–13'. (Thesis in the Redpath Library, McGill University.)

[2] To Buxton, July 6, 1903.

[3] To Buxton, July 15, 1903.

[4] To Buxton, November 20, 1905. 'I came to the conclusion that I had better not sign the Balkan Committee's Memorial to Lord L(ansdowne).'

[5] Buxton and his friends seem to have remained unperturbed by evidence, even when it came from their own allies, that the non-Turkish peoples of the Balkans were not immaculate. In June 1909, while blaming the Greeks and the Servians for maintaining bands in Macedonia, Bourchier reported that 'the Bulgarians are divided into three parties all at war with each other and a good deal of murdering is going on'. At the end of the year, he wrote that he was 'enlightening *The Times* with regard to the Young Greek movement which is more or less an understudy of the Young Turk one'. In April 1914, he found Macedonia under the Greeks and Servians 'a perfect hell', but a month earlier, having written that 'it is only a mockery to abolish Turkish rule in the Balkans if it is to be succeeded by what is worse tyranny in many ways', and having recited the tale of massacres perpetrated by the Greeks, he concluded 'that the influence of our Court is all powerful in their favour, and Constantine's butcheries have never been revealed'. During the Balkan Wars, Arthur Moore (one time Secretary of the Balkan Committee) wrote, in April 1913: 'I don't really think the Turkish atrocities in the war have been more than a drop in the ocean in comparison with the Christian performance.' When the Great War came, Edith Durham who, in 1911, had made poignant appeals to the Committee on behalf of Albanian refugees from Turkish oppression, wrote to Buxton that she was appalled (May 17, 1917) by the infamy of the cruelties practised by Servians on Montenegrins, and vice versa.

On March 29, he had made the shrewd judgment that 'My own brief visit to Macedonia convinced me that the population feared the comitadjis even more than any mis-government by Turkish officials. Against the terrorism of the former they have no resource—against the latter they have already partial and I hope eventually will have complete securities.'

For the Social Democratic Federation, H. M. Hyndman was far from temperate:[1]

> Strange as it may seem to you, I find that I have quite enough to do with reference to the appalling poverty of the large masses of our own countrymen here at home, directly due to the cruelty and the indifference of the Tory and Liberal factions who agree to pay no attention whatever to the inevitable result of the social and economic domination by which their leaders and followers in the House of Commons alike profit. I also consider that British rule in India is in many respects more infamous and more injurious, for an almost infinitely greater number of the human race, than is Turkish rule in the Balkans, about which you and your Committee are so greatly exercised. I do not observe, however, that any member of your Committee has, at any time of his life, devoted any considerable amount of his time to helping the 12,500,000 British people whom Sir Henry Campbell Bannerman, Leader of the Liberal Party in the House of Commons, avers are constantly on the brink of starvation; nor do I note that any of them has ever vigorously endeavoured to put an end to the bleeding to death of our greatest dependency, and to the deliberate manufacture of famine on an ever-increasing scale for the greater part of the 230,000,000 under direct British rule in Hindustan.

It was what Taylor saw as the 'pro-Bulgarian' attitude of the Buxton's[2] which formed the link between the period before 1914 (when the Balkan

[1] To Buxton, A. Moore, and R. Yerburgh, March 4, 1905. Intermediate between Percy and Hyndman, was H. F. Lynch whose chief concern was for the Armenians. He wrote (March 5, 1906) that 'the policy of futile pinpricks' stood condemned 'even on humanitarian grounds' as having resulted in 'abominable butchery'. We could only exercise a real influence on Turkey if we resumed our old ascendancy over her, and he believed this to be still possible. As to 'the Salisbury attitude' that we had put our money on the wrong horse, 'my answer to that is that the winning of a race depends quite as much upon the jockey as upon the horse. Rather a poor horse, I admit; but the German jockey is riding him not only with great advantage to himself, but in some respects with benefit to the horse'. England could never follow the German policy of leaving the Sultan a free hand with his Christian subjects, but there was no need to abdicate in this way. 'If he cannot hope to obtain . . . assistance from us, he will naturally resist our demands. . . . We can well say to him: "No reforms, no assistance"; but we cannot say to him: "Reforms and no assistance." '

[2] On January 10, 1913, Aubrey Herbert resigned from the Committee on the ground that 'I have, for some time past, been out of sympathy with the partizan attitude of the Balkan Committee, which favoured the Bulgarian at the expense of the Greek and Moslem inhabitants in Macedonia'. Pointing out that '. . . the Servians have massacred Albanians wholesale' and 'that Bulgarian Committees are exterminating the Moslem women & children in Macedonia with the object of establishing a claim to inherit the land', he thought that 'the least your committee could do . . . is to declare your disapproval of such . . . savagery, before passing resolutions which deal with the apportionment of the spoil & the inheritance of the murdered'.

Committee acted as, in Bryce's phrase, a body 'formed for the sake of awakening and focussing public interest and of supplying accurate information and just views, to a too ignorant public'[1]) and the period of the Great War when Buxton and his friends virtually put themselves forward as an alternative Foreign Office with respect to the Balkans.

As early as the spring of 1904, Buxton was already so confident of the position and influence of the Balkan Committee that he was writing to Lansdowne, on behalf of 'the leaders of the Macedonian insurgents', to ask for explanations of the Secretary of State's pronouncements in the House of Lords;[2] but it was in connection with his plans of 1914–5 to bring Bulgaria into the war on the Allied side that he and his friends expressly asserted their claim to special knowledge of, and special influence in, the Balkans. In identical notes to Grey and to Lloyd George, on September 30, 1914, Buxton described himself as 'having special sources of information regarding political factors in Bulgaria' and, in the following June, he actually asked to be supplied with the Foreign Office telegrams on the Balkans.[3] In the same month, he submitted, to Cecil, a private memorandum on 'the working of the Foreign Office as I have seen it in connection with the Balkan question'. He complained that the information of the Office about Bulgaria was 'defective'; that 'special evils' had sprung from the 'constant and ostentatious' sympathy of the Minister at Sofia (Bax Ironside) for the Serbs, and that the First Secretary (O'Reilly), who had done most to repair the damage done by Bax Ironside, had been recalled. 'Not only was he not put into the War Department (where his knowledge would be of daily use) but he was not even seen by Grey or Nicholson on his return.' Buxton's dealings with Grey had left, he said, 'an impression of amateurishness' and, in sum: 'Seeing the undoubted ability and personnel of the Foreign Office, one is puzzled by the apparent failures in its action. One hears various reasons suggested, e.g. the traditions of short-sighted circumspection which weighs small risks and ignores great ones, and of unwillingness to risk rebuff, however slight, ingrained in time of peace.'

There were obvious difficulties in the way of Buxton's plan, chief of them, the fact that the rulers of Bulgaria were convinced that Germany was going to win the war so that, as Amery wrote: 'I cannot help thinking that what the other side has to offer Bulgaria is in many ways so much more attractive than what we have to give, including as it very easily might not only Skoplye but

[1] To Buxton, July 25, 1903.

[2] Sanderson (Permanent Under-Secretary) to Buxton, May 2, 1904.

[3] Crewe replied (June 30, 1915): 'It would not be possible to send you all the telegrams on the Balkan question, as this would involve telegrams from and to France, Russia and Italy with whom we are in frequent consultation. Necessarily action in the Balkans depends to a great extent on the general position of the war, and if only a certain number of telegrams reached you you would receive an incomplete and one-sided view of what was going on, so that the conclusions you came to might not be such as full knowledge would enable you to form.'

North Albania and Pirot and Nish. Meanwhile the news which poor Bourchier has reluctantly had to send from Sofia confirms what I have all along thought, that the chief use that Bulgaria is making of our offers is to get something out of the Turks.'[1] Moreover, Buxton's plan required that Greece, Servia, Roumania and Turkey should give back to Bulgaria the territories which she had forfeited at the end of the second and third Balkan wars; and this was something which they had no intention of doing; a fact which led Buckmaster to ask of Buxton 'Are we to fight the people who refuse to relinquish these territories?'[2]: and which led Wickham Steed to protest: 'I am convinced that the policy of unmitigated courtship of Bulgaria without heed to the danger of alienating other sympathies would doubly defeat its object.'[3] There must have been many to agree with Robert Cecil that 'At present the difficulty of making any of the Balkan States even moderately reasonable appears very great. Montenegro is a shade the worst, but Serbia, Bulgaria and Greece are only just behind.'[4] And one who, like Buxton, thought diplomacy to be an integral part of warfare, cannot have been consoled by Ian Hamilton's note: 'My business is war not diplomacy, yet I cannot help having at the back of my mind a shrewd suspicion that our Balkan diplomacy has been anything but brilliant. Never mind, fighting men will put it all right in the long run.[5]

But, to the Balkan Committee, this episode was the final demonstration of the incompetence, or worse, of the Foreign Office. Bryce was always wholeheartedly in favour of Buxton's project, minimising its difficulties and pressing it, by letter and by interview, on both Grey and Crewe[6]: but, by the autumn of 1915, he was writing to Buxton: 'It seems to me doubtful if the F.O. will wish to use you—you know what their traditions are and how they don't like what they regard as interference and trust their own official channels only.'[7] Arthur Moore admitted that ' to be fair to the F.O., I should say that *the Allies* made a break, for at that time Russia was certainly a great obstacle in the way of any heart to heart talk with Servia'[8]; and Arthur Evans saw that there was no real help in, or for, Bulgaria save in a revolt which should overthrow and expel King Ferdinand[9]; but most of the group remained convinced that only Grey's bungling had pushed Bulgaria into Germany's arms. Ignoring Maurice de Bunsen's point that 'we had gone to very great lengths in our

[1] To Buxton, July 27, 1915.

[2] To Buxton, July 29, 1915.

[3] To Buxton, July 8, 1915.

[4] To Buxton, August 2, 1915. Masterman wrote to Buxton, July 16, that 'Bob Cecil will at least listen and argue—*o si sic omnes*': but added, next day, that 'Cecil has absolutely no influence at the F.O. and is completely sidetracked by the officials and Grey'.

[5] To Buxton, June 30, 1915.

[6] Bryce to Buxton, February 7, March 29, April 14, May 29, and July 16, 1915.

[7] September 5, 1915.

[8] To Buxton (n.d.). Written when he was with the Salonika Expeditionary Force.

[9] To Buxton, February 17, 1916.

promises to Bulgaria',[1] Sir Edward Boyle found that 'Every Bulgarian I have met is miserable about it and justifiably bitter as to our diplomacy'. 'I will not tell you', he concluded, 'what I think of Grey and the F.O.'[2]

The most impervious to difficulties, perhaps, was Lord Newton. His letter to Buxton, of May 22, 1915, breathes the hardy Dissenting assumption that the ambitions of other Powers, large and small, will give way to the demonstrable disinterestedness of British purposes. 'It is quite intelligible', he wrote, 'that both Greece and Serbia should refuse to cede voluntarily any territory now in their possession, but it is not improbable that they might do so if pressure were put upon them from the outside. I gather from Hadji Mischeff that the difficulty in doing so arises chiefly from excessive consideration for our allies (France and Russia) but surely we could afford to take the initiative, and I understand that pressure from us would be less resented than from any other Power, because our disinterestedness is largely recognized.' It is fair to add that this letter is minuted by Buxton: 'less cogent than previous note.'

The whole episode reflected a perennial differrence between Dissent and Government. Governments deal with Governments. As Charlesworth wrote from the War Office: 'The Bulgarian Government is a Government in being and apparently can carry the army with it against the wishes of the people. There is at present no sign of King Ferdinand's position being seriously assailed or that of M. Radoslavoff.'[3] Buxton and his kind, as Dissenters, thought in terms of, and expected everything from, Dissenters on the other side. Just as, in the later and much larger question of the Germany of Ludendorff and the Germany of Hitler, Buxton was to be always discerning a 'liberal' Germany in opposition, so, in all the Balkan correspondence, everything was expected from 'encouraging' a Bulgarian Opposition. Buxton and Bourchier and Fitzmaurice seldom challenged the F.O.s estimate of the probable intentions of King Ferdinand and his Government: they simply thought that estimate to be irrelevant when they were sure that they had friends and correspondents in Bulgaria who would throw out the Bulgarian Government if only they could be 'encouraged' by London. In out-and-out Dissenters (such as Edith Durham and the passionately philo-Montenegrin MacKellar) such a faith was tenable: but, for a Gladstonian such as Buxton (to whom Taylor's description of Gladstone—'He was by nature an interferer, by training a man of Power'—applied literally) this position and the results were bound to be ambiguous. Paul Cambon thought Buxton's notes 'tout à fait tendencieuse', and wrote, flatly: 'Quant à forcer la main au Roi Ferdinand, cela n'était au pouvoir d'aucun homme ni d'aucun partie en Bulgarie et les personnes visées dans votre note n'étaient pas, à mon avis en état de diriger la politique de leur pays.'[4]

[1] October 6, 1915.
[2] To Buxton, October 5/17, 1915.
[3] To Buxton, October 6, 1915.
[4] To Buxton, October 9, 1915.

Once more, therefore, criticism came both from the side of Government and from that of a section of Dissent with different preoccupations. Sir John Simon wrote: 'Forgive me for saying that you will not expect me quite to accept Lord Newton's proposition of the "intense futility" of British diplomacy in the Balkans, even though you tell me that those best qualified to understand the Balkan situation share Lord Newton's opinion. We must put up with such instruments as we have, and I confess to thinking that Edward Grey understands something about it!'[1]

On the other hand, E. D. Morel lifted[2] the argument to another plane:

> Now if I read you aright, your main object is to urge Roumania, Bulgaria and Greece to join in this war, and, of course, on the side of the allies. Of course you see in the victory of the allies (consumated by that means) the only way of an eventual settlement calculated to ensure a permanent solution of the political and racial difficulties peculiar to the Balkans, and of placing the future peace of Europe, thereby, on a stable foundation. In effect, you urge that 1,300,000 more males should be flung into the inferno (with all the attendant and incidental miseries which the non-fighting population of those States will suffer) because you think that their sacrifice now will prevent further and larger sacrifices of human life later. If I judge accurately, that is your case. As I am sure you loathe war and all its bestialities as much as I do, I am bound to assume that you could not assume the immense moral responsibility involved in urging such a course of action, unless you were absolutely persuaded that the effect of it would be such as you anticipate. It is on that assumption I convey to you—for what they are worth, and they are probably worth very little—the doubts and difficulties I experience in accepting your thesis.

Starting from Buxton's hope of settling the Balkans on lines of nationality, Morel went on to depict a Serbia willing to surrender Bulgarian Macedonia only if allowed 'to carve up' Austria; a Greece burying the hatchet with Bulgaria only if allowed to expand in Asia; a Roumania ceding territory to Bulgaria only if allowed 'to smash' the Magyars; a Russia yielding up Bessarabia in compensation for—what?—Constantinople?—or Galicia? 'But is a Russified Galicia going to help humanity? With all its faults, the Dual-Monarchy has made of Galicia the only Polish oasis, and has given the Ukrainians privileges which Russia not only denies to them in Russian Ruthenia but which she has taken from them in such parts of Galicia as she has occupied since the war.' Beyond this, he asked, what of Germany? 'Johnson closes Africa to her. The Australians close the Pacific. You close the Near East. We dictate her world policy owing to our surface command of the sea (not, apparently, the last word in sea command). Is it not comparable to putting champagne in a bottle and omitting to wire the cork?'

Charles Buxton minuted Morel's letter: 'He was very sound, I think. Destroy when read.' But Noel minuted it: 'No! *We* were sound—proved now.'

[1] To Buxton, June 3, 1915. [2] To Buxton, May 17, 1915.

After the ironies of Morel, it is with a sense of anti-climax that one reads G. W. Prothero's note to Buxton of March 1, 1916: 'The question involves so many intricacies and so much that is still uncertain with regard to Bulgaria's attitude at different periods that it is hard to make any statement against which something cd [*sic*] not be said.'

*

There has always been a type of Dissenter to whom actual and immediate decisions in foreign policy are the Great Irrelevance. Some day, the Apotheosis will arrive, Radical or Socialist and, on that day, wars will cease. Until then, governments will, as Mr Mantalini said of foreigners, be as God made them; and the Elect will be wise to expect the worst. Taylor pointed out that the Radicals of the French Revolutionary period 'drew from Tom Paine the moral that foreign policy did not concern them. It was a conspiracy run by the old order and would disappear with the triumph of Radicalism.' R. B. McCallum[1] saw that many Socialists shared this attitude in the years after the Great War: 'According to the high theory of Socialism the actual details of the Treaty did not matter. There was nothing surprising in it. Thus did imperialist-capitalist powers behave after they had won a military victory . . .; indeed it mattered little who had won the war, for the processes of history are not stayed by the mere incidents of history.

This was never Buxton's temper. Nothing in him was sounder (as against, for example, Lloyd George) than his realisation, often reiterated, that means affect ends, so that the shape of tomorrow's New Order would be very substantially affected by the choices which were made today. But, if it never occurred to him, with one strain of Dissent, to leave the improvement of Anglo-German relations or the settlement of the Balkans to await some social or economic millennium, he kept equally clear of that other strain in Dissenting action, popular agitation. There are no 'Midlothians' in the Buxton pattern. His method was to influence the already influential; to do this by the untiring submission of memoranda of information and argument, and by the machinery of committee and deputation. The recipients of the memoranda and of the deputations were the politically established and the culturally articulate.

Indeed, as one reads his correspondence, one has the growing sense that something is missing; and then one realises why this is so; it is because of the almost total absence of the North. Scottish peers write to him and even, on occasion, a Scots commoner.[2] A Trevelyan, of course, writes from North-

[1] *Public Opinion and the Last Peace* (London, 1944).

[2] T. Millar to Buxton, July 21, 1917: 'Edinburgh is an apathetic place mostly occupied by people who live at the expense of other people's labour power and educated by a Press whose chief ability has always been the advertising of the virtues of the State, the Church and the Governing Classes generally. . . . I hope that the views of the Decisive Settlement Committee are gaining ground in London. The people one comes across here are all sick of the business of war and exploitation but they will require a lead from London.'

allerton but, for the rest, the euphonious southern English addresses accumulate: The Manor House, Cheselbourne; Longworth Rectory, Farringdon; Lollards Tower, Lambeth; Whitburn, Youlbury; Lymore End, Lymington. It is a world redolent of Cambridge Combination Rooms and bishop's palaces, of rectories and deaneries in the Home Counties and of manor houses in the Cotswolds; a world for which England north of the Trent exists only to provide safe Liberal seats. Any northcountryman would recognise the tone in which (à propos of Buxton's short occupancy of the seat for Whitby) we learn that 'of course, our Yorkshiremen are splendid'. In some such tone, no doubt, a Roman centurion once wrote of Illyrian auxiliaries.

These two characteristics of Buxton (aspects of his nature as a 'Man of Power'), his understanding of the importance of present action and his method of working through the already influential, are particularly exemplified in his role during the First World War. The line which he adopted was exactly that which Taylor ascribed to the Radicals of the time of the Boer War: to argue that the war was not so much wrong as unnecessary, in that all its essential aims could be achieved by negotiation. It was a line which, as Taylor wrote, made it 'possible to be a Dissenter and a patriot at the same time'.

Buxton called his policy 'A Decisive War Policy' and, out of it, came 'a Decisive Settlement Committee' under the leadership of himself and Lord Parmoor. Its essential aim was that proclaimed by President Wilson as interpreted by Frank Cobb, the editor of *The World*; to separate the idea of 'peace without victory' from that of 'war without victory' and to set it over against a policy of war without end. 'Peace without victory', Cobb had written, 'means simply that no permanent peace can be imposed by the sword. It does not mean that the Allies shall not crush Germany's military power if they can; it does not mean that they shall not crumple up the German armies and occupy Berlin if that be possible. It places no limitations on the extent or completeness of military occupations, but it emphatically affirms that the terms of peace ought not to be dictated by the success of such operations. Peace without victory does not imply war without victory, but most certainly implies that a durable peace must be a peace of justice and humanity and not merely a peace of the sword.'

All Buxton's speeches and writings, during the war, were variations on this theme. At the only large, public meeting which he had addressed, up to that time, he told an audience in the Central Hall, Westminster, on March 19, 1917, that 'This is not a Pacifist meeting. It is not a meeting to advocate peace at a low price. It is a meeting to urge the efficient conduct of war policy according to principles of reason. It is a meeting to discuss what are the true methods of destroying militarism.'[1]

[1] He added: 'There was a time when we thought that public discussion was not to the public advantage. We are distinguished in that from some who from the very first discussed war aims and urged negotiation. We think that in war time the ideal is efficiency with silence. But now the time has come, in our judgment, for a meeting like this, for several reasons.'

In pursuit of these purposes, Buxton worked parallel to, but was never completely identified with, many allies: among organisations, the League of Nations Society (founded in 1915), the Civil Union for the Right Understanding of International Interests,[1] the League to Abolish War,[2] the League to Enforce Peace (American), the National Peace Council which invited Buxton to become its Chairman,[3] the Universal Fraternity and Sisterhood of Nations: among journals, particularly Lowes Dickinson's *Cambridge Magazine* and F. W. Hirst's *Common Sense*: and, among individuals, more especially, Lord Parmoor and Col. Josiah Wedgwood. But it is significant of his sense of the practicable that he steered clear of a compromising association with E. D. Morel's Union of Democratic Control. To Sir Edwin Pears (January 25, 1917) he wrote: 'There is a definite proposal for a meeting on the terms of settlement & America, & I am willing to speak if we can do so together. A friend of mine suggested it & would get it up at the Central Hall on a Monday evening. The sooner the better after the two next Mondays, at 8 o'clock. No Pacifist or U.D.C. person to be concerned.' On May 31, 1917, H. G. Tanner supplied him with 'a list of names of persons to whom I think it might be useful for you to send any literature issued in connection with the Decisive Settlement Movement. The names represent people who may generally be said to have a fairly open mind but who have not been willing to join the U.D.C.': and, at about the same time, F. W. Hirst, in sending a list of 'possible sympathisers' (4 Tory M.P.s, 31 Liberal M.P.s and 8 Peers) wrote:

> There is a public ready to back negotiation, if it is not ostensibly U.D.C. vide leader of Labour Party & leader of Liberal party at Manchester. The latter subscribes to U.D.C. secretly, & the former says Trade Unionists mainly pacific now, but anti-U.D.C. How to arrange meetings? U.D.C. is in touch with men who will organise on these lines & would patriotically help without credit to U.D.C., as e.g. re Central Hall Meetings (March 1917). How to provide platform? M.Ps loth to leave London except on Fridays, but many would be anxious to promote pro-negotiation & pro-Lansdowne movement, especially if a good show can be made. Organisers report that they can arrange meetings if a peer will speak. Snobbery still a force in pacifist movement as elsewhere.

That snobbery was not the only human failing among pacifists appears from Mr J. King's note (March 4, 1917) that 'Seton Watson has now joined the R.A.M.C.—thanks to me. I hope this may curb his baneful activities.'

Much as he had claimed special information with respect to Bulgarian

[1] Norman Angell, Mrs Geo. Cadbury, Erskine Childers, Lady Courtney, Rt Rev. Lord Bishop of Hereford, J. A. Hobson, Philip Morrell, Alfred Noyes, Charles Sarolea, H. B. Lees-Smith.

[2] Rt Hon. G. N. Barnes, Sir Rabindranath Tagore, Rt Hon. C. W. Bowerman, Rt Hon. Thos. Burt, Rt Hon. W. Dickinson, the Bishop of Carlisle, Lowes Dickinson, H. W. Massingham.

[3] Carol Heath to Buxton, January 16, 1917.

affairs, Buxton tended, especially after his visit to the U.S. in mid-1916, to lay claim to a special knowledge of responsible American opinion.[1] In the early days of the war, he hoped for American mediation to end it. Then, and for so long as the first and second Asquith Governments lasted, he worked to get such a public statement of the Allies' war aims as would enlist American enthusiasms and supply ammunition to German 'moderates'. In the third stage and after the formation of the Lloyd George Administration, he worked to defeat the policy of 'the knock-out blow' or 'war to the bitter end'. And, at each stage, he was tireless in supplying the Press and, still more, persons in position with material for the shaping of opinion. A note in his correspondence shows that copies of his Central Hall speech went to all M.P.s, to one hundred selected Peers and to a number of selected ambassadors and editors: and that the pamphlet, 'America, Russia and the War' (prepared by Lowes Dickinson on the basis of Buxton's speech, with the addition of material from the *Cambridge Magazine*), went to 31 Ministers, 42 Peers, 62 M.P.s, 14 ambassadors and 27 Trades and Labour Councils, as well as to various editors.

Buxton's role, once Lloyd George had come to power, illustrates Taylor's dictum that 'the true controversy of Dissent was . . . rarely with the Conservatives . . . The serious argument went on within the Left . . . attacks on a Liberal or Labour government when it was in office; debate as to future policy when the party was in opposition.' He never seems explicitly to have adopted Morel's view that it was *because* Asquith and Grey were contemplating a negotiated peace, in the autumn of 1916, that they were replaced by Lloyd George but, in practice, he acted on this assumption. Late in 1916, he and Wedgwood prepared an appeal to Asquith:

> We desire with all respect to lay before you a view which is held by many members of the Liberal party in the House and in the country with regard to the question of war aims. It is felt by a large number of those who have been most loyal to the Liberal party and its traditions, that the Liberal attitude towards the problems of the settlement at which the war is aimed differs of necessity from that of Conservatism, and there is a keen desire that the distinction should be voiced in the utterances of Liberal leadership. Liberals now realise that the present Prime Minister is necessarily under the sway of influences which represent not merely the Conservative, but the Ulster tradition. They feel a desire for a statement of principles and aims distinct from those of the Government, because they are conscious that those of Liberalism cannot be as similar to those of the Government as at present they appear to be. They note that even among Conservatives there is a strong body of feeling hostile to extravagent aims such as the destruction of Austria,

[1] His *Confidential Memorandum* of July 1916: 'The President's actual influence in framing foreign policy is very much debated. Judging from the information of those who are intimate with him, it appears to extend even to the details of diplomatic action. A set of men numbering not more than ten appear to be his confidants and advisers in this sphere. I had the advantage of meeting this group of men; and also the President himself, Colonel Roosevelt and leading Republicans; and I formed opinions as to the official attitude and official information on many points.'

and they are deeply puzzled when they understand from your own utterances that while the Government has tended to follow the more moderate section in this matter, the Liberal leader takes the extreme view. We know for a fact that a considerable section of the most active Liberals, feeling the want of material for the exercise of party loyalty and enthusiasm are tending to sever their party ties . . . We believe in the party truce, but the party truce applies to the conduct of the war, not to the statesmanship which deals with the settlement. There the rival principles which in the main characterise our two great parties cannot be avoided . . . It will not be denied that if your own support were given to the argument in regard to war aims which we have described as the Liberal argument, the vast majority of the public would in the near future express the same view. We cannot help appealing to you, for to you the party still looks with a hope which is now, as to the keenest section of the Liberals, puzzled and bewildered.

This memorandum went to all Liberal M.P.s, with the confidential note from its authors:

It seems to many Liberals important that the liberalism of this country should express itself on the ultimate peace settlement. Too much influence is exercised by conservatives with Prussian traditions. At present we have to rely on America to ensure a settlement on really liberal lines. Can we not get Mr. Asquith to give us a lead? Will you look at the enclosed and let us know if you could join in sending it to Mr. Asquith?

It is possible to trace replies from thirty-five recipients, twenty-one of whom were prepared to sign the memorandum and fourteen of whom were not. Some of those who declined to sign did so because they thought the memorandum was being sent to the wrong address. Thus, R. D. Denman (December 11, 1917) wrote: 'My one mental reservation is that I'm not in the least either "puzzled" or "bewildered" by Asquith's attitude. It's just exactly what one would expect! One positive suggestion; is it not possible to get a somewhat similar note signed for presentation to Ll.G.? Personally I am anxious to keep him in the Liberal fold, or at least not to split the Party by compelling him to lean on the Tories. An appeal of this sort to A. & not at the same time to Ll.G. looks, at the least, like cold shouldering the latter.' More grudgingly, E. J. John (December 1917) said that he was willing to sign but that he considered Asquith's 'position infinitely less satisfactory than that of say, Lord Lansdowne and I am disposed to think that in Wales, the liberals who have withstood militarism will elect to form an alliance with Labour on the lines of an Independent Welsh Nationalist Labour Party. I have therefore not much prospect of identifying myself with a merely "Asquithite" Group.'

The more fundamental objections came from George Greenwood, H. W. Carr Gomm and A. F. Whyte and their objections illustrated the perennial conflict in Dissent between the desire for peace and the desire for righteousness.[1] Greenwood agreed that there was something to be said for a re-statement of

[1] To Buxton from Geo. Greenwood, H. W. Carr Gomm, and A. F. Whyte on, respectively, December 9, December 10, and December 10.

Allied aims but pointed out that Lord Lansdowne's famous letter had put forward *negative* propositions. It had stated what we did not want to do. But we did want, Greenwood pointed out, 'the complete restoration of Belgian independence and such compensation as we could obtain for her: the same for Serbia: the restoration of Alsace and Lorraine, or at any rate a great part of them: a just and much needed rectification of the Italian frontier.' Was there any chance, he asked, at that time, of Germany meeting these demands? Beyond this, he agreed that the dismemberment of Austria-Hungary did not form part of our terms but added: 'I think if it be possible to obtain the deliverance of the misgoverned Slavs under Austrian rule, & not to leave them under that rule, humanity would be immensely benefited.' And he concluded: 'Why am I not a Liberal—and a "keen" one—if I am so convinced? I am a "Pacifist"—so strong a "Pacificist" that I think Peace worth fighting for—a real peace, a conclusive peace, & a permanent peace—And the nation that endureth to the end the same shall be saved. Liberavi animum meum!'

Whyte agreed with Greenwood on the subject of the Dual Monarchy:

> Where I join issue with you most assuredly is in your prognosis about Austria. I do not cherish what you call 'extravagant aims such as the destruction of Austria' but I think it wrong to suggest as is often done now that we have no quarrel with the Habsburg Monarchy. Doubtless the extent and depth of the quarrel depends on the relations of Vienna with Berlin but as long as they remain as they are now and as long as the whole system of Government is unchanged in Austria—and especially in Hungary—the Monarchy will be a menace to European peace.

Carr Gomm wrote:

> You ask Asquith to propound a Liberal as opposed to a Government policy, so far as I can grasp your meaning. Is not this most unwise? For it emphasizes the fact that there are two policies and by underlining the importance of the Liberal policy it will invite reprisals from the Ulster-Tory spirits in the Government. I am for 'laying' the Junker ghost in England not for provoking it. You imply however a still more dangerous theory and this is that our War Aims should be altered in view of some military disappointments which may have occurred recently—e.g. the failure of the Russian Campaign. Our aims and objects in 1914 were good enough for the Liberal Party to fight for. What is wrong with them in 1917? By all means resist any attempt to make them Imperialistic but don't start at this moment or even help in starting the see-saw of rival Peace programmes.

But although this initiative by Buxton and Wedgwood had failed to get general Liberal support, some Liberals remained disquieted. On May 5, 1917, Eleanor Acland wrote to Buxton to deplore the 'supine attitude of the present Liberal party', 'specially after the revelation about the Austrian peace overtures in 1917'; and to ask 'if there is any prospect of any other Coalition being formed, which people like myself (and thousands of other new women-voters) could support—people who may not be prepared at the moment to swallow the whole I.L.P. programme, but who yet want to protest against the methods and dreary policy of the Government coalition.' The plan to enlist Asquith was not dropped and, on April 16, 1918, Buxton took advantage of the military reverses in France to propose, to the *Manchester Guardian*, that:

> Indignation against the Government for this almost irremediable failure at the final crisis is only restrained by the despairing sense that no alternative government exists. Doubtless the task of taking over the knock-out policy, when its bankruptcy has just been proved, is not attractive, but the moment may be near when a change of leadership will be both intensely desired by a majority in the country and intensely urgent for national welfare.

He went on to suggest a Government led by Lansdowne, Asquith and Henderson, with Grey, Sir William Robertson and Lord Jellicoe, as representing 'the three main technical functions connected with war policy', as the other members of the War Cabinet. But, on July 14, Richard Holt (who had helped F. W. Hirst to launch *Common Sense*) wrote that 'To be frank—I have not made any progress:—the men on whose judgment I place most reliance are averse from any action very largely from a feeling that it is useless to put any further pressure on Asquith while at the same time there is the strong feeling that it is no good trying to do anything without him.'

Buxton was not ready to accept this verdict and, in a last flutter of king-making, before Foch's victories swept such plans away, appealed, on June 19, to Runiciman:

> We feel it our duty to lay before you our view regarding the influence of the Liberal Party in reference to War Policy and War Aims. We desire to express our thanks for the services you have done in counteracting the defection of supporters of the Liberal Party which is taking place owing to the widespread feeling that the Liberal Party has failed to express the Liberal view in regard to the war. We are fully conscious of the difficulty of going beyond the leader of the Party in expressing opinion during the present crisis and we specially appreciate the independence and courage which you have shown in deprecating the committal of this country to extravagant aims in regard to Alsace-Lorraine. There is a widespread feeling that not only is inaction a national disaster, but it is endangering the future of the Liberal party in particular. We desire earnestly to suggest that you and your colleagues, whose anxiety must be at least as great as our own, should realise the necessity of freely expressing the Liberal view and of refusing to be bound to silence by the individual opinion of the present Leader of the Party.

In the last resort, Buxton had no convincing answer to the dilemma which Taylor saw confronting the Radicals at the time of the Boer War. Possibly, war might have been avoided by more moderate men on both sides. Possibly, the wrong-headed on the other side owed their triumph to the wrong-headed on ours. But what if the enemy's people were now behind their wrong-headed leaders? 'The Radicals refused to answer, refused even to contemplate, this question.'

It was an essential counterpart to Buxton's urgings, in season and out,[1] that the Allies should proclaim moderate war aims, that he should have remained fixed in the belief that, at all stages of the war, there was a body of 'Dissent' in Germany which was prepared to satisfy the purposes for which Britain had gone to war: the evacuation of, and restitution for, Belgium, by Germany; the securing of France against the threat of aggression; the placing of the rights of small nations upon an unassailable foundation and the destruction of military domination of Prussia. That there were Germans who did not share all the ambitions of the extreme militarists is certain: it is equally certain that, until Ludendorff had come to believe that the war could not be won, such Germans were either not prepared, or not in a position, to overthrow their rulers. One may think (with the advantage of hindsight) that it would have been better had the war ended in a 'negotiated' peace in 1916 or 1917: one may agree that some of the fruits of victory to which the Allies had become attached in the course of the war represented a large extension of the original war aims of Britain: but the ineluctable fact is that, until Germany's military collapse was impending, no one in power in Germany gave any sign of meeting those original aims. There was no one whom Buxton delighted more to quote, to his own countrymen, on the subject of war aims, than Colonel House; and it was House who wrote to Wilson, at the end of May 1917: 'It is, I think, evident that the German military clique have no intention of making peace upon any other basis than that of conquest. . . . The Kaiser and his civil government are taking the gambler's chance. If they are able to hold what they have, then the German liberals can be defied, for the mass of the German people will be satisfied with the outcome of the war.'[2]

Buxton, on the other hand, never abated his belief that there was a Dissenting Germany which, if encouraged, could and would reject Germany's rulers. As a matter of tactics, and because, of course, until 1917, the U.S. was still represented diplomatically in Berlin, he usually offered this conclusion to his own countrymen as being the opinion of 'responsible Americans'. In his 'Notes on American Opinion regarding the War' (drafted October 1916 but sent in December), he assured the Cabinet that 'the policy of aggression and the influence of the military leaders (i.e. in Germany) are discredited already'. Five days after the submission of this memorandum, he told the Commons that the Americans were looking to 'the mass of sane and anti-militarist and anti-Junker influence in Germany'. From the autumn of 1916 on, in all accessible quarters, he kept citing testimony that 'an influential section', under Delbrueck was 'now in favour of constitutional reform and international peace machinery';

[1] In the spring of 1917 (May 24), Buckmaster had pointed out that, as a result of Russia's exit from the war, British failures in Palestine and Mesopotamia and the growing exhaustion of France and Italy, 'the Germans are more confident of victory than they have been for many months past—probably more so than at any time during the last two years.' A year later (April 17, 1918) C. P. Scott wrote to say that the current German victories made it no time at which to approach the Central Powers.

[2] *The Intimate Papers of Colonel House* (Boston and New York, 1928), vol. III, p. 132.

and, as late as February 1918, he was transmitting to Ministers the view of 'a neutral diplomat in close touch with German affairs' who was certain that, if the Allies were to offer peace on the basis of 'no annexations and no indemnities', such an offer would, itself, represent such a defeat for the aims of German militarism that it would suffice to separate the German people from the German Government. 'If the Allies', Buxton quoted the diplomat as saying, 'would accept such a moderate peace, all they have got to do is to say so, and sit down to wait for the plain people in Germany to do the rest.'

Few of Buxton's old leading associates of the days of the Balkan Committee and the 'Grey-must-go' campaign, after Agadir, shared his confidence in 'the other' Germany. One or two historians did. W. H. Dawson took refuge in the evasion that we should 'tame Germany with decent treatment and a democratic constitution' and suggested that, if she would surrender Alsace-Lorraine, Britain should compensate her elsewhere[1]: and Professor Eileen Power (in contrast to her Cambridge colleague, G. C. Coulton) thought that 'no one who looks at the extracts from the foreign press printed in the *Cambridge Magazine* could fail to see that it is Mr Lloyd George's 'knockout' speech and the Paris economic policy which is keeping up (very naturally) the German ardour for the war', though she added: 'I think that it is probably true that the German military successes are at present too great for them to be likely to consider reasonable peace terms.'[2] Loreburn wrote in the old high, vague and unhelpful Gladstonian terms[3] but many older friends were doubtful. On August 1, 1916, Bryce had told Buxton that American mediation, at that time, would mean that Germany would keep all her conquests. 'We will not make peace on a *status quo* ante basis', he wrote, and he saw little to be done 'till the Germans are in a much more chastened frame of mind.' A week later, he wrote 'that nothing but Defeat can discredit in the German mind that association of War with national prosperity which has become the curse of Germany': and, on October 22, 1916: 'I cannot believe that the Germans are yet prepared to concede what we think essential. For instance, I myself would never make peace (unless of course I despaired of success) till Belgium had been fully compensated and the young Turks utterly smashed.' The old Balkan Committee days were long gone when T. P. Conwell-Evans could minute this letter, from the Committee's first president: 'Oh! what a diehard.'

That other staunch ally, Lord Courtney, had to inquire (August 19, 1916): 'How did you get the notion that the Germans might be prepared to give up Metz. I have seen nothing to indicate this. If it were true and if we on our part were prepared to set up again the Declaration of London or something like it as the future code of International Law I should think peace near at hand; but these are two very great ifs.'

Sir John Simon wrote a conciliatory note to Charles Buxton, on December

[1] To Buxton, March 8 and 18, 1917.

[2] To Buxton, December 11, 1916.

[3] To Buxton, November–December 1916.

30, 1916, accepting the idea of a negotiated peace, but concluded: 'The point on which I feel most inclined to differ from you is your proposition about further humiliation provoking resentment and a feeling of revenge. Is Germany humiliated at present at all? No one reading Bethmann-Holweg's speech would think so, and there is a strain of vanity in the German character which will assert itself, if we too readily assume she is already humiliated.' Buckmaster, having pointed out that Buxton's campaign was untimely because of Allied defeats and Russia's defection, added that 'The result is serious. It means that no longer is it possible for us to obtain by voluntary offer on the part of Germany terms that would even involve the restoration of Belgium and the evacuation of France. Their temper is hardened and our chance of negotiation not only seems more remote, but the prospect of opening it up appears even more difficult of attainment.'[1]

J. A. Spender, who had stood by Grey in the days of Buxton's Liberal Foreign Affairs Group, now dismissed Buxton's idea of the 'two Germanies'. 'I wish I could see', he wrote, 'any evidence that Germany is or was willing to conclude a peace on the basis of no annexations, and indemnities. No doubt a considerable number of the German people are, but to my mind all the evidence goes to show that the people in control always intended to get plunder in the East or the West, and preferably in both.'[2] From the Department of Information, John Buchan thanked Buxton for his evidence of German anxiety for peace but added: 'I have evidence of the same kind, and I have evidence also of the opposite view. It is a tangled business guessing at the psychology of our foes.'[3] And even George Barnes, of the League to Abolish War, wrote: 'I am in receipt of your letter of the 27th February, and have read the statement made by a neutral diplomat in close touch with German affairs on the question of democratisation in Germany. I cannot help feeling the gravest doubt upon the statement that "Germany would have been ready to make a peace on the 'No annexations, No indemnities' basis". The recent developments in Russia do not support that proposition.'[4]

It had been left to Hilton Young to strike the older Radical note. Having said that 'it might have been better for the country if the Liberal Party had split over the recourse to war and left the responsibility for it to a Coalition', he reverted to the older line of Hobhouse or Hyndman. 'The force that has sent us to war', he wrote, 'is I suppose the preference of the ruling class for war and their prejudice against Germany. The first has its origin in internal politics the second in international. This force is quite incapable of making a satisfactory settlement after the war and I see no influence or inspiration or interest either in Parliament—the Foreign Office or the Press likely to steer it away from diplomatic formulae onto sound democratic principles.'[5]

Early in 1917, Crewe had pointed out to Buxton that 'I see considerable

[1] To Buxton, May 24, 1917. [2] To Buxton, February 27, 1918.
[3] To Buxton, February 8, 1918. [4] To Buxton, February 28, 1918.
[5] To Buxton, August 12, 1914.

difficulty even in a private communication to the American Government of the joint terms expected by the Allies, whether the maximum be set out or the minimum. To state the maximum obtainable by a complete victory might appear arrogant, if not actually grasping; while the minimum would involve a long preliminary discussion between the different Allies to decide by whom the sacrifice of what each regards as a just individual claim should be made.'[1]: and it must be admitted that Buxton became progressively ready 'to decide by whom the sacrifices of what' should be made. That he should hold that Russia's defection had relieved the Allies of any obligation to her in the matter of Constantinople, or that he should have protested against the extension of British aims to include the dismemberment of Austria-Hungary, was legitimate enough: but, as time went by, he became increasingly equivocal even about Belgium and Alsace-Lorraine.

In a draft of 'Peace Terms', dated October 1916, he included, under the heading of 'Defeat of Aggression', the evacuation of Belgium and compensation to her by Germany. But his Central Hall speech was a subtly-worded affair. To his audience, it must have seemed that the Belgian question was straightforward. He, first, gave what he called 'a sane interpretation' of the last Allied Note as covering 'the restoration of Belgium', and he went on to say that the set of terms 'which, upon the highest possible authority, was obtainable a few weeks ago', was 'identical with the sketch of terms which in our view would be a decisive set of terms'. But, as we now know, the German terms to which he referred had suggested, not the evacuation and restoration of Belgium, but only the 'restitution of Belgium *under guarantees for the safety of Germany*: and, as late as July 1918, the German High Command's conception of those 'guarantees' was, as we know, totally incompatible with the survival of an independent Belgium, much more with her full restoration. Did Buxton know this, then, or had he misunderstood, or been misled by, his American friends? If the latter, a curious light is thrown on his claim, to the Editor of the *Daily News*, that satisfactory terms could 'in the opinion of President Wilson's *highest authorities* have been got from the German Government a few months ago'.[2]

Similarly, in his draft of October 1916, under the heading of 'Adjustments to Meet National Claims', he proposed that France should receive 'Metz and district' or, alternatively, that Alsace-Lorraine should form a buffer State. In the months which followed, however, he was collecting material to throw doubt upon the French claims, and this issued in a paper for the *Manchester Guardian*, of July 27, 1917, in which he fell well below his own level: 'The sympathies of Alsace are predominantly German, and in West Lorraine they are as strongly French, but everywhere you have a section whose attitude is changing because of the economic benefits brought by German rule. Anyone who has motored along the Lorraine frontier & crossed

[1] To Buxton, January 2, 1917.

[2] January 15, 1917.

& recrossed between French & German territory will have noticed the superior prosperity & cleanliness of the villages on the Eastern side.' He went on to argue that support for the French claim really came from the wish to deprive Germany of the coal and iron of Lorraine. In December 1916, Wedgwood had prepared a memorandum on 'America and the Peace' in which he asked: 'Can America be induced to make the sacrifice of her isolation & safety? President Wilson, being a typical Liberal with no special reluctance to being hailed as the saviour of the world, may be trusted to do it,—if he thinks he can persuade America & the Senate. (I presume it could not be done by presidential fiat, & would require the endorsement of the Senate). The following suggestions are made, with all the diffidence of a non-American, as to conditions whose appeal to sentimental & business feeling in America might secure their willigness to pay the price.' He went on to list among 'other terms of settlement in which America is not so directly interested', a provision to add Alsace 'as a canton to Switzerland' and to divide Lorraine between Germany and France. By January 15, 1918, he was writing of 'settling the Alsace-Lorraine question on the basis of making it a separate state in the German Empire on the same status as Saxony and Bavaria, possibly with freedom from military service and some such similar arrangement for Prussian Poland' . . . 'Such a settlement for Alsace-Lorraine could be well interpreted as reparation for the injury of 1871 and of course it is favoured by the Socialists in Germany now and by many liberals.' Yet it was Gladstone who had thought the German annexation of Alsace-Lorraine 'hard to reconcile with considerations of equity; and . . . repulsive to the sense of modern civilization.'

At the time of Buxton's Central Hall speech, both the *Daily Chronicle* and the British Workers' National League pressed him for enlightment as to the terms on which, as he claimed, a satisfactory peace could have been made[1]; and, to the latter, he wrote (March 24, 1917):

> With regard to my authority for the statement I am very glad to send you a reply, the matter being as you say of vital importance. When in America I had the advantage of seeing a considerable number of the highest official authorities in connection with the matter of foreign policy, who have the closest possible information as to the situation (in the highest quarters) in Berlin. You will readily understand that none of them would wish to be mentioned by name. No set of men, either in the belligerent States, or in the minor neutral States, has been in such an advantageous position as these Americans to know the truth. Their evidence is therefore the best available. As they have devoted the utmost possible attention to the matter, it is also evidence of the highest order. The opinions which I reported in regard to the terms which have been possible were the result of the most exhaustive consideration & deliberate conviction, (based upon confidential statements made in Berlin) on their part.

[1] Buxton's account of the terms and the question of his authority for claiming that they had been available, raised a lively curiosity among those who were looking for a speedy end to the war but who wished to know the source of his confidence. For an interview, with Buxton, in elaboration of his speech, see the issue of *Common Sense* for May 12, 1917.

In its combination of candour with concealment, the explanation was eminently Gladstonian.

*

Taylor more than once noticed (especially, for example, with reference to David Urquhart and E. D. Morel) the tendency of too many Dissenters to self-righteousness; and there are times when the rest of us are exasperated into feeling that this tendency to believe that those who disagree with them are not only mistaken (which is possible) but also necessarily wicked (which does not follow) is their chief, single characteristic. Buxton was pleasingly free from this trait. Too many of his correspondents betray the Morley-like sense that they are a misunderstood élite of the enlightened, preserving their virtues against a happier season, and that a population which supported other policies than theirs must be, by definition, 'unthinking'. The older Gladstonians among them, in particular, repeatedly deplored the decline of spiritual energy inside and outside of Parliament. Buxton was either too serene or too busy a spirit for this sort of thing. There is in him none of the acidity of Morley or of A. G. Gardiner; none of the acerbity of a Hirst, a Hyndman or a Morel. In his draft for his *Autiobiography*, he wrote of the family houses which he visited as a youth as representing 'a combination of public spirit with a determination not to claim any more of it than other people.' It is a happy description of his own temper.

GEORGES BONNIN

Les Leçons du Putsch de Hitler de 1923

GEORGES BONNIN

Les Leçons du Putsch de Hitler de 1923

LE Putsch de Hitler à Munich a été une tentative de prise du pouvoir qui n'a pas réussi. Il est utile d'analyser les causes de cet échec. Les nazis eux-mêmes ont, en effet, établi un parallèle entre 1923 et 1933 et Hitler a toujours prétendu qu'il aurait pris le pouvoir dès 1923 s'il n'avait pas été 'trahi'. Par qui avait-il été trahi? Par le général von Lossow, chef de la Reichswehr bavaroise, et par von Kahr, Generalstaatskommissar et pratiquement dictateur de la Bavière.

Il y a, certes, des points de ressemblance entre 1923 et 1933. Dans les deux cas, l'événement faisait suite à une crise économique et financière profonde: en 1923, l'inflation; en 1933, le chômage et les autres conséquences de la crise mondiale de 1929. Ces données, cependant, ne contribuent guère à éclaircir le mystère, bien au contraire. La 'solution Hitler' aux difficultés économiques de l'Allemagne apparaît malgré tout improbable et elle l'était à l'époque. Le 26 janvier 1933, Hindenburg déclarait qu'il ne songeait nullement à faire du caporal autrichien le ministre de la guerre ou le Chancelier.[1] Hitler essayait en 1923 comme en 1933 de se présenter comme étant à la tête d'un mouvement de masse et cela était plus vrai en 1933 qu'en 1923.

La version officielle du Putsch

Lorsqu'il s'agit de tirer les leçons du Putsch, les historiens, ainsi que les biographes de Hitler sont généralement influencés par le récit rédigé par le général von Lossow. Cette 'version Lossow' fut en quelque sorte une version officielle, imprimée à 150 exemplaires ou plus, et circulée parmi les 'hautes autorités du Reich'. Elle tendait à exonérer Lossow et Kahr de toute responsabilité dans le Putsch et à exonérer en même temps l'armée, la police et les milieux conservateurs.

Pour les historiens, la leçon du Putsch est simple: Hitler a échoué parce qu'il était en conflit avec l'armée, et Hitler décida après le Putsch qu'il n'essaierait jamais plus de marcher contre l'armée. En généralisant ces conclusions, les

[1] Conversation avec le général von Hammerstein, alors à la tête de l'armée (v. Bracher. Die Auflösung der Weimarer Republik. 2 ème éd. 1957. p. 733). Sans doute, pour Hindenburg, le ministère de la guerre et la Chancellerie étaient des postes 'nobles' au sein du gouvernement; il pouvait, malgré cette affirmation, songer quand même à une participation des nazis au gouvernement.

tenants de la science politique arrivent à la formule suivante: pas de Putsch réussi sans l'armée et vice versa; seule l'armée peut renverser une dictature.

Il s'agit là de vérités premières. Les réalités du Putsch sont plus complexes. En y regardant de près, on s'aperçoit que le conflit entre Hitler et l'armée a été plutôt accidentel et que la version Lossow a été un écran de fumée destiné à cacher le rôle de l'armée dans cette affaire.

Il n'y avait pas en 1923 de profonde opposition entre Hitler et l'armée. Les archives et la documentation de l'époque prouvent au contraire que dès les premiers mois de l'année, Hitler etait en étroit contact avec les chefs de l'armée et les dirigeants bavarois. Il eut même une longue conversation avec le général von Seeckt. Jusqu'en novembre 1923, les sections d'assaut nazies étaient entraînées dans les casernes de la Reichswehr, sous l'uniforme et avec des armes de l'armée régulière.

Avant comme après le Putsch, Hitler a maintenu et répété qu'il n'avait pas, qu'il n'avait jamais eu l'intention de marcher contre l'armée. Sa déclaration finale au procès qui suivit le Putsch, contient un passage qui est devenu fameux:

> L'armée, elle grandit de jour en jour, d'heure en heure toujours plus vite. Même maintenant, j'ai le ferme espoir qu'un jour l'heure viendra, quand ces bandes tumultueuses deviendront des bataillons, les bataillons des régiments, les régiments des divisions, quand la vieille cocarde sera tirée de la boue, quand les vieux drapeaux claqueront à nouveau devant nous.

Les nombreux auteurs qui citent ce passage, veulent y voir une évocation prophétique du futur réarmement et du relèvement militaire de l'Allemagne. En fait, Hitler ne faisait que reprendre les projets poursuivis de concert *avant* le Putsch par la Reichswehr et les organisations para-militaires.

La technique même du Putsch de 1923 est révélatrice: il ne s'agissait pas de s'emparer des casernes en tirant sur la troupe mais en s'y introduisant à la faveur de l'intimité régnant dans les rapports entre Reichswehr, Sections d'Assaut nazies et autres organisations para-militaires. Hitler, le soir du Putsch, n'a pas arrêté le général von Lossow seulement pour l'empêcher d'agir mais pour le persuader de se joindre au Putsch, appelé 'Révolution Nationale'.

Hitler, enfin, ne s'est-il pas décidé le 6 novembre à lancer le Putsch lorsqu'il eut la conviction que l'armée serait de son côté? Röhm lui avait affirmé que les cadres de l'armée, en particulier les jeunes officiers, s'associeraient à l'action projetée.

L'intervention de Hitler à la Bürgerbräukeller fut un succès. Le Putsch avait réussi puisque le général von Lossow et von Kahr s'y étaient ralliés. Ce n'est qu' au milieu de la nuit du 8 au 9 novembre que Lossow décida de se désolidariser de Hitler et d'écraser le Putsch. Par la suite, dans son récit des événements, Lossow choisit d'affirmer que dès la première minute, il avait été contre le Putsch, qu'il avait prétendu se rallier à la 'Révolution Nationale', parce qu'il était sous la menace du pistolet de Hitler, mais qu'il n'avait fait que 'jouer la comédie', qu'il en allait de même pour von Kahr et von Seisser, le chef de la police bavaroise, avec lesquels il s'était entendu dès leur arrestation en échangeant des clins d'oeil qui voulaient dire 'Jouer la comédie!'

Ce récit n'est guère convaincant. En réalité, Lossow s'est rallié à la Révolution Nationale, lorsque le général Ludendorff fit son apparition aux côtés de Hitler. Lossow voyait Ludendorff reprenant la tête des armées allemandes et se lançant dans une nouvelle offensive contre la France. Von Kahr s'était fait prier un peu plus longtemps avant de donner son assentiment.

Le général von Lossow quitta la Bürgerbräukeller pensant que la 'Révolution Nationale' était en train. Il reprit contact avec les réalités lorsque le général von Danner, commandant de la ville, l'accueillit par ces mots: 'Ce n'était que du bluff, mon général?' Lossow fut mis alors au courant de mesures déjà prises par la Reichswehr contre les Putschistes, qui n'avaient pas réussi en définitive à s'emparer des casernes. Lossow comprit qu'en s'alliant à Ludendorff et à Hitler, il avait commis précisément l'erreur qu'il avait décidé depuis longtemps d'éviter: s'engager dans une affaire condamnée d'avance à l'échec, un Putsch semblable à celui de Küstrin qui avait si misérablement échoué.[1]

Hitler n'avait pas entièrement tort lorsqu'il prétendait qu'il avait été 'trahi' par le général von Lossow, par von Kahr et par von Seisser. Certes, sur le plan juridique on ne pouvait pas appeler trahison le geste de Lossow refusant de se faire plus longtemps le complice de Hitler, mais le général von Lossow ne voulait pas avouer avoir lâché ses compagnons lorsque l'affaire risqua de mal tourner. C'est pourquoi il affirma avoir fait des réserves mentales dès le début.

Au procès, Hitler maintiendra qu'il ne pouvait pas être accusé d'avoir commis un acte illégal puisqu'il avait agi de concert avec les autorités légitimes de la Bavière: von Lossow, von Kahr et von Seisser, non seulement le soir du Putsch mais depuis bien longtemps.

Le parallèle entre 1923 et 1933 est ici aussi remarquable, car lors du 10 ème anniversaire du Putsch, Hitler, désormais Chancelier, déclarait qu'il avait 'conquis le pouvoir par la voie légale'.

II. Le phénomène Hitler

Depuis la guerre, Hitler est resté une énigme et est devenu un bouc émissaire. Comment fut-il possible à un petit bonhomme ridicule et gauche, sans formation intellectuelle, de devenir Chancelier du Reich? Il exerçait, paraît-il, sur les foules un effet hypnotique, mais cela n'explique pas pourquoi le 'caporal autrichien' fut nommé Chancelier par le maréchal von Hindenburg. Hitler était un sans-métier, un déclassé et il avait peu de respect pour les valeurs traditionnelles. Comment a-t-il pu prendre le pouvoir ou plus exactement le recevoir des mains des conservateurs?

[1] Le septembre 30, 1923, le commandant Buchrucker avait voulu utiliser ses troupes de la 'Schwarze Reichswehr' à Küstrin pour forcer la main au gouvernement du Reich. L'affaire n'avait pas duré trois jours.

Les explications les plus diverses et les plus fantastiques ont été avancées. On s'est demandé sérieusement si Hitler n'était pas possédé du démon, ou du moins s'il n'avait pas un pouvoir 'démonique'. C'était la thèse de l'avocat de Schacht au procès de Nuremberg, thèse qui reposait sur une citation de Goethe. Elle provoqua des réactions bruyamment ironiques sur le banc des accusés, en particulier de la part de Goering et de Ribbentrop. Ce n'était pas le Hitler qu'ils avaient connu. A chacun son Hitler. Si l'on énumérait les interprétations proposées, on arriverait à une étrange litanie: Hitler autodidacte, Hitler profond penseur politique, Hitler fascinateur, Hitler stratège de génie, Hitler dément, Hitler réaliste, Hitler idéaliste, Hitler grand simplificateur de l'Histoire, Hitler européen, Hitler rempart contre le Bolchévisme, Hitler expansionniste, Hitler totalitaire, Hitler rendu possible par les nouvelles techniques de communications . . . On est loin d'une explication 'totale' de Hitler.

Même les auteurs qui ne veulent pas s'embarrasser de complications et qui présentent une image d'Epinal de Hitler, sont bien forcés d'admettre une contradiction dans le portrait qu'ils traçent: d'un côté le déclassé, le dévoyé, le paresseux, l'autodidacte, l'homme qui vit dans un monde imaginaire de sa création; d'un autre côté, comme il faut bien rendre compte des succès très positifs qu'il a remportés, on lui attribue un sens politique sans égal, qui lui permettait d'exploiter toutes les situations, et comme cela ne suffit pas encore, on lui attribue aussi un talent extraordinaire d'organisateur.

Pour gratuites que soient ces affirmations, elles illustrent l'existence du paradoxe de Hitler: un homme, selon toutes les apparences, médiocre, mais qui a obtenu des résultats inouïs sur le plan politique. Plus on examine le rôle de Hitler dans le détail, plus l'analyse offre des contradictions. Finalement, Hitler apparaît tellement multiforme qu'on peut se demander s'il possédait une personnalité bien marquée on même bien définie. La passion de l'orateur dans le tumulte des réunions de masses, les idées les plus banales rassemblées pêle-mêle dans ce capharnaüm intitulé *Mein Kampf*, tout cela n'aboutit pas à déterminer un 'caractère'. Dire que Hitler possédait un don hypnotique revient à expliquer le mystère par le mystère.

La multiplicité des explications incline au scepticisme. On a l'impression de tourner autour du problème. Or la tendance de la littérature d'après-guerre est claire: tout ramener à la personne de Hitler pour le charger de toutes les responsabilités et de toutes les culpabilités. Hitler est devenu le bouc émissaire.

La thèse inverse a été soigneusement évitée, parce que peu politique. Les auteurs se sont bien gardés de dire: Hitler était le produit de son temps et de son milieu, l'écho des aspirations profondes de l'Allemagne; il s'est intitulé le Führer, le guide, alors qu'il ne faisait que suivre la poussée de ses troupes.

Cette thèse ne pourrait que blesser les susceptibilités; elle serait hérétique aussi bien en Allemagne qu'à l'étranger. Seuls les pro-nazis sont prêts à s'y rallier aujourd'hui, car elle suggérerait que Hitler a joui dès le début d'un appui très positif de la population. Néanmoins, pour inadmissible qu'elle paraisse, la thèse 'Hitler, écho des aspirations de l'Allemagne' rendrait plus plausible certains aspects de Hitler. Ainsi, au lieu de parler d'un pouvoir de fascination exercé sur les foules, on parlerait d'une sorte de 'dialogue' entre la foule et l'orateur, celui-ci sachant exprimer ce que la foule sent profondément sans oser ou sans pouvoir le dire.

Le ton et la substance des discours de Hitler ont changé au cours des années. Ils ont changé selon le public et l'actualité. En 1923, Hitler s'en prenait au gouvernement et au système parlementaire. Les conservateurs le jugeaient alors dangereux, 'révolutionnaire'. Mais pendant les années précédentes, la propagande qu'il poursuivait était d'un nationalisme impeccable et ne donnait pas lieu à inquiétude: Hitler choisissait pour cible les Juifs, les Marxistes et aussi naturellement le traité de Versailles. Citons par exemple ce discours de 1922:

> Que l'on ait fait de Rathenau un ministre des affaires étrangères, c'est vraiment le comble (interruption: 'Rathenau, Die Judensau'). Cela, vous n'avez maintenant plus le droit de le dire, parce que, depuis qu'il est ministre, il est à nouveau un homme que l'on peut offenser.
>
> Nos jeunes filles sont séduites par les juifs et le peuple est infecté. Tout juif que l'on surprend avec une jeune fille blonde, on devrait . . . (interruption: 'le pendre!') . . . je ne veux pas dire de le pendre, mais il devrait y avoir un tribunal qui condamne ces juifs à mort (Applaudissements) . . . Nous ne pourrons lutter efficacement contre les juifs et les vaincre que si tous les Allemands se mettent ensemble.
>
> Le peuple allemand va déjà mieux. On bâtit![1] Dans quelques mois, ça ira encore mieux! (Rires) Et ainsi, ça ira toujours de mieux en mieux, jusqu'au moment où le bâtiment pourri finira par s'écrouler, jusqu'au moment où nous, nous resterons, comme un roc, un bloc de granit, en dépit des autres partis (Applaudissements). Alors, nous bâtirons et nous bâtirons pour le bien du peuple (Longs applaudissements).[2]

Il y avait foule à Munich pour écouter de tels discours. Ce n'étaient pas ses 'idées' qui pouvaient assurer le succès de Hitler, même si certains ont voulu depuis voir en lui un profond penseur politique. Hitler jouait sur les émotions des masses et l'on voit assez clairement le procédé dans cette période: provoquer l'indignation des auditeurs.

L'atmosphère nationaliste de Munich après la guerre n'avait pas été créée par Hitler. L'ineptitude de ses discours indique bien qu'il n'avait pas besoin d'informer, de convaincre ou de persuader son auditoire. Son éloquence apportait une excitation. Pourquoi ne pas le reconnaître? Hitler était un agitateur, qui trouvait en Bavière et plus tard en Allemagne un milieu réceptif. Il savait d'ailleurs s'adapter à son auditoire et obtenait le même succès dans la conversation en tête à tête. Il avait l'art d'exprimer et de libérer les désirs de ses interlocuteurs.

[1] Allusion ironique aux socialistes qui voulaient 'bâtir' une nouvelle société.

[2] Compte-rendu de police du discours de Hitler du 2 février 1922. in Haupstaatsarchiv, München; Allgemeines Staatsarchiv. Sonderabgabe 1480.

En 1923, les dirigeants bavarois, et aussi le représentant diplomatique de Berlin à Munich, Haniel von Haimhausen, ne redoutaient pas la propagande nationaliste de Hitler mais ils voyaient en lui et ses partisans un mouvement tourné uniquement vers l'action et l'action immédiate. Hitler était un révolutionnaire, un homme prêt à tout, qui allait s'emparer du gouvernement par la force.

Hitler lui-même, par les vastes réunions qu'il organisait, encourageait la diffusion du mythe 'Hitler entraîneur des masses et homme d'action'. Cependant, au jour de l'action véritable, il pouvait mettre en ligne non pas des 'masses' de 200,000 hommes, mais 2 ou 3,000 hommes seulement, et encore le Ier mai comme le 8 novembre 1923 devait-il faire appel à plusieurs autre 'organisations patriotiques' pour supplémenter ses propres troupes.

Le recours de Hitler à la violence tenait plus de l'action psychologique que de l'emploi de la force pure. La prise du pouvoir ne pouvait pas s'effectuer par les masses inorganisées, même si l'éloquence de Hitler provoquait chez elles un enthousiasme délirant. Ce n'étaient pas non plus les petites formations para-militaires qui auraient pu s'emparer du pouvoir par la force; elles ne pouvaient rien contre l'armée régulière et la police. La réussite dépendait du degré de sympathie que Hitler rencontrait dans les milieux non-extrémistes, dans les milieux conservateurs et plus particulièrement dans l'armée. Hitler tenta un coup d'état de l'intérieur par une action psychologique qui cherchait à décider les chefs politiques et militaires.

Goebbels, dans son discours du 8 novembre 1933 au cirque Krone à Munich discutait, à l'occasion du 10 ème anniversaire du Putsch, la question de savoir si la 'Révolution Nationale', qui avait désormais pris place, était une révolution par en-haut ou une révolution par en-bas:

> Les révolutions ont leur propre légalité et leur propre dynamique. Lorsqu'elles ont passé un certain stade de leur évolution, elles échappent au pouvoir des hommes et n'obéissent plus qu'à la loi selon laquelle elles sont intervenues. Il y a des révolutions par en-haut et il y a des révolutions par en-bas. Les révolutions par en-haut n'ont pour la plupart qu'une courte durée, car il est difficile, sinon impossible, de dicter d'en-haut une nouvelle légalité à un peuple.
>
> Par contre, les révolutions qui viennent d'en-bas, survivront les siècles, car le peuple lui-même se fait le support de la révolution. C'est pourquoi, la révolution que nous avons faite, est une véritable révolution . . .

On perçoit bien ce que Goebbels voulait faire croire: que la prise du pouvoir en 1933 était une révolution, une révolution par en-bas, une révolution, enfin, qui survivrait les siècles, parce qu'elle avait l'appui du peuple. Autan d'affirmations, autant de contre-vérités. Ni en 1923, ni en 1933, il ne s'agissait de 'Révolution' à proprement parler, même si l'on proclamait la 'Révolution Nationale'.

III. L'intégration de Hitler

Toute la vie politique bavaroise était teintée de particularisme et les dirigeants de Munich ont cherché à utiliser la crise d'octobre 1923 avec Berlin pour marquer de nouveaux points sur le tableau de l'autonomie.

Cependant, le crise elle-même n'avait pas son point de départ ni son point d'arrivée dans le particularisme bavarois. Elle fut causée par 'l'affaire Lossow', par le refus du général von Lossow en octobre 1923 d'empêcher par la force la publication du *Völkischer Beobachter*, l'organe des nazis. Le général von Seeckt, alors à la tête de l'armée allemande, en avait fait une question personnelle: le *Völkischer Beobachter* avait insulté sa femme en prétendant qu'elle était juive. Lorsque le général von Lossow, qui commandait la Reichswehr en Bavière, refusa d'exécuter l'ordre pour éviter d'entrer en difficultés avec le gouvernement bavarois, Seeckt, ainsi que le ministre de la Reichswehr, Gessler, ne voulurent voir dans l'affaire Lossow qu'un refus d'obéissance. Les autorités bavaroises prirent alors fait et cause pour le général von Lossow, que Seeckt voulait limoger. Ils regardèrent l'attitude de Berlin comme une ingérence dans les affaires intérieures bavaroises et 'l'affaire Lossow' prit un tour particulariste marqué.

La crise dans les rapports Berlin-Munich ne doit cependant pas faire illusion. Hitler, le 6 novembre, décida de faire le Putsch à un moment où le gouvernement de Berlin avait déjà pris la décision de se réconcilier avec Munich et, comme gage de ses bonnes intentions, avait expulsé les socialistes du gouvernement, pour se gagner les bonnes grâces des dirigeants munichois qui trouvaient que le gouvernement de Berlin n'était pas assez 'national'.

Les intentions profondes des dirigeants bavarois, fin octobre-début novembre, n'allaient pas dans le sens d'un conflit avec Berlin. Il s'agissait de bien autre chose. Von Kahr et le général von Lossow se plaçaient résolument sur le plan de la politique allemande et non pas bavaroise. Ils obéissaient à un réflexe social et se révélaient hommes de droite et conservateurs avant d'être bavarois. Ils voulaient se mettre au service d'un 'Directoire', qui serait créé à Berlin, ayant à sa tête le général von Seeckt.

Le 24 octobre 1923, au moment où la rupture avec Berlin semblait consommée, le général von Lossow et von Kahr convoquaient les représentants des organisations para-militaires et en particulier des formations dans l'obédience de Hitler. Ils leur proposaient d'envisager une mobilisation: les membres des 'organisations patriotiques' seraient incorporés dans la Reichswehr. Les effectifs de l'armée régulière pourraient être ainsi triplés du jour au lendemain. Les représentants de Hitler acceptèrent.

Pourquoi cette mobilisation, cette intégration des troupes de Hitler dans la Reichswehr? L'ordre rédigé par Lossow, l'ordre IA 800, commençait ainsi: 'Au cas de troubles intérieurs . . .' A quels 'troubles intérieurs' songeaient von Lossow et von Kahr? Cela apparut clairement le 6 novembre lorsque les représentants des formations para-militaires furent à nouveau convoquées. Cette fois, on ne leur dit pas: 'Marchez-vous avec nous?' Au contraire, on leur interdit de bouger, de prendre l'initiative d'un coup d'état. Certes, Kahr et Lossow étaient prêts quant à eux à participer, s'il le fallait, à un 'coup d'état', mais pas à une entreprise condamnée d'avance à l'échec et qui s'écroulerait dans les trois jours. Lossow était obsédé par le souvenir récent du coup manqué de Küstrin.

Le général von Lossow voulait que la Reichswehr bavaroise, renforcée par les organisations patriotiques, joue le rôle d'un 'bâton de police' au service du Directoire de Berlin. Plusieurs documents donnent des précisions sur ce projet de Directoire. Nous avons, par exemple, la lettre de Seeckt à Wiedfeldt, l'ancien directeur de Krupp, alors à Washington, lui proposant, au nom de Ebert, le Président du Reich, de faire partie du Directoire. Il s'agissait de donner à l'Allemagne un gouvernement de fortes personnalités venant de l'armée, de l'industrie, de l'agriculture, gouvernement d'origine extra-parlementaire et qui gouvernerait sans le Parlement.[1]

A Munich, on attendait avec impatience la formation du Directoire, mais Seeckt n'avait pas l'audace nécessaire. Il avait bien été voir Stresemann, le Chancelier, début novembre, pour lui dire que l'armée n'avait plus confiance en lui: 'Retirez-vous, faites donc ce sacrifice pour la patrie', lui avait dit Seeckt, mais Stresemann avait refusé et s'accrochait au pouvoir. Seeckt en restait là.

Finalement, les dirigeants bavarois envoyèrent aux nouvelles à Berlin un des leurs le Colonel von Seisser, chef de la police d'état bavaroise. Les interlocuteurs berlinois de Seisser, le 3 novembre, sont représentatifs des milieux conservateurs qui voulaient s'emparer du pouvoir sous le couvert du Directoire. Il y avait parmi eux Minoux, le représentant de Stinnes, chef d'un empire industriel aux ramifications étendues. Il y avait également les représentants des associations de propriétaires terriens, dont l'attitude était particulièrement importante à ce moment car la famine était menaçante et les propriétaires terriens pouvaient décider de ravitailler ou non les grandes villes. Il y avait aussi le chef des organisations patriotiques et il y avait le général von Seeckt lui-même.

Seisser reçut partout à peu près la même réponse: il n'était plus question de Directoire pour l'instant, car Seeckt n'arrivait pas à se décider. En fait, Seeckt avait les plus hautes ambitions, il convoitait le pouvoir suprême. Il avait préparé ses batteries de longue main et il avait même un programme de gouvernement. C'était au tout dernier moment qu'il se dérobait.

L'attitude de Stinnes, telle que l'on peut la discerner dans les propos de Minoux, est à ce moment remarquable: attendre l'hiver, attendre que les populations souffrent du froid et de la faim, alors une révolte sera inévitable. C'est par ce machiavélisme que les conservateurs, si on leur en donne l'occasion, peuvent creuser leur propre tombe.

A la suite de la mission de Seisser à Berlin, les dirigeants bavarois convoquèrent à nouveau, le 6 novembre 1923, les représentants des organisations patriotiques, dont le Kampfbund de Hitler pour dire que le coup était remis à plus tard, que le Directoire se constituerait d'ici peu et qu'il s'agissait de savoir si Seeckt se déciderait. Le jour J était désormais le 11 novembre.

[1] Sur ce dermier point, cependant, Ebert n'avait pas donné son accord.

En présence de ces hésitations, aussi bien de Berlin que de Munich, Hitler décida le soir même de lancer son coup d'état à lui. Il voulait provoquer *le* coup d'état qui avait été préparé par les milieux conservateurs, et dans lequel on ne lui avait assigné qu'un rôle secondaire. En déclenchant l'avalanche, Hitler voulait jouer la vedette.

On ne comprend pas comment Hitler a pu avoir l'idée de faire un Putsch à Munich et de prendre en même temps le pouvoir à Berlin, si l'on ne sait pas qu'un coup d'état conservateur était sur le point de se produire dans toute l'Allemagne. Hitler, faisant le Putsch, était le fruit d'une situation qu'il n'avait pas créée.

Pour les milieux conservateurs dirigeants, Hitler était un allié occasionnel que l'on pouvait utiliser à certaines besognes mais un allié méprisé qui devait se contenter de tâches secondaires: ses troupes pouvaient servir à renforcer les effectifs de l'armée; lui-même, en raison de son talent d'orateur pouvait jouer un rôle de propagandiste.

Quels étaient les buts essentiels des conservateurs, et plus particulièrement de l'armée après 1918? Faire échec au socialisme et reprendre les armes contre la France.

Les conservateurs étaient en tout premier lieu obsédés par le danger socialiste. Un document révélateur à cet égard est la lettre que le général von Seeckt écrivait le 14 mai 1926 au Maréchal von Hindenburg. Seeckt croyait nécessaire d'ouvrir son coeur à son ancien chef pour lui faire part de ses craintes qui en 1926 étaient les mêmes qu'en 1918 et avant 1918:

> Des observations les plus diverses, j'ai gagné l'impression que nous sommes à la veille d'une seconde révolution. Votre Excellence se rappellera que déjà pendant la guerre, j'ai attiré de bonne heure l'attention des autorités suprêmes du Reich et de l'armée sur le mouvement révolutionnaire à l'intérieur et présenté des propositions positives pour écarter ces dangers. Pour n'en citer que quelques-unes: interdire au front le *Berliner Tageblatt*, la *Frankfurter Zeitung*, *Vorwärts*; punir sans pitié les parlementaires (chefs USPD) qui participèrent à la première mutinerie de la marine; adopter une politique de salaires raisonnable à l'égard des ouvriers des usines de munitions; enfin, intervenir brutalement contre les milliers de tire-au-flanc et de permissionnaires qui flânaient à l'arrière. Dans ce but organiser de nouvelles unités aux principaux centres ferroviaires et les amener immédiatement au front par des marches à pied.
>
> Je ne mentionne ces choses, qui appartiennent au passé, que parce que déjà sur la base de mes observations j'étais arrivé de bonne heure à la conviction selon laquelle un mouvement révolutionnaire à l'intérieur ne pouvait pas être arrêté si les mesures proposées par moi n'étaient pas exécutées et si la guerre devait durer assez longtemps. Les mesures proposées ne furent pas exécutées et la conséquence en fut le déclenchement de la honteuse révolution de 1918.
>
> Les choses se présentent, à mon avis, d'une façon tout à fait semblable aujourd'hui. Le parti de la gauche (y compris les Démocrates) travaille systématiquement à une deuxième révolution. En partie inconsciemment—mais aussi pour la plus grande part consciemment—les principaux ressorts de ce mouvement sont d'une

nature purement bolchévique. L'agitation contre nos Hohenzollern, contre la magistrature, contre la propriété foncière agricole, en définitive contre toute propriété, n'est qu'une préparation systématique de la bolchévisation de l'Allemagne.

Le gouvernement socialiste en Prusse, personnifié dans ces deux hommes, Braun et Severing, dont franchement j'admire dans un sens négatif l'intelligence et le travail méthodique, a déjà accompli d'importants préparatifs en vue de gagner les fonctionnaires prussiens et une grande partie de la Schutzpolizei à la venue de la révolution de gauche. Je pourrais citer des centaines de faits pour appuyer cette affirmation. La création de la Reichsbanner[1]—sous la conduite de l' 'excellent' Hörsing—était déjà un signe d'orage à prendre très au sérieux. Cette Reichsbanner, qui ne personnifie qu'extérieurement les couleurs noir, rouge et or[2] et qui depuis déjà très longtemps a élevé sur le pavois le drapeau rouge, donne sa forme à la révolution qui approche, de concert avec le Frontkämpferbund et les organisations communistes. Par contre, pour maintenir l'autorité de l'Etat, il y a encore la Reichswehr, de minces fractions de la Schutzpolizei et les organisations patriotiques. La Reichswehr serait excellente et sûre, mais cent mille hommes, ce n'est pas beaucoup en présence d'un peuple qui compte des millions. Seules de minces fractions de la Schutzpolizei pourront être prises en considération lorsqu'il s'agira d'écraser la révolution rouge. Enfin, les organisations patriotiques; c'est une bien triste histoire. Premièrement, il n'y a pas d'unité de commandement et deuxièmement toutes ces organisations souffrent du manque d'argent.

Pour des raisons de politique extérieure, nous avons conclu un nouvel accord avec la Russie soviétique comme moyen de pression contre les prétentions inouïes de l'Entente. Certes, un coup très habile. Mais nous devrons certainement payer cher cet accord par des concessions que nous ferons à Messieurs les Bolchéviques. A nouveau, la porte est grande ouverte pour la propagande bolchévique et il est clair pour moi qu'un gouvernement socialiste en Prusse qui n'a qu'une pensée: 'L'ennemi est à droite!', n'opposera aucune résistance à cette propagande. Pour donner un exemple, puis-je me contenter de citer le cas à Berlin du film de la révolution: 'Cuirassé Potemkine'? Tous les soirs, on y montre à des milliers de personnes comment des matelots assassinent leurs officiers. Contre cela, *le gouvernement ne fait rien*. Si cela n'est pas une préparation à la révolution à venir, alors je ne sais pas.

Juste avant de commencer cette lettre, je lis dans le journal la chute de Luther. Un nouveau signe d'orage!

Votre Excellence peut croire qu'il ne m'a pas été facile de vous écrire ces pensées qui sont les miennes. Je sais que votre Excellence est animé par la pensée de réconcilier les oppositions existant dans notre peuple. Vous avez cru—ou croyez même encore maintenant—à une communauté dans le peuple. Personnellement j'ai cessé d'y croire. Il ne s'agit plus ici d'un compromis entre les oppositions, mais il s'agit tout simplement de décider brutalement dans une lutte de conceptions fondamentales (Weltanschauungen). D'un côté, il y a tout ce que jadis nous avons aimé et tenu pour sacré: un vigoureux sentiment national, une

[1] Fondée en 1924 par les sociaux-démocrates Hörsing et Höltermann, cette association d' 'anciens combattants et de républicains' se proposait de défendre la république de Weimar.

[2] Couleurs de la république.

vigoureuse autorité de l'Etat, un sens élevé du devoir, un labeur désintéressé pour la Patrie. De l'autre côté, il y a le pacifisme international, la soi-disant Liberté, le persiflage de toute autorité et dernier maillon de la chaîne: le Bolchévisme.

Il est encore temps pour un gouvernement résolu, qui est prêt à utiliser brutalement ses pouvoirs, de s'opposer à ces tendances dissolvantes. Mais le temps presse et il est grand temps sans aucun doute. Si cela n'a pas lieu, alors je vois venir une guerre civile sanglante, dont personne ne peut prévoir l'issue, mais qui mettrait en tout cas notre patrie pour de longues années dans un état désespéré de dissolution économique et politique.[1]

Il s'agit là, à n'en pas douter, d'une argumentation ad hominem. Seeckt voulait influencer le vieux maréchal von Hindenburg, qui avait gardé la nostalgie du monde d'avant 1914, période idyllique où sous les Hohenzollern les vertus traditionnelles du soldat étaient chéries et respectées. Comme Hindenburg était aussi devenu grand propriétaire terrien, Seeckt évoquait le danger bolchévique menaçant la propriété foncière et toute propriété en général. On voit comment Hindenburg a pu se laisser berner par les personnalités apparemment les plus respectables des milieux conservateurs, jusqu'au jour où il a fait appel à Hitler comme Chancelier. La nomination de Hitler, en effet, se situe dans la perspective de la situation politique allemande telle qu'elle était analysée par Seeckt: situation caractérisée par le danger d'une révolution d'inspiration bolchévique, avec d'un côté la gauche, une gauche énorme et redoutable, qui comprenait même les Démocrates et bien entendu tous les pacifistes et les internationalistes, une gauche qui dominait la Prusse gouvernée par des socialistes comme Braun et Severing, dont l'intelligence perverse frayait méthodiquement les voies au Bolchévisme. De l'autre côté, se trouvaient seulement la Reichswehr, peut-être quelques éléments de la Schutzpolizei et enfin les 'organisations patriotiques'. Pour Seeckt, il n'était pas question de vouloir réconciler la gauche et la droite; il n'y avait pas de compromis possible entre internationalistes et nationalistes. Il fallait choisir. Le choix de Hitler découlait d'une telle analyse.

Nous trouvons la même analyse de la situation le 29 janvier 1933, la veille de la 'prise du pouvoir', dans une conversation entre le général von Hammerstein, alors chef de l'armée, et le général von Schleicher, le Chancelier sortant:

'Il nous était clair à tous deux que seul Hitler était possible comme futur Chancelier. Tout autre choix conduirait à la grève générale, sinon à la guerre civile, et ainsi à une intervention extrêmement indésirable de l'armée à l'intérieur dans deux directions à la fois, contre les nationaux-socialistes et contre la gauche.'[2]

En 1933, comme en 1923, Hitler était considéré comme un homme d'action prêt à tout, prêt à s'emparer du pouvoir par la force. Il n'eut pas à

[1] Papiers Seeckt. Freiburg in Breisgan. Archives Militaire.

[2] Compte-rendu de Hammerstein de sa conversation avec Schleicher. in Bracher, Die Auflösung der Weimarer Republik. 2ème éd. 1957. p. 733.

faire la preuve de sa résolution. On lui donna le pouvoir. Il réussit en 1933, là où il avait échoué en 1923, à 'conquérir le pouvoir par la voie légale'.

Sur le plan militaire, contrairement à la réputation qui lui a été faite, le général von Seeckt avait des vues courtes. Ses plans étaient à brève échéance. Il ne voulait pas organiser une armée qui se battrait dans dix ou vingt ans. Il voulait en 1923 se battre tout de suite contre la France, du moins dans quelques semaines ou quelques mois. Pour Seeckt, Hitler était un homme capable de fournir immédiatement des troupes en vue de compléter les effectifs de la Reichswehr. Hitler était un patriote, un ennemi du traité de Versailles et il était anti-marxiste. Cela suffisait, Seeckt intégrait son mouvement à l'Organisation. Telle est la cause profonde du Putsch de 1923.

Les conservateurs n'ont pas compris avant 1933 le danger que constituait Hitler pour l'Allemagne. Certains ne l'ont compris qu'en 1939 ou en 1943.[1]

[1] Pour ne citer qu'un exemple, le comte Schenk von Stauffenberg, qui devait être en 1944 l'âme du complot du 20 juillet, se mettait en 1933 à la tête de ceux qui célébraient à Bamberg la prise du pouvoir par Hitler.

ISAIAH BERLIN

Lewis Namier: A Personal Impression

ISAIAH BERLIN

Lewis Namier : A Personal Impression

THIS account of Sir Lewis Namier is based upon no research and is composed purely from memory. Namier was one of the most distinguished historians of our time, a man of fame and influence. His achievement as an historian, still more his decisive influence on English historical research and writing, as well as his extraordinary life, deserve full and detailed study. For this task I am not qualified. My sole purpose is to describe to the best of my ability the character and some of the opinions of one of the most remarkable men that I have ever known. I was not at any time one of his intimate friends; but his immediate intellectual and moral impact was such that even those who, like myself, met him infrequently but regularly, and spoke with him, or rather were addressed by him, on matters in which he was interested, are unlikely to forget it. It is this impression that I should like to record for the benefit of those who did not know him and may be curious about the kind of man that he was.

I first came across his name as an undergraduate at Oxford, in, I think, 1929. Someone showed me an article by him, in either the *New Statesman* or the *Nation*, on the condition of the Jews of modern Europe. It was the best and most arresting piece on that subject that I or, I suspect, anyone had ever read. Much was being written on that topic then. For the most part it was competent journalism: a combination of intellectual power, historical sweep and capacity for writing clear and vigorous prose was seldom, if ever, to be found among the writers on this subject, whether Jews or Christians. This essay was of an altogether higher quality. In reading it one had the sensation—for which there is no substitute—of suddenly sailing in first-class waters. Namier compared the Jews of Eastern Europe to an iceberg, part of which remained submerged and still frozen; part of which had evaporated under the influence of the rays of the Enlightenment; while the rest had melted and formed violent nationalist or socialist-nationalist torrents. He developed this thesis with incomparable imagination and a power of incisive historical generalisation that was at once factually concrete and had great historical sweep, with no attempt to play down disturbing implications. I wondered who the author might be. I was told that he was an historian whose work had caused some stir in the world of learning, at most a respected specialist, but not a scholar of the same order as Tout or Barker or Fisher, not to speak of Halévy or Trevelyan. That was that: the author was a minor historical expert with a fairly high reputation in his own profession. I heard no more until 1932 when I was elected to All Souls.

There I found that a higher opinion of Namier was entertained by my new historical colleagues—G. N. Clark, Richard Pares, A. L. Rowse and others. From them I learnt something of Namier's real achievement. My election to All Souls had evidently intrigued Namier, who had failed to secure election himself some years before the First World War.[1] I received a note in which, in huge majuscule letters, the author informed me that he proposed to call on me one afternoon in the following week and hoped that I would be free to receive him. The letter was signed L. B. Namier. When he arrived, he said in his slow. deliberate, ponderous voice, that he wished to see me because his friend Richard Pares had told him that I was interested in Karl Marx, of whom he held a low opinion. He wished to know why I was engaged in writing a book about him. He had some respect for the Fellows of All Souls. He believed them, for the most part, with certain exceptions which he did not wish to mention, to be intellectually qualified to do genuine research work. Marx appeared to him unworthy of such attention: he was a poor historian and a poor economist, blinded by hatred. Why was I not writing about Freud? Freud's importance for historical and biographical science had still been insufficiently appreciated. Freud's books were, unlike those of Marx, works of genius and far better written. Besides which, Freud was still alive and could be interviewed. Marx fortunately, was not; his followers, especially in Russia, which was now intellectually dead, had used up far too much printer's ink, comparable in this respect with German philosophers who suffered from an equal lack of sense of proportion and of literary talent and taste.

He stood in the middle of my room and spoke his words in a slow, somewhat hypnotic voice, with great emphasis and in a continuous unbroken drone, with few intervals between the sentences, a strongly central European accent and a frozen expression. He kept his eyes immovably upon me, frowning now and then, and producing (I realised later that this was how he drew his breath without seeming to do so) a curious mooing sound which blocked the gaps between his sentences and made interruption literally impossible. Not that I dreamt of interrupting: the entire phenomenon was too strange, the intensity of the utterance too great; I felt that I was being eyed by a stern and heavy headmaster who knew precisely what I was at, disapproved, and was determined to set me right and to get his instructions obeyed. Finally he stopped and glared in silence. I begged him to sit down. He did so, and went on glaring. I made a halting defence of what I was, in fact, doing. He scarcely listened. 'Marx! Marx!', he kept intoning, 'a typical Jewish half-charlatan,

[1] 'I have always had a certain grudge against Grant Robertson, who, as examiner, had preferred Cruttwell to myself', Namier said to me in the late thirties, 'but when I think of what he has done for the German Jewish refugees—I forgive him.'

who got hold of quite a good idea and then ran it to death just to spite the Gentiles.' I asked whether Marx's origin seemed to him relevant to his views. This turned out to be the stimulus that he needed to plunge into his own autobiography. The next two hours were full of interest. He spoke almost continuously.

He told me that he was born the son of a man called Bernstein (or Bernsztajn) the Jewish administrator of a large Polish estate, and that his father had been converted to Roman Catholic faith, which, he said, was common enough in his family's class and circumstances. He had himself been given the education of a young Polish squire, for his parents believed that assimilation to a Polish Catholic pattern was a feasible and desirable process if one wanted it strongly enough. They supposed that the only barrier between Jews and Gentiles was the difference of religion, that if this were abolished, the social and cultural obstacles which it had historically brought about would fall with it. Conversion could bring about the total integration of the Jews into the prevailing social texture, and would put an end to the insulation, ambiguous status and, indeed, persecution of Jews sensible enough to follow this rational course. His parents' theory was essentially the same as that which had moved Börne and Heine, as well as Heinrich Marx and Isaac Disraeli—two fathers of famous sons—to embrace Christianity. The hypothesis was, in his view, baseless and degrading; and he, Ludwik Bernsztajn as he then was, came to understand this when he was still quite young, sixteen or seventeen. He felt himself in a false position, and realised that the converted Jews in his circle lived in an unreal world—had abandoned the traditional misery of their ancestors only to find themselves in a no-man's land between the two camps, welcome to neither. His father's conventional, bourgeois outlook repelled him in any case. He decided to return to the Jewish community—at any rate in his own mind—partly because he believed that to attempt to cut oneself off from one's own past was self destructive and shameful, and in any case, impracticable; partly because he wished to show his contempt for his family and their unworthy ideals. His father thought him ungrateful, foolish and perverse, and refused to support him. He went to England, which to him as to many Central and Eastern European Jews appeared the most civilised and humane society in the world, as well as one respectful of traditions including his own. As part of his general revolt against his father's way of life, which was in his mind associated with the mixture of corruption, hypocrisy and oppression by which the Austro-Hungarian Empire was governed, he was attracted to socialism. The false and humiliating lives lived by his parents and their society seemed to him largely due to systematic delusion about themselves and their position, and, in particular, the attitude towards them of the Poles, whether Austrianised or nationalist, among whom they lived. Marxism was the leading philosophy which attempted to explain away and to refute such liberal fantasies as so many disguises intended to conceal an irrational and unjust social order, and one based on ignorance or misinterpretation of the real (largely economic) facts.

When he arrived in London, he became a student at the London School of Economics, then dominated by the Webbs, Graham Wallas and their followers, who, if not Marxists, were socialists and militantly anti-Liberal. However in due course, he realised that he had simply left one set of delusive ideologies for another. The principles and generalisations of socialism were as silly and unrealistic as those it sought to supplant. The only reality was to be found in the individual and his basic desires—conscious and unconscious, particularly the latter, which were repressed and rationalised by a series of intellectual subterfuges, which Marxism had detected, but for which it had substituted illusions of its own. Individual psychology, not sociology, was the key. Human action—and social reality in general—could be explained only by fearless and dispassionate scientific examination of the roots of individual human behaviour—basic drives, permanent human cravings for food, shelter, power, sexual satisfaction, social recognition and so on. Nor was human history, and in particular political history, to be explained in any other way.

He was not disappointed in England. It took, as he had supposed, a humane, civilised, and, above all, sober, undramatised, empirical view of life. Englishmen, seemed to him to take account, more than most men, of the real ends of human life—pleasure, justice, power, freedom, glory, the sense of human solidarity which underlay both patriotism and adherence to tradition; above all they loathed abstract principles and general theories. Human motives could be illuminated by attention to unexamined, occult causes which Freud and other psychologists had begun to investigate. Nevertheless, even such overt considerations as were present to the mind of an average Englishman, far more than to that of, say, an average German or an average Pole, accounted for a great deal of human behaviour—a far larger sector of it than had been explained by the 'ideologists'. At some point in this discourse—delivered with a kind of controlled ferocity, Namier spoke—as he often later spoke—of the absurdity of those who attempted to account for human behaviour by invoking the influence of ideas. Ideas were mere interpretations by the mind of deep-seated drives and motives which it was too cowardly, or too conventionally brought up, to face. Historians of ideas were the least useful kind of historians. 'Do you remember?' he asked me, 'what Lueger, the anti-semitic Mayor of Vienna, once said to the municipality of Vienna when a subsidy for the natural sciences was asked for? "Science? That is what one Jew cribs from another."[1] That is what *I* say about *Ideengeschichte*, history of ideas.' Perhaps he saw a discontented expression on my face, for I well remember that he repeated all this again in still more formidable accents, and emphasised it over and over again in a slow, heavy, drawling voice, as he often did on later occasions.

The London School of Economics was not the England that he had admired from afar, and he felt this still more strongly when he met it face to face. It was a pathetic offshoot of the worst continental nonsense. He migrated to Balliol College, Oxford, and was there taught history by A. L. Smith and

[1] He quoted this with much relish in German: 'Was einer Jude vom andern Juden abschreibt.'

others. Oxford (he continued) had less truck with ideologies: here he could freely profess what he thought to be the deepest factor in modern history—the historically grounded sense of nationality. The notion that rational men, Jews or Gentiles, could live full lives either by dedication to a religion (organised falsification—rabbis were worse than priests, and lived on and by deception) or by abandoning their religion, or by emigrating to lands beyond the sea, or by any means other than those by which all other human communities had done so, that is, by organising themselves into political units and acquiring a soil of their own—all such notions were sheer nonsense. Self-understanding was everything, both in history and in individual life; and this could be achieved only by scrupulous empiricism, the continuous adaptation of one's hypotheses to the twisted and obscure windings of individual and social lives. Hence his respect for Freud and other psychological theorists—including graphologists, in whom his faith was very strong; and his lack of respect for Marx, who had, indeed, correctly diagnosed the disease, but then had offered a charlatan's nostrum. Still, that was better than Burke or Bentham, who peddled mere ideas rooted in nothing, and were rightly distrusted by sensible, practical politicians. He returned to his autobiography: he had not been too well treated by England. He deserved a permanent post in Oxford which he had not obtained. Scant recognition had been shown him by many established scholars, because they knew that he could 'show them up'. Nevertheless, it was the only country to live in. It was less fanatical and closer to empirical reality than other nations, and there was in its political tradition a certain realism—some called it cynicism—which was worth all the vapid idealism and idiotic liberalism of the Continent. There were Englishmen who were taken in by continental 'isms'—here followed names of some eminent contemporaries—but they were relatively few and not too influential: the majority wisely went by habit and well tried practical rules and kept clear of theory, thereby avoiding much nonsense in their ideas and brutality in their action. He could not talk to English Jews about Zionism. The Jews of England were victims of pathetic illusions—ostriches with their heads in some very inferior sands—foolish, ridiculous creatures not worth saving. But Englishmen understood its appeal and its justification. The only Jew whom he had ever met, who in this respect could be compared to an Englishman was Weizmann—indeed, he was the only Zionist for whom he had complete respect. Upon this note he ended, and having, as must be supposed, diagnosed me sufficiently—although he took not the slightest notice of my occasional queries—he marched out of my room to tea with Kenneth Bell of Balliol, 'whose family is very fond of me' he added.

I felt flattered by his visit, as well as deeply impressed and slightly bewildered by his lecture. In the five or so years before the war I met him more than once. He spoke bitterly about the policy of appeasement. He felt that their sense of reality and their empiricism had evidently deserted the ruling classes in England: not to understand that Hitler meant everything he said—that *Mein Kampf* was to be taken literally—that Hitler had a plan for a war of conquest—was self-deception worthy of Germans or Jews. The Cecils were 'all right', they understood reality, they stood for what was most characteristic of England. So was Winston Churchill. The men who opposed Zionism were the same as those who were against Churchill and the policy of national resistance—Geoffrey Dawson, the editor of *The Times*, Chamberlain, Halifax, Toynbee, the officials of the Foreign Office, Archbishop Lang, the bulk of the Conservative Party, most trade unionists. The Cecils, Churchill, true aristrocracy, pride, respect for human dignity, traditional virtues, resistance, Zionism, personal grandeur, no nonsense realism, these were fused into one amalgam in his mind. Pro-Germans and pro-Arabs were one gang. He spoke a good deal about Zionism to me, no doubt because he thought (rightly) that I was sympathetic. Gradually I became convinced that this was the deepest strain in him: and that he was fundamentally driven into it by sheer pride. He found the position of the Jews to be humiliating: he disliked those who put up with this or pretended that it did not exist. He wanted a free and dignified existence. He was intelligent enough to realise that to shed his Judaism, to assume protective colouring and disappear into the Gentile world, was not feasible and a pathetic form of self-deception. If he was not to sink to the level of the majority of his brethren (whom on the whole he despised), if he had to remain one of them, as was historically inevitable, then there was only one way out—they must be pulled up to his own level. If this could not be achieved by slow, gradual, peaceful, kindly means, then it must be achieved by rapid, and, if need be, somewhat drastic ones. He had not believed this to be wholly possible until he had met Weizmann, whom he admired to the point of hero-worship: here at least was a Jew with whom he did not find it embarrassing to associate, indeed, even to follow. But the other Zionist leaders appeared nonentities to him and he did not trouble to conceal this. He called them 'the rabbis' and said that they were no better than priests and clergymen—to him, then, terms of abuse. His Zionist colleagues valued his gifts but could scarcely be expected to enjoy his open and highly articulate contempt. Despite Weizmann's favour, he was never made a member of the World Zionist Executive—a fact that rankled with him for the rest of his life. Despite all his talk of realism and his historical method, he had the temperament of a political romantic. I am not sure that he did not indulge in day-dreams in which he saw himself as a kind of Zionist D'Annunzio riding on a white horse to capture some Trans-Jordanian Fiume. He saw the Jewish national movement as a *Risorgimento*; if he was not to be its Garibaldi, he would serve as the adviser and champion of its Cavour—the sagacious, realistic, dignified, Europeanised, the almost English, Dr Weizmann.

Privately I used to think that in character, if not in ideas, Namier was not wholly unlike his *bête noire*, Karl Marx. He too was an intellectually formidable at times aggressive, politically minded intellectual—and his hatred of doctrine was held with a doctrinaire tenacity. Like Marx, he was vain, proud, contemptuous, intolerant, quick to give and take offence, master of his craft, confident of his own powers, not without a strain of pathos and self pity. Like Marx he hated all forms of weakness, sentimentality, idealistic liberalism; most of all he hated servility. Like Marx, he fascinated his interlocutors and oppressed them too. If you happened to be interested in the topic which he was discussing (Polish documents relating to the Revolution of 1848, or English country houses), you were fortunate, for it was not likely that you would again hear the subject expounded with such learning, brilliance and originality. If, however, you were not interested, you could not escape. Hence those who met him were divided into some who looked on him as a man of genius and a dazzling talker and others who fled from him as an appalling bore. He was, in fact, both. He aroused admiration, enthusiasm and affection among his pupils and those who were sympathetic to his opinions; uneasy respect and embarrassed dislike among those who did not. If he came across latent anti-semitism he stirred it into a flame; London clubmen (whom he often naïvely pursued) viewed him with distaste. Academics and civil servants, whom he bullied, loathed and denigrated him. Scholars looked on him as a man of prodigious powers and treated him with deep, if, at times, somewhat nervous, admiration.

I never experienced boredom in his company, not even when he was at his most ponderous. All the subjects that he discussed appeared to me, at any rate while he spoke about them, interesting and important; when in form he spoke marvellously. He spoke with sovereign, and often wholly unmitigated, contempt about other scholars, and indeed most other human beings. The only living persons wholly exempt from his disparagement were Winston Churchill, who could do no wrong; Weizmann, in whose presence Namier was simple, childlike, reverent, uncritical to the point of worship; and his great friend Blanche Dugdale, Balfour's niece. He was said to be transformed in her presence, but I never saw them together. Nor do I know how he felt and what he said in the country houses which he visited for the purpose of examining their muniments and family papers. His pleasure in staying in them was part of the romantic Anglomania which remained with him to the end of his days. The English aristocracy was for him bathed in a heavenly light. His interest in history is certainly not alone sufficient to explain this radiant vision. Rather it is probably the other way about: his interest in the history of individual members of the English Parliament during a time when many of them were members of (or closely connected with) a powerful and gifted Whig aristocracy, was due to his idealisation of this style of life. He has, at times, been accused of being a snob. There is something in this; but Namier's snobbery was of the Proustian kind—peers, members of the aristocracy, rich, proud, self-possessed, independent, freedom loving to the point of eccentricity—such Englishmen were for him works of art which he studied with devoted, indeed, fanatical attention and discrimination. He was not carried away by the fascination of this world as Oscar Wilde, or even Henry James, appear to have been. He was content to remain an outsider. He gloried in his vision of the English national character, its strength and its foibles, and remained a life-long passionate addict to a single human species, to the analysis, and, inevitably, celebration of which, his life—for psychological reasons which Freud had certainly not helped him to understand—was devoted. He studied every detail in the life of the English governing class, as Marx studied the proletariat, not in detail, but as a social formation; in each case from an outside vantage point which they did not bother either to emphasise or deny.

His origins obsessed him. His morbid hatred of obsequiousness, which may have had something to do with his memories of Poles and Jews in Galicia, often took ferocious forms. Meeting me in the corridor of a train, he said, a propos of nothing: 'I have been visiting Lord Derby. He said to me: "Namier you are a Jew. Why do you write our English history, why do you not write Jewish history?" I replied, "Derby! There is no Jewish history, only a Jewish martyrology, and that is not amusing enough for me." ' He spoke of Jews as 'my co-racials', and clearly enjoyed the embarrassing effect which this word produced on Jew and Gentile alike. In All Souls one afternoon someone in his presence—he was in the Common Room at tea as a guest—defended the German claim to colonies, a topic then much in the air. Namier rose, glared round the room, fixed a basilisk-like eye on one of his fellow-guests whom he had, mistakenly as it turned out, assumed to be a German, and said loudly '*Wir Juden und die andere farbigen meinen anders*'.[1] He savoured the effect of these startling words with great satisfaction. He was an out and out nationalist, and did not disguise his far from fraternal feelings towards the Arabs in Palestine, about whom his position was more intransigent than that of the majority of his fellow Zionists. I well recollect a meeting to interview candidates for a post in English in the University of Jerusalem, at which Namier would fix some timid lecturer from, say, Nottingham, with his baleful, annihilating glare, and say: 'Mr Levy, can you shoot?' The candidate would mutter something—'Because if you take this post, you will have to shoot. You will have to shoot our Arab cousins. Because if you do not shoot them, they will shoot you.' Stunned silence. 'Mr Levy, will you please answer my question: can you shoot?'. Some of the candidates withdrew. No appointment was made.

As the thirties wore on and the position of the West steadily deteriorated, Namier grew steadily gloomier and more ferocious. He would visit me in All Souls, and later in New College, and say that as war was now inevitable, he proposed to sell his life as dearly as possible, and painted imaginary pictures involving the extermination of a good many Nazis by all kinds of diabolical means. The position of Zionism—one of the victims of British foreign policy at this time—depressed him further. The villains in his eyes were not so much the Conservative leaders—some of those were members of the aristocracy and as such enjoyed a certain degree of exemption from blame—but the Arab-loving 'pen-pushers of the Foreign Office' and the 'hypocritical idiots of the Colonial Office'. He would lie in wait for these—particularly the latter,

[1] 'We Jews and the other coloured peoples think otherwise.'

in the Athenaeum. There he would drive some unsuspecting official into the corner of the Smoking Room, where he would treat him to a terrifying homily which the victim would not soon forget, and which would probably increase his already violent antipathy to Zionism in general and Namier in particular. Sir John Shuckburgh, then the Permanent Under-Secretary of the Colonial Office, was a not infrequent target for Namier when he was on the war-path. I was once present when Namier, in his soft but penetrating and remorseless voice, addressed Shuckburgh who made every effort to escape; in vain. Namier followed him out of the room, onto the steps, into the street, and so on—down the Duke of York's steps, probably to the door of the Colonial Office itself. Politically he was as great a liability to his party as he was an asset to it intellectually. His final and most savagely treated victim was Malcolm MacDonald, the Colonial Secretary himself. In 1939, after the Chamberlain government's White Paper on Palestine, which seemed to put an end to all Zionist hopes, Namier came to lunch with Professor Reginald Coupland at All Souls. Coupland was the effective author of the Peel Report on Palestine, probably the most valuable document ever composed on that agonising subject. Coupland had spoken bitterly of the shameful betrayal of the Palestine Jews by the British Government, and said that he would write a letter to *The Times* pointing out the shortcomings of both Chamberlain and Malcolm MacDonald. Namier said that he had his own method of dealing with such cases. He had met Malcolm MacDonald somewhere in London. 'I spoke to him. I began with a jest. I said that in the eighteenth century peers made their tutors Under-Secretaries, whereas in the twentieth Under-Secretaries made their tutors peers. He did not seem to understand. I did not bother to explain.[1] Then I said something he would understand. I said to him, "Malcolm"—he is, you know, still Malcolm to me—I know him quite well—"I am writing a new book." He said, "What is it, Lewis?" I replied, "I will tell you what it is. I have called it *The Two MacDonalds: A Study in Treachery*."' I do not know whether Namier had actually said this; he supposed that he had and was certainly capable of it. It was, again, not unlike Karl Marx at his most vindictive, and, like Marx's insults, was intended to draw blood. Yet he was surprised by the fact that he was feared and disliked so widely.

In 1941 I was employed by the Ministry of Information in New York, and there I met a man who threw a good deal of light on Namier's younger days. His name was Max Hammerling, and his father had been associated with Josef Bernsztajn, Namier's father, in the management of his estate near Lemberg in Galicia, long before the First World War. The younger Hammer-

[1] Only Namier would have supposed that the average educated Englishman (or Scotsman) would realise that he was referring to the fact that the philosopher Locke had been made an Under-Secretary by his ex-pupil, Lord Shaftesbury, and that Mr Godfrey Elton, who had been Malcolm MacDonald's tutor at Queen's College, Oxford, had recently been elevated to the peerage.

ling was a warm sympathiser with the British cause, and got in touch with me to offer his help at a time when Britain was fighting Hitler alone. In the course of general conversation he asked me if I knew a man called Professor Namier, and was surprised to hear that I did. He said that he used to see him in earlier years, but that since then the connection had ended and he was anxious to hear what had happened to the son of his father's associate. Hammerling Senior had, so his son told me, emigrated to America and acquired control of one or more of the foreign language periodicals of New York in the years before the First World War. The young Namier first arrived in New York in 1913 with very little money—supplied by his father—to engage in research on the American War of Independence. Josef Bernsztajn had made an arrangement with his old associate under which Hammerling engaged Namier to write leading articles to be syndicated and translated for a section of his publications. Namier wrote these articles at night, and worked in the New York Public Library in the day-time, and in this way kept body and soul together. According to Max Hammerling, Namier viewed the continued existence of the Dual Monarchy with extreme disfavour, and was a vigorous champion of the *Entente cordiale*. Hammerling senior had many Roman Catholic readers and had no great wish to alienate the Roman Church in the United States which was on the whole pro-Austrian and isolationist. When Namier's articles became too violently interventionist, he was told to moderate them: he ignored hints and requests; matters came to a head, and his employment came to an end in the spring of 1914. It was then that Namier, without any obvious means of subsistence, returned to England and was given a grant by Balliol College which enabled him to continue his research. Namier told me that the news of the assassination of the Archduke Franz Ferdinand was brought to the Editor of *The Times*, Geoffrey Dawson, in All Souls after dinner. Namier who happened to be there too, announced to Dawson and his friends that war was now imminent. Dawson indicated that he did not believe this (he laboured under similar delusions in 1938–9) and turned to other topics.

When war was declared Namier volunteered for the British Army. He was evidently not a perfect soldier. Some intelligent person took him out of the army, and put him into the Foreign Office as adviser on Polish affairs attached to the Historical Adviser to the Foreign Office, Sir John Headlam-Morley. 'I remember', said Namier to me, 'the day in 1918 when the Emperor Karl sued for peace. I said to Headlam-Morley: "Wait." Headlam-Morley said to Balfour: "Wait." Balfour said to Lloyd George: "Wait." Lloyd George said to Wilson: "Wait." And while they waited, the Austro-Hungarian Empire disintegrated.[1] I may say that I pulled it to pieces with my own hands.'

Apart from feeling convinced that the Polish National Democratic Party was plotting his assassination, Namier enjoyed his work in the Foreign Office. The Foreign Office showed no desire to retain Namier on its staff after the war, nor did the Treasury, with which he also was temporarily connected.

[1] Namier pronounced this word very slowly, syllable by syllable, which heightened the dramatic climax of his narrative.

Nor did Balliol College, Oxford, which made him a temporary lecturer for a while, his most devoted Oxford pupils date from this period. Thereupon he left England for Vienna, and there made a few thousand pounds. In the early twenties he came back to London with his exiguous capital. Here his extraordinary character showed itself at its fullest. He did not do what others might have been tempted to do: he did not try to spend as little as possible while looking for a means of subsistence: he knew that he had it in him to write an original and important book and decided to do so. He spoke of this to friends and allies (some of them connected with the Round Table group of Liberal Imperialists with whose ideas Namier had been in sympathy during the war). He told them that he needed money to write a book; he held out no promise of repayment; the money was to be regarded as an investment in learning and in that alone. Philip Kerr, who was among those approached, told me (in Washington in 1940 where he was by then Lord Lothian and British Ambassador) that he did not find Namier congenial company, but was overawed by his leonine personality and felt him to be a man of unusual intellectual power. He and his friends obtained a grant for him; he was also supported by at least one private person. Namier felt no false shame in accepting such patronage: this was usual enough in that best of all periods, the later years of the eighteenth century. He felt that he had as good a claim as Burke, or any other talented writer of the past, whom the rich and the powerful should be proud to support; and he bound his spell upon his 'patrons', who as he had always known, had no cause to regret their generosity. The books that he wrote did what he wished them to do: they transformed the standards of historical scholarship (and to some degree the style of historical writing) in England for at least a quarter of a century.

Having discharged this intellectual obligation, Namier threw himself, in the later twenties, with passion and ferocity into political work in the Zionist Organisation. This gave full play to his formidable gifts: his polemical skill, his sense of history, his pride, his nationalism, his passion for exposing weakness, cowardice, lies and unworthy motives. He derived deep satisfaction from those labours. In the course of them, he managed to irritate and humiliate his less talented collaborators, to impress some members of the British intelligentsia, astonish and anger others, and permanently upset and infuriate a number of influential officials in the Foreign and Colonial Offices. After the Second World War, when it became plain that his unwavering and withering contempt for most of his Zionist colleagues had made it certain that if an independent Jewish establishment ever emerged he would not be amongst its guides, he turned his back upon Zionist politics, without changing his moral or political convictions. He returned to the study of history. He hoped and expected, not without reason, that he might yet be appointed to a post by his *alma mater*. This was not to be. Whenever a Chair in History (or International Relations, on which, too, he had made himself a leading expert), fell vacant, his name inevitably came up and was duly dismissed. Those responsible for such appointments in Oxford often said that it was a crying shame that some other group of electors had failed to appoint Namier to one or other of the three or four Chairs for which his distinction fitted him pre-eminently. But when their own turn came, such electors or advisers acted precisely like their predecessors. He was invariably passed over. Various reasons were adduced: that his field of specialisation was too narrow; that he was politically intemperate, as his Zionism or his low opinion of pre-war British foreign policy plainly showed; that he would be too arrogant to his colleagues or too exacting to his students; that he would be a terrible bore, intolerable at meal times to the Fellows of this or that college. The quality of his genius was not seriously disputed: but this was not regarded as a sufficiently weighty factor. He had made some implacable enemies. Yet, despite his acuteness, he was an unworldly man, and in personal matters clumsy, innocent and childlike. He was easily deceived: he took flattery for true coin. He often had no notion of who was covertly working against him: he was totally incapable of manoeuvre or intrigue. He achieved everything by the sheer weight of his huge intellectual armour. He misjudged motives and often could not tell friends from ill wishers. He fell into traps and remained to his dying day unaware of this. He was an Othello who retained confidence in more than one minor academic Iago. His failure to obtain an Oxford Chair ate into his soul, as it has into those of others similarly treated. 'I will tell you how they make professors in Oxford,' he said bitterly to me during the period when he was delivering the Waynflete Lectures at Magdalen College shortly after the end of the Second World War. 'In the eighteenth century there was a club called the Koran Club. The qualification for membership was to have travelled in the East. Then it was found that there were various persons whom it was thought desirable to make members of the club and who had not travelled in the East. So the rules were changed from "travelling in the East" to "expressing a wish to travel in the East". That is how they make professors in Oxford. Do not', he added, 'let this story go too far.' He continued to teach at Manchester, but finally moved to London and was entrusted with the formidable enterprise of the History of Parliament to be done in his own fashion—by means of detailed, microscopically examined lives of all who ever were members of it. Honours were showered upon him in England and abroad, but nothing made up for the Oxford disappointment. Balliol made him an Honorary Fellow. Two honorary doctorates were conferred upon him by the University. He delivered the Romanes Lecture. But although this pleased him, as did his knighthood, the old scar remained and troubled him.

It was at this period that he married for the second time (his first marriage had not lasted long—his wife is said to have been a Muslim and died during the second war). He was converted to the Anglican faith, and his marriage to Julia de Beausobre finally ended the period of acute loneliness and bitter personal unhappiness, mitigated by rare moments of pride and joy, which had begun for him after the First World War. Dr Friedrich Waismann, an eminent Austrian philosopher whom he had met during his years in Vienna, told me that he had never in his life met an intellectually more gifted, penetrating and fascinating man, or one more deeply plunged in the most hopeless misery and solitude.

His conversion to Christianity cost him the friendship of Dr Weizmann, who did not wish to examine the reasons for this step, but reacted instinctively, as his fathers would have done before him, to what he regarded as an act of apostasy for which no decent motive could exist. This, of course, hurt Namier deeply, but his marriage had created a new life for him and he bore such things more easily. He visited the state of Israel after Weizmann's death, was profoundly moved, but remained implacably opposed to the rabbis and complained of clerical tyranny. When I made light of this to him he turned upon me sternly and said 'You do not know rabbis and priests as I do—they can ruin any country. Clergymen are harmless. Nobody ever speaks of being in the hands of the clergymen as they do of the Jesuits and, I fear now, should do of rabbis.' During this period I would receive occasional visits from him in Oxford. He had grown mellower with age; he was happier because his domestic life was serene, and because adequate recognition had been given him at last. He took criticism as painfully as ever: when his friend and disciple Alan Taylor wrote an insufficiently respectful review of a collection of his essays in the *Manchester Guardian*, he, like Marx, took this as a symptom of failing powers on the part of the critic. He invested a great deal in his few personal relationships, and breaches were particularly painful to him. His relations with Taylor suffered further deterioration, in large part as a result of the role which Taylor believed him to have played in the choice of the successor to Professor H. V. Galbraith as Regius Professor of History in Oxford. Taylor was not appointed; he blamed Namier for failing to support him sufficiently when he could have done so, and broke off relations. Namier was genuinely fond of him—fonder of him than of most men. He told me that some of his happiest hours had been spent at Taylor's house; that one must be careful—more careful than he had been—in one's human relations; but that Taylor, whose gifts were so extraordinary, had disappointed him by what he considered his addiction to popular journalism. 'And if I have hurt *your* feelings', he said to me, 'I apologise also. I am not always too careful': this was a touching and handsome reference to the fact that I had sent him the printed version of a lecture on an abstract subject, which he had acknowledged with the words 'You must indeed be a very clever man to understand what you write'. This was a characteristic gibe aimed at the philosophy of history—a subject which he believed to be bogus, and which had been the subject of my lecture. I was delighted by his letter, which could not have been regarded as offensive by any normal person, still less by anyone who knew Namier and took pleasure in his prejudices and absurdities. E. H. Carr, who was a common friend, came to visit me on the day when I received it, and I read him Namier's letter with great relish. Carr was somehow responsible for the appearance of Namier's comment in a gossip column of the *Daily Express*. Namier was horrified, and wrote to me immediately to explain that he had not, of course, meant to insult either me or the subject of my lecture. My reassurances did not convince him: it had been very wrong of E. H. Carr to stoop to supplying tittle tattle to the *Daily Express*—serious journalism was, of course, another matter. How could such serious, learned, gifted men, Taylor, Carr, Fellows of the British Academy, who had it in them to give so much to historical study, compromise the dignity of their calling—and of academic life generally—by associating with the enemies of learning, however entertaining and informative? And in so public a fashion? At least Professor Butterfield, than whom no one was more mistaken, did not dabble in this. My defence fell on deaf ears: an idealised image, which he had carried with him for the greater part of his life—the image of the scholar, and perhaps also of the Englishman—had in some way been damaged, and this was almost more painful than a personal attack.

He spoke often of the dignity of learning: of the need to keep scholarship pure, of protecting it from its three greatest enemies: amateurism; journalistic prostitution and obsession with doctrine. 'An amateur' he declared in one of his typical apophthegms, 'An amateur is a man who thinks more about himself than about his subject', and he mentioned a younger colleague whom he suspected of a wish to glitter. He passionately believed in professionalism in every field: he denounced fine writing: and still more, a desire to startle or shock the reader, whether he was a member of the general public or of the world of scholars. He spoke with indignation about those who had accused him of wishing to reassess the character and historical influence of George III out of a desire to dish the Whigs and attack their values and their heroes. He would solemnly and with deep sincerity assure me that his sole purpose was to reconstruct the facts and explain them by the use of well tested, severely empirical methods; that his only reason for distrusting party labels and professions of political ideals in the eighteenth century was his conviction—based on incontrovertible documentary and other factual evidence—that such labels and professions disguised the truth, often from the agents themselves. His own psychological tenets, on which these exposures were in part based, seemed to him confirmed over and over again by the historical evidence—the actual transactions of the politicians and their agents and their kinsfolk—which were susceptible of one and only one true explanation. Whether or not he was mistaken in this, he believed profoundly that he was guided not by theories but by the facts and by them alone. As for the question of what was a fact, what constituted evidence, this was a philosophical issue—something from which he shied with all the force of his whole abstraction-hating, anti-philosophical nature. Journalism—the desire to *épater*, to entertain, to be brilliant—was, in a man of learning, mere irresponsibility. 'Irresponsible' was one of the most opprobrious terms in his vocabulary. His belief in the moral duties of historians and scholars generally was Kantian in its severity and genuineness. As for doctrinaire obsessions, that again appeared to him as a form of culpable self indulgence—wanton escape from the duty of following minutely wherever they led, the often complex, convoluted empirical paths constituted by the 'facts', into some symmetrical pattern invented by the historian to indulge his own metaphysical or moral predilection; alternatively it was a quasi-pathological intellectual obsession which rendered the historian literally incapable of seeing '*wie es eigentlich gewesen*'. Hence Namier's distaste for, and ironies at the expense of, philosophical historians; and the emphasis on material factors and distrust of ideal ones. This was odd in a man who was himself governed by so many ideals and indeed prejudices: nationalism and national character, love of traditional 'roots', *la terre en les morts*, disbelief in the efficacy of intellectuals and theorisers, faith in individual psychology, even in graphology, as a key to character and action. But it was so.

It is not perhaps too extravagant to classify his essentially deflationary tendency—the desire to reduce both the general propositions and the impressionism of historians to hard pellet-like 'facts', to bring everything down to brass tacks—to regard this as part of the dominant intellectual trend of his age and milieu. It was in Vienna, after all, that Ernst Mach enunciated the principles of 'economy of thought' and tried to reduce physical phenomena to clusters of identifiable, almost isolable, sensations; that Freud looked for 'material', empirically testable causes of psychical phenomena; that the Vienna Circle of philosophers generated the verification principle as a weapon against vagueness, transcendentalism, theology, metaphysics; that the Bauhaus with its clear, rational lines had its origin in the ideas of Adolf Loos and his disciples. Vienna was the centre of the new anti-metaphysical and anti-impressionist positivism. Whether he knew this or not—and nobody could protest more vehemently against such ideological categorisation—this was the world from which Namier came. Its most original thinkers had reacted violently against German metaphysics and had found British empiricism sympathetic. In philosophy they achieved a celebrated and fruitful symbiosis with British thought. Namier was one of the boldest and most revolutionary pioneers of the application of this very method to history. The method—especially in the work of his followers—had been criticised as having gone too far—'taken the mind out of history'. This kind of criticism has been levelled no less at the corresponding schools of philosophy, art, architecture, psychology. Whether the charge is just or not, even its sharpest critics can scarcely deny the value and importance of the early impact of the new method. It opened windows, let in air, revealed new horizons, made men see what they had not seen before. In this great constructive—destructive movement Namier was a major figure.

Namier's most striking personal characteristics were an unremittingly active intellectual power, independence, lack of fear and an unswerving devotion to his chosen method. This method had yielded him rich fruit, and he would not modify it merely because it seemed extreme or fanatical to eclectics or philistines. Like Marx, like Darwin, like Freud, he was severely anti-eclectic. Nor did he believe in practising moderation or introducing qualifications simply in order to avoid charges of extremism, to please men of good sense. Indeed, anxiety to please in any fashion, still less appeasement of critics, was remote from his temperament. He believed that objective truth could be discovered, and that he had found a method of doing so in history; that this method consisted in a sort of *pointillisme*, 'the microscopic method', the splitting up of social facts into details of individual lives—atomic entities, the careers of which could be precisely verified; and that these atoms could then be integrated into greater wholes. This was the nearest to scientific method that was attainable in history, and he would adhere to it at whatever cost, in spite of all criticism, until and unless he became convinced by internal criteria of its inadequacy, because it had failed to produce results verified by research. This psychological Cartesianism was his weapon against impressionism and dilletantism of every kind. Kant had said that nature would yield up her secrets only under torture, only if specific questions were put to her. Namier believed this of history. The questions had to be formulated in such a way as to be answerable. He was a child of a positivistic, deflationary, anti-romantic age, and his deep natural romanticism came out in other—political—directions. Dedicated historian that he was, he deliberately confined himself to his atomic data. He did indeed split up and reduce his material to tiny fragments, then he reintegrated them with a marvellous power of imaginative generalisation as great as that of any other historian of his time. He was not primarily a narrative historian, and he did, perhaps, underestimate the importance and the influence of ideas. He admired individual greatness, he despised equality, mediocrity, stupidity; he worshipped political and personal liberty. His attitude to economic facts was at best ambivalent: and he was a very half hearted determinist in his writing of history, whatever he may have said about it in his theoretical essays. Materialism, excessive determinism, were criticisms levelled against him, but it fits better those historians who, using the method without the genius, tend towards pedantry and timidity, where he was boldly constructive, intuitive and untrammelled. He thought in large terms. The care with which he examined and described the individual trees did not obscure his vision of the wood for the sake of which the huge accumulation and the minute analyses had been undertaken; the end, at any rate in the works of his best period, is never lost to view; the reader is not cluttered with detail, never feels that he is in the grasp of an avid fact gatherer who cannot let anything go, a fanatical antiquary who can no longer distinguish between the trivial and the important. Perhaps, towards the end of his life, trees and even shrubs did begin to obscure his vision of the wood. But when he was at his best he might well have said, echoing Marx, for whom he had so little respect and by whose method he was in practice much influenced: '*Surtout, je ne suis pas namieriste*'.

PAUL EINZIG

The Financial Crisis of 1931

PAUL EINZIG

The Financial Crisis of 1931

ENGLISH people have always had a soft spot for dilettantism. In no other country are brilliant dabblers in subjects outside their spheres of competence looked upon with so much indulgence as in Britain. The German cult of the specialist is proverbial. In the United States, too, he is a pampered favourite and untold millions of dollars are spent on providing the expert with almost any factual and statistical material he chooses to ask for. In Soviet Russia, where worship of efficiency forms part of the Communist religion, the specialist is even forgiven for not being a Communist. France and Italy have long lived down their pre-war reputation for easy-going dilettantism. In none of these countries are dilettants tolerated and encouraged to anything like the same extent as in Britain.

This British attitude towards dilettantism, which has been clearly noticeable ever since the eighteenth century, has become increasingly evident in our days, largely as a result of the combined efforts of the B.B.C. and of the popular Press. Admittedly, it would be difficult for anyone who started life as a dilettante to achieve fame as a dilettante. In order to be listened to when pontificating on subjects about which one knows little or nothing, one has first to achieve a reputation—or at any rate a notoriety—of some kind. But once somebody's name has become a household word on any subject, Broadcasting House and Fleet Street go out of their way to publicise his views on subjects on which he has no more real knowledge than most of his listeners or readers.

Parlour-games, in which celebrities answer questions or participate in debates on subjects entirely outside their special interests, are indeed very popular among viewers and listeners. The explanation lies in human nature. We all enjoy seeing or hearing our betters make fools of themselves, and it is therefore a real pleasure to catch them out when laying down the law on some subject about which we happen to know more than they do. They are blissfully unaware of the comic figure they cut when talking pompous nonsense in the grand manner of condescending to give away pearls of world wisdom. Admittedly, if some of these distinguished broadcasters, instead of taking part in such parlour-games, were to stand on their heads in Trafalgar Square, surrounded by a multitude of beats and pigeons on a sunny Sunday afternoon, it might be even funnier than some of their answers—but only marginally so.

As for the popular Press, the magic of a famous name commands high fees even if the subject of the article is not one on which the pronouncements of the contributor deservedly commands respect. If his name is sufficiently familiar to the general public his article is bound to be read by millions, which helps the circulation of the paper. In one instance at any rate, it also helped a Press Baron towards achieving his main ambition in life—to increase his nuisance-value.

Thanks to the combined exertions of the B.B.C. and Fleet Street, a generation of famous dilettants has emerged in our midst—prominent personalities who are highly respected scholars when broadcasting or writing on subjects they really know about, but who are mere dabblers when broadcasting or writing on other subjects.

Mr A. J. P. Taylor may be regarded as one of the outstanding instances to illustrate the point. He is generally and rightly admired and respected as one of the leading authorities of our generation on various periods of history. Instead of being content with that, he cannot resist the temptation at times to write or broadcast on subjects with which he is unfamiliar. He is doing this in the same cocksure tone that he employs with every justification when discussing his own special subjects. The worst of it is that he is a brilliant writer and broadcaster, and his readers and listeners, fascinated by his presentation of his facts and interpretations, are liable to accept them without scrutiny. I must confess that I derive much pleasure from reading him even on subjects on which I disagree with him. When it comes to 'neutral' subjects I have to be very much on my guard to avoid coming under his spell.

'I am not an economist, just as I am not a general, but I can describe battles and I think I can describe this strange economic crisis.'[1] This sentence, uttered with disarming candour by Mr Taylor in a broadcast lecture dealing with the financial crisis of 1931—surely one of the most complex human experiences in modern times, that has baffled two generations of highly qualified experts—could well serve as an eternal signature tune to introduce dilettante pronouncements.

It is hardly surprising that Mr Taylor selected economics for his dilettantist exercise instead of venturing into the realms of, say, higher mathematics, or nuclear physics, or biochemistry. For the preserves of economics invite trespassing by the layman simply because the ordinary language of economics is familiar to any intelligent reader of the daily Press. It is true, in more recent years pure economists have invented a language of their own. If and when it should come to be generally adopted as the only permissible language for discussing economic subjects it will of course effectively bar the dilettante. But at what a cost! The futile obscurantism of that language and, to quote a remark made to me by the late Henry Whitehead, the 'pseudo-intellectual masturbation' of mathematical economics that goes with it—and this is almost praising it compared with what some other genuine mathematicians think of the question-begging performances of their imitators among economists—is so

[1] A. J. P. Taylor, 'The Great Depression', the *Listener*, March 22, 1962, p. 505.

repellent that even some occasional dilettante, dabbling in the 'dismal' discipline must be deemed as a distinctly less distressing disaster.

I really feel that dilettants, if they want to get away with bluffing on economics, might at least familiarise themselves with the elements of that subject. Mr Taylor is of course right in claiming that historians who undertake to describe battles need not necessarily be generals. But surely they must know enough about military science to avoid mistaking battalions for divisions or Very pistols for rocket-launchers. Yet in his description of the financial crisis of 1931 Mr Taylor disclosed a comparable lack of elementary knowledge on finance.

Mr. Taylor's experiment in describing an economic crisis pursues the end of blaming merchant bankers for the financial crisis which brought down the Labour Government and the pound in 1931. His attack is not directed at bankers in general, but at merchant bankers. While it is said to have taken the combined effort of nine tailors to ring the bells for the dead, one Taylor appears to have been sufficient to resurrect a dead legend—that of the alleged responsibility of London merchant bankers for the sterling crisis of 1931. The 'bankers' ramp' myth of the 'thirties, long dead and buried and almost forgotten, has now been brought to life by Mr Taylor in a brand-new streamlined form. Having a well-deserved world-wide reputation as one of the greatest historians of our generation, and being widely known also as a popular journalist and broadcaster, his words were bound to receive attention both among the learned élite and among a wide public, even though on the present occasion he talked about a subject with which he was unfamiliar.

In the broadcast lecture quoted above Mr Taylor treated his listeners to a very strange version of the crisis that had led to the suspension of the gold standard. Never in all my experience, extending over some half a century, have I come across any published material which contains so many factual inaccuracies and errors of interpretation per column inch as is contained in Mr Taylor's broadcast when read in cold print in the *Listener*.

The least important among Mr Taylor's mistakes is his opening sentence stating that the Wall Street crash started on October 15, 1929. After all, he is out by a mere fortnight. But one should have thought that the date of the Wall Street slump, October 29, 1929, marking as it did the beginning of the economic crisis which was to bring Hitler to power, was important enough for a historian covering that period to make sure of its accuracy.[1]

Mr Taylor's account of the role played by merchant bankers in 1931 reads as follows:

> The merchant bankers had . . . borrowed from the French at 2 per cent and *lent it to the Germans at* 8 . . . The German banks could not pay the money which they owed to the London banks. The London banks then could not pay

[1] In his new book, *English History* 1914–1945 (p. 284), Mr Taylor does quote the correct date.

> the money they owed the French. *The London banks admitted that they owed £250 million: other calculations are that they owed as much as £600 million.* On all honest calculation they were bankrupt too. They turned to the Bank of England. The Bank of England then, though they tell me not now, was itself run by merchant bankers. So the Bank of England naturally went to the rescue of the merchant bankers. And *when the merchant bankers could not pay their debts to the French the Bank of England handed them out gold.* This, though it seems incredible, is the financial crisis of 1931. The whole thing was an operation to rescue a lot of London banks which had got into trouble . . . *You would think that the thing was to tell the merchant banks to close their doors.* No, . . . the Labour Government would have shrunk with horror from the idea that there should be any challenge to the repute of the City of London.[1]

I think I can claim to have criticised merchant banks in the 'twenties and early 'thirties as much as any living human being for having lent too much to Germany. Nor can I expect any thanks from them for raising here this subject which, they feel, had better be allowed to fade into oblivion.[2] But I feel that I must defend them, whether they like it or not, because Mr Taylor's attack on them, based as it is on wrong figures and imaginary facts, calls for a detailed refutation.

It is a great pity that Mr Taylor omitted to ascertain the true facts and figures and to acquire some elementary knowledge of the system of acceptance credits, foreign deposits, foreign exchanges and gold movements before writing on a subject about which it is impossible to talk sense without some such knowledge. A general historian could not be expected to be familiar with highly technical subjects relating to banking and currency. But then he should not write on them with a misleading display of assurance.

Mr Taylor's observations quoted above contain, among others, the following factual errors:

(1) Merchant banks did *not* lend for Germany before 1931 at anything like 8 per cent. They charged on acceptance credits a commission of ½ to 1 per cent p.a., and the bills accepted by them were placed by the German borrowers in the London discount market at between 2 and 2½ per cent p.a. during the twelve months preceding the crisis of 1931. In the late 'twenties even German long-term loans were issued in London on a 5 per cent basis, which was the same as the yield on British long-term loans.

(2) It is quite incorrect to say that the merchant banks were unable in 1931 to repay the French deposits without aid from the Bank of England. No such aid was in fact asked for, received, or needed by any merchant banks *in 1931.* What Mr Taylor may possibly have had in mind was the official aid given to a number of them *in 1939*, after the outbreak of the war, about which more will be said later.

(3) London merchant banks never admitted having owed to the French

[1] The *Listener*, p. 507 (My italics).

[2] The Accepting Houses Committee actually destroyed in 1960 all its files relating to German standstill credits.

£250 million in 1931. They could admit no such thing, considering that the *total* of foreign deposits held by merchant banks *and* clearing banks together on March 31, 1931, was £142.2 million, according to the Macmillan Report.[1] Only part of these deposits belonged to the French, and in any case it is a reasonable assumption that the clearing banks held the bigger share of these £142 million.

(4) Mr Taylor was completely misled, whether through his informants' fault or through misunderstanding them, about the alleged 'other calculations' putting the total of French deposits with merchant banks at £600 million. What his informants had presumably in mind was the revised figures for 1931 published after the war, which included not only the deposits held by merchant banks but also those held by foreign bank branches and subsidiaries in London and by London banks operating mainly overseas. Since Mr Taylor's attack was directed exclusively against merchant banks who were singled out for criticism, these larger figures, representing as they did the total overseas deposits held by the London banking community as a whole—and including, incidentally, large amounts held by residents in countries with currencies based on sterling—were utterly irrelevant to his argument.[2]

(5) In any case, the total involved in the German default was a mere fraction of Mr Taylor's 'calculations' of the French deposits. German standstill credits of merchant banks, which became frozen in 1931, were understood to have amounted to less than £40 million at the outbreak of the war.

(6) The freezing of the German credits did not and could not prevent merchant banks from meeting their liabilities to French depositors *in 1931*, for the simple reason that they were not called upon to meet their German acceptances *until 1939*. Meanwhile their names commanded sufficient confidence for the bills accepted by them to be taken freely in the London discount market. I propose to explain this technical point later.

(7) The Bank of England did *not* at any time 'hand out gold' to the merchant banks to enable the latter to repay French deposits. Those were sterling deposits pure and simple, and were repayable not in gold but in sterling. What did happen was that French depositors sold in the foreign exchange market the sterling they had withdrawn from the merchant banks, and the resulting weakness of sterling made it necessary for the Bank of England to intervene in support of sterling by drawing on its credits obtained from the U.S. and French authorities.

These are Mr Taylor's seven deadly factual sins. In addition he was guilty

[1] Report of the Committee on Finance and Industry (Cmd. 3857) 1931, p. 42.

[2] In his *English History*, 1914–45 (p. 289), Mr Taylor repeats his high estimates of deposits and even increases them tentatively to '£600 or £700 million'. But this time he refers to *foreign* deposits in general and not to French deposits, and to 'the City' in general instead of merchant banks only, which is quite a different story. It includes hundreds of millions of pounds held in London by banks of the Commonwealth, Latin America and the Far East, unrelated to borrowing from France or to lending to Germany.

of false interpretations, due to his lack of background knowledge, on the following points:

(1) When talking about merchant bankers having 'lent' to Germany he showed himself understandably unfamiliar with the system of acceptance credits under which the creditor does not actually provide the money borrowed by his debtor but merely authorises the latter to draw on him bills of exchange which he 'accepts', thereby guaranteeing their payment. As a result of his acceptance, his debtor is able to have the bills discounted in London at a very favourable discount rate—the rate for 'fine bank bills'. The creditor does not have to part with any cash whatsoever at any time. The debtor remits the amounts to him before maturity, so that when the bills are presented to the merchant banks for payment they are paid with the aid of the funds provided in advance by the debtor for that purpose.

Alternatively, a debtor whose creditor has agreed to renew the credit sends to his creditor new bills to the same total amount, and the maturing bills are paid by the merchant bank out of the proceeds of the sale of these new bills. It is only if and when the debtor ever failed to provide either cash or marketable new bills—in other words, if he defaulted on his debt—that the creditor would have to part with his own cash. This situation did *not* arise in 1931. Default was avoided, thanks to the Standstill Agreement which was concluded in July 1931, and was renewed every year. Under its provisions the German debtors replaced the maturing bills by new bills every three months and the creditors accepted these bills and sold them in the discount market, so that they were always able to secure the amounts necessary for meeting the maturing bills they had accepted.

The difficulty which Mr Taylor thought arose in 1931 did not in fact arise until September 1939 when, owing to the outbreak of the war, no new German bills were forthcoming any longer, and in any case bills issued in an enemy country ceased to be marketable in Britain. Then and not before did it become necessary for the merchant banks to meet the outstanding bills out of their own resources. Then, and only then, did it become necessary for the Bank of England to assist them by providing sterling, but *not gold*, to enable a number of merchant banks to meet the maturing bills. This was done by rediscounting these bills and keeping them in 'cold storage' for the duration, or until the merchant banks were in a position to redeem them.

(2) Mr Taylor's background knowledge was also deficient in respect of the system of 'borrowing' from the French. He seemed to imagine that this was done on purpose in order to be able to re-lend the borrowed money to Germany. We already saw above that there was no need for the merchant banks to acquire additional cash resources in order to be able to grant acceptance credits to Germany. They received French deposits, and indeed other foreign deposits, mainly as a result of the relatively high interest rates prevailing in London compared with other financial centres—Paris, New York, Amsterdam or Zurich. It was all done on the initiative of the depositors themselves, and the

operation had no connection whatsoever with the granting of acceptance credits to Germany. While it is true that the London banking community *as a whole* borrowed from France and lent to Germany, this was not necessarily true of any individual merchant bank. Some of them may possibly have invested part of the French deposits in German sterling bills, but in all probability the bulk of those deposits was invested in other forms, and the bulk of the German bills was acquired and held by others.

(3) Mr Taylor's idea, that merchant bankers, who had indeed controlled the Bank of England in their capacity of its stockholders before its nationalisation in 1946, misused in 1931 their position for securing benefits for their respective banks, is entirely mistaken. As I said above, no occasion for obtaining the Bank of England's support arose at all in 1931. And when it did arise eight years later, the terms on which support was granted were of quite exceptional severity. Instead of charging the official rediscount rate charged to ordinary borrowers, the Bank charged to its own stockholders 2 per cent above that rate, *with a minimum of 6 per cent*. Since the Bank rate was kept down at 2 per cent for quite a number of years, throughout that period the merchant banks controlling the Bank paid interest to the Bank at 4 per cent above the Bank rate. They charged themselves *three times* the interest rates the Bank charged to its ordinary customers during the same period. This could be quoted as an outstanding instance of self-inflicted penalty. The merchant bankers, through their control of the Bank of England, could easily have secured much more lenient terms for themselves. Nobody could have blamed them if they had charged themselves the Bank rate. Instead they chose to charge themselves 6 per cent. And it is these men whom Mr Taylor accuses of having wrecked sterling in order to save their own skins at the cost of sacrificing sterling.

(4) Mr Taylor believes that the run on sterling could and should have been stopped by 'telling the merchant bankers to close their doors'. He seems to be completely unaware of the disastrous self-aggravating effects of a banking crisis. Had banks whose name had been household words for generations suspended payments, the public might have lost confidence in all banks without exception. Additional pressure on sterling that would have been caused by the resulting panic would have been many times larger than the French deposits whose withdrawal would have been prevented if the merchant banks had suspended payments. It is a mystery to me how a man with Mr Taylor's outstanding intellect could possibly believe that a run on the banks, superimposed on all our other troubles in 1931, would have saved the pound. As is generally known, it was precisely such a banking crisis in the United States that was mainly responsible for the flight from the dollar in 1933, leading to the suspension of the American gold standard in spite of the immense superiority of the American gold reserve compared with the British.

One should have thought that, once the attention of a scholar of Mr Taylor's high standing was directed to gross factual errors such as those exposed above, he would take the earliest opportunity to make amends, especially since he had used the incorrect facts as a basis for unfair allegations against merchant bankers. But Mr Taylor did not recant. In the *Listener* of March 29 I challenged him to quote his authority for the merchant banks' alleged admission that they owed £250 million to the French and for the alleged 'other calculations' according to which they owed £600 million. In addition, I also wrote to him, to make sure that my challenge had not escaped his attention, and I repeated my challenge in the April 19 *Listener*, placing on record the fact that I had written to him. But Mr Taylor, who is usually anything but bashful in answering criticisms, chose to keep silent this time.

By refraining from admitting this mistake, Mr Taylor has provided, for the purposes of political propaganda, a legend that London merchant banks, by their inability to repay £600 million of French deposits they were supposed to have re-lent to Germany, were responsible for the 1931 crisis that culminated in the suspension of the gold standard.

Admittedly, in his recently published scholarly work quoted above, Mr Taylor goes some way towards making good the harm he had done. He recognised that the City 'strove to restore the economic life of Central Europe by generous lending'. He even credits the City with helping Central Europe 'from the highest motives'—although his compliment assumes a distinctly backhanded character in the second half of the same sentence in which he repeats and even aggravates deliberately his incorrect broadcast allegation that the City, having borrowed from the French at 2 per cent, 'lent to Germans "at 8 or 10 per cent" '.[1] It seems probable that for each person who will read the modified version of Mr Taylor's account of the crisis there were scores who listened to his broadcast account. And in any case even his more scholarly version of the crisis is far from having repaired the damage caused by his dilettante version. The legend he created in his broadcast account undoubtedly survives.

An outstanding example of how such legends are apt to establish themselves in spite of their flagrant falsity was provided by another historian-journalist, belonging to a totally different class, Mr John Gunther. In 1936 he made the charge that the National Government, having gone to the country 'on a promise to stick to gold' dishonoured that pledge as soon as it was re-elected with a large majority.[2] Although this howler escaped the attention of all his reviewers but one, I did point out in the *Financial News* that the gold standard was suspended in September 1931 while the general election was not held until October 1931. But the publicity received by my review was of course negligible compared with that received by Mr Gunther's factual mis-statement which was reprinted unchanged in subsequent editions of his best-seller. He had thus created a legend which was repeated uncontradicted on a

[1] *English History*, 1914–45, p. 289.

[2] John Gunther, *Inside Europe* (London, 1936), p. 257.

number of occasions in recent years, in the House of Commons and elsewhere.[1] Mr Taylor, by his unwillingness to admit his mistake, stands a good chance of emulating Mr Gunther's achievement.

I had a somewhat similar experience with another general historian who, having achieved a high reputation in his own sphere, found himself out of his depth when venturing into the economic sphere without adequate preparation. Gordon Childe, when dealing with the invention of coinage in his popular book *What Happened in History*, remarked: 'Greek tradition attributes to Croesus of Lydia . . . the initiation of this practice about 700 B.C.'[2] Whatever else may or may not have happened in history, this could not possibly have happened, for the simple and obvious reason that Croesus reigned between 560 and 546 B.C. In fact, the first adoption of coinage is attributed by Greek tradition not to him but to his great-great-grandfather, Gyges.

When I challenged Professor Childe to quote his authority he simply ignored my challenge, just as Mr Taylor did some fifteen years later. In his case, however, I think I did manage later to recall his source. The self-same mistake occurred also in H. G. Wells' *Outline of History*. So now we know at any rate one of Childe's original sources. It occurred to me at the time that it might be a good idea if the literary executors of the late H. G. Wells changed the title of his deservedly popular work to *Childe's Guide to History*.

I yield to no one in my sincere and enthusiastic admiration, bordering on hero-worship, for Mr Taylor's scholarly work as distinct from much of his popular journalism and broadcasting. I even enjoy much of his popular output, for he always has something interesting to say, and the very irritation he causes is stimulating to thought. But the discovery of mistakes such as those quoted above leaves me with an uneasy feeling. I cannot help wondering if, were I to take the time and trouble to make a thorough study of the subjects on which he is a recognised authority, I could not catch him out on some factual inaccuracies, inadequacy of background knowledge and errors of interpretation comparable with those of which his description of the financial crisis of 1931 proved to have been guilty? Most probably not. Anyhow, he certainly deserves to be given the benefit of the doubt. Even so, he should not give cause for doubt. I cannot help remembering how before the war enthusiastic British readers and reviewers of *Inside Europe* used to say: 'Of course, much of what he says about England is nonsense, but he says some very interesting things about [say] Poland.' Presumably his Polish readers and reviewers were lost in admiration for the interesting and well-informed things he said about England but thought rather less highly of what he said about Poland.

[1] I myself heard it repeated by the prospective Chancellor of the Exchequer, Mr James Callaghan, M.P., in the House of Commons in 1956. Nobody on the crowded Conservative benches corrected him, which gives an idea of the extent to which Gunther's legend came to be accepted as the correct version of what happened in 1931.

[2] Gordon Childe, *What Happened in History* (Penguin Edition). London, 1942, p. 192.

Even allowing for the admittedly very remote possibility that my admiration for Mr Taylor's serious work may be due not so much to his prodigious knowledge of its subjects as to my abysmal ignorance of them, I feel that the highest tribute is due to him, without any reservations whatsoever, for the way in which he presents his material. I enjoy reading him more than any other historian apart from Gibbon. But precisely because he is capable of producing such superb material, he has the duty to himself, as well as to his readers, to abstain from displays of dilettantism that are liable to undermine the faith of some of us even in his serious writings. And it is time he is made to realise the risk that his popular writings and broadcasting—*not* only those dealing with the financial crisis of 1931—might endanger his reputation as a historian. Should he be unfortunate enough to be found out repeatedly in the way in which he was on the crisis of 1931, it might do irreparable harm to his standing as a scholar, which, after all, must surely matter to him a great deal more than his popularity among the large number of semi-morons and nincompoops in whose eyes he can simply do no wrong.

Of course he stands a reasonable chance of getting away with mistakes resulting from superficial work for popular consumption, even if they be mistakes of the same order as those quoted above. Possibly he may think it was sheer bad luck that his story about the financial crisis of 1931 happened to come into my firing line, and that such an accident is not likely to recur. No doubt he discovered long ago that most reviewers never notice any real mistakes. They criticise a book if they disagree with its author's political or scholarly views or if they dislike him personally; or if they themselves have just published or are about to publish a rival book on the same subject; or if they want to get even with him for some long-forgotten unfavourable review of their book; or if their name does not appear in his index or his bibliography in which practically all reviewers hasten to look for their names as soon as the review copy reaches them; or they are longing to show just how smart they are, or how daring they are, in attacking one of such high reputation; or if they happen to think of a devastating wisecrack at the author's expense; or if they are just green with envy about the immense superiority of the author's achievements compared with their own. In any such instances many reviewers have indeed a remarkable ability to persuade themselves, by a subconscious process, that his is a thoroughly bad book which it is their duty to discredit, and they are too busy trying to do just that on safe general grounds to find time for engaging in some hard and honest research work in order to check the accuracy of its facts.

Such practices are all too prevalent in post-war book reviewing, and readers of Mr Taylor's unfavourable reviews ought to discount them. The intelligent section of the reading public is in fact vaguely familiar with the willingness of so many reviewers to sacrifice unhesitatingly truth and fairness for the sake of smartness and/or smugness. Hence the frequency of instances in which books with a more or less unanimously bad Press sell remarkably well.

On the other hand, it is equally necessary for readers of Mr Taylor's books to discount favourable reviews to some extent. After all, some reviewers may possibly praise him simply because they like him; or because they belong to the same political camp; or because it is fashionable to praise him; or because he is a formidable book reviewer himself, and, since they judge others by themselves, they are afraid of reprisals; or because they are quoted in his book extensively and with approval; or even because they are anxious to sell their review copy in Charing Cross Road before the time limit for the payment of the favourable price allowed for review copies of recently published books expires, and have therefore no time to read it sufficiently thoroughly to criticise it adversely without taking undue risk.

Possibly Mr Taylor's knowledge that most critics are not sufficiently thorough to be able to discover genuine mistakes may have been largely responsible for the absence of any effort on his part to ensure the accuracy of his facts and figures in his broadcast account of the crisis of 1931. But he would be well advised to bear in mind that, even though he might be able to get away with similar mistakes in the case of most reviewers all the time and in the case of all reviewers some of the time, he is not necessarily a hundred per cent safe in assuming that he can get away with it in the case of all reviewers all the time. I am quite certain that he is big enough not to reject this well-intentioned if tactlessly expressed advice out of hand merely because of any resentment he may feel over the style of my criticisms.

In conclusion I should like to assure him with the utmost emphasis that, were it not for the critical but nonetheless genuine admiration I feel for his work when he is at his best, I would certainly not have deemed it worth while to criticise his display of dilettantism. And perhaps it might conceivably mitigate his resentment over my present essay in the gentle art of making enemies if I confessed here and now that this highly inadequate attempt to imitate his own superb fighting style of writing when he is on the warpath is really meant to be, if not exactly the highest form of flattery, at any rate a very warm tribute to a truly great writer and historian.

HUGH THOMAS

Anarchist Agrarian Collectives in the Spanish Civil War

HUGH THOMAS

Anarchist Agrarian Collectives in the Spanish Civil War

AT the beginning of the Spanish war in 1936, large sections of Spain fell under the control of a movement usually described as anarchist. The movement itself would refer to itself as federalist or syndicalist, and certainly the purist would say that the use of the word anarchist *tout court* is always wrong where Spain is concerned. In full civil war, a leading intellectual of the movement, Federica Montseny, remarked that her intellectual formation derived less from Bakunin than from the nineteenth-century federalist, Pi y Margall. The facts are that there was a large general labour confederation, the CNT (National Confederation of Labour), in which anarchist or federalist ideas prevailed, which was loosely organised and whose membership is difficult to estimate accurately: possibly there were 350,000 actual members, who could however count on the sympathy and, in times of crisis, the support of a million more. Springing out of the CNT there had been formed nine years before a smaller group, the FAI, the Iberian Anarchist Federation, whose main purpose was to sharpen militancy among the CNT, to provide the CNT with an élite leadership and in some respects to alter the actual goals of the CNT's activity: for instance, it was not till the FAI succeeded in gaining effective leadership of the CNT in the early 'thirties that the CNT's agrarian policy was changed from the idea of the distribution of the great estates to that of formation of collectives. The FAI's numbers before the civil war was estimated by the CNT historian, Peirats, at about 30,000.

In July 1936, after many false starts and warnings the Spanish officers rose against the centre-left minority government. It was not a Fascist rising, except in the sense that any explicit anti-democrat activity can be described as Fascist. The actual Spanish Fascists, the Falange, knew what was planned, but, though their leadership had made an agreement of a kind with the officers, they had generally no hand in the plans. The Government was not the main force which caused the rising in many places to fail. This was organised labour, that is, the activity of the CNT and FAI and also of the socialist General Union of Workers (UGT). Immediately after the defeat of the officers (in over half Spain), these organisations, together with the local representatives of the political parties of the popular front, became the masters of society. To say that they were the government would be misleading since during the defeat of the officers the conventional expressions of the centralised state had in most places disappeared. The civil guard, the priest, the barracks, and, in larger places, the café or club where the upper classes might have been expected to gather, existed no longer.

This situation found the anarchist movement (as I shall persist erroneously in calling it) in a considerable quandary. First, it had never been supposed by anarchists that their great opportunity would occur where they would be allied with other working-class movements and even political parties, even bourgeois political parties. Secondly, the anarchists had naturally not expected to gain power in the middle of what was (as was evident from early on) a real war. And thirdly, even without these confusing factors, the anarchist movement was not really united on aims at the time they had this chance to apply them. In May there had been a show of unity when a faction of the movement, the treintistas (in 1931 expelled for their criticism of the FAI) had been received back into the fold. At Saragossa a long programme of action to be enacted after the revolution, prepared by Doctor Isaac Puente (killed afterwards by the army in Logroño), had been adopted, making clear that collectivisation rather than distribution of land was the official CNT plan. But how far was this everywhere accepted? Not, as will be seen, everywhere, even by anarchists themselves.

Meantime, even at the outbreak of the civil war, a number of collectives had already been set up. One had even been formed in the suburbs of Madrid: on May 9, 1936, Salomon Vázquez and Provencio Roque formed a collective after four market gardeners had been sacked and after the land had been found neglected. The local syndicate agreed to hand over the land to the peasants, and twelve men set out, finding at the end of the day that wages could be raised from 6.25 to 8.25 pesetas a day. After three weeks there was a fund of 3,500. At this point the revolution began. There were other collectives in Cataluña and Extremadura formed in the spring.

Quite quickly after the outbreak of war, the anarchist leadership made a general agreement to share power with their allies. According to the most reliable commentator, Abad de Santillan, this was done specifically so that while a seat on the governing committee would have to be given to the Communists and Socialists even where the anarchists were powerful, the anarchists would, as a *quid pro quo*, get a similar seat in places where their strength was less—such as in Castile. In the first weeks, the anarchists and left-wing Socialists made the political pace. However, the middle-class parties, the right-wing Socialists, and the Communists, made themselves the champions of the revival of the State. The demands of war and incessant defeats in southern and western Spain led to the gradual victory of this point of view. The anarchist movement (though not all the rank and file, by any means) explicitly accepted this, however much it meant the abandonment of what Malraux referred to as *l'illusion lyrique*: in September the anarchists entered the Catalan government, in November they joined the central government. Though their four ministers resigned in May 1937, they continued to collaborate with the government, anarchists serving in official positions in administration till the end of the war. In April 1938 an anarchist, Segundo Blanco, from Asturias, returned to the cabinet and remained there till the end of the war.

The entry into the government posed a great revaluation of aims and motives for those anarchists involved, and it is clear they entered not simply to help the war effort but also to try and prevent the total destruction of the movement by the Communists. In this they were fairly successful. A number of anarchist leaders continued in the reorganised Republican Army. At the end of the war, as events at the time of Colonel Casado's anti-Communist coup were to show, a considerable number of the commands in the central and southern zones of Spain were held by anarchists. By and large, the demands of war forced the gradual abandonment of the large variety of anarchist types of control in industry. As early as July 20, 1936, the anarchist leader, García Oliver, nominated Eugenio Vallejo to start a munitions industry in Catalonia, and the necessity of collaboration with the State and political parties was implicit from the start. By the end of the first year of war, most large industries had had to accept a lesser or greater extent of state direction even if they continued to operate under nominally anarchist management.

On the land, there was never any real resolution of the tension between the Revolution and the State. Most detailed observation of the collectives in the countryside and small towns of Republican Spain is by anarchist writers. The most complete series of accounts of the life of the collectives appears in the anarchist press, and this is far from complete and not unprejudiced. Two anarchist writers, Peirats and Gaston Leval (a Frenchman who was incidentally one of the five men to represent the CNT in Moscow in 1921 when they were discussing whether or not to join the Comintern) gathered information on the activities of a number of collectives, but the details they give only extend to an apparently arbitrarily chosen selection of about eighty collectives out of what appear to be about 1,500 in all. Much of even their information comes from newspapers at the time. Some writers went to a number of collectives at the time, but most were either (like Alardo Prats and Agustin Souchy) commited in favour of them or (like Borkenau and Kaminski) visited them in the early months, before they had had a chance to show how they would work after the exultant enthusiasm for the revolution in the early days had passed away. All the famous descriptive books on the anarchist collectives seem in fact to have been published in 1937, usually recounting events in 1936—the exception being Alardo Prats (whose book appeared in 1938).[1]

[1] There are many references to the collectives in Bolloten's *The Grand Camouflage*, and some interesting quotations, but even here there is little interpretation and analysis; though Bolloten (as a good anti-Communist) is apparently attracted, we don't really learn whether he thinks that the collectives were making out well or badly, considered in themselves. In fact of course he tells us that he did not set out to give a complete picture of life in the anarchist towns—and *his* book only deals with events up to May 1937.

In the winter of 1936–7 there were well over 1,000 agricultural collectives in Republican Spain. They were agricultural in the sense that the work they carried on was mainly concerned with the land, but they were concentrated on the towns, small or big, which serve in most of Spain as the homes of agricultural workers and their families. Many of these collectives ran primitive forms of industry like wine and olive presses or flour mills, but their main activity was the land. In Aragon, there were 450 collective towns, comprising about 433,000 persons, about 75 per cent of the population in Republican hands.[1] The average Aragonese collective therefore consisted of about 960 members. Three hundred and fifty of these were totally collectivised towns, in the 100 others there were free or *individualista* elements. In the Levante, there were about 340 collectives, of which most were mixed.[2] In the centre and in the area of Andalucia still part of the Republic, there may have been 250 more, and in Catalonia another 200.[3] Possibly a majority of persons even in areas where there were collectives remained outside collective control.

The size of the collectives varied greatly. That at Tomelloso (Ciudad Real) had 5,000 members; that at Villas Viejas (Albacete) consisted simply of two farms taken over by about twenty families (92 persons) who worked there. The national average was probably smaller than the Aragonese one of 960.

The majority of collectives were organised by an alliance of CNT and UGT. Whatever differences continued on a national level between their leaders, at many small places local relations continued good throughout the war.[4] The first stage towards the formation of a collective was usually the constitution by the local CNT and UGT of a united union, *sindicato unico*. A council of administration (*consejo de administración*) would be constituted. It was customarily composed of a president, secretary, vice-secretary and treasurer, together with a number of other *vocals* (voters) or *delegados* responsible for specific questions such as statistics, cattle, food, the olive crop and so on. There would also be various technical advisers who were not part of the *consejo*. Schoolmasters were often found as accountants (as at Masroig in Tarragona province).[5] Usually the collective as such would be formed after the *consejo*, and very often this would not be for several months after the beginning of the war: many collectives seem only to have been formally constituted in the winter of 1936 or early 1937. None of the members of these governing bodies of the collective were professional administrators; they

[1] Prats, *Vanguardia y Retaguardia de Aragòn*, p. 81.

[2] The Regional Congress of Farm Workers of the Levante in November 1937 gave this figure (Peirats, vol. I, p. 340).

[3] These figures are a guess based on the number of towns, since no proper estimate for this figure has been found.

[4] There were some places (e.g. Los Hinojosos) which had, however, two collectives, one CNT, one UGT. Almagro had two CNT collectives, though one was industrial.

[5] Peirats, I, p. 309.

had to find time for civic responsibilities after their own work for the day was over. (Work was compulsory, over the age of fifteen as a rule.) To avoid suspicion that personal advantage could be served through membership of the *consejo*, in some places (such as Tomelloso) the *consejo de administración* got less pay than other workers.[1]

At the heart of each collective there existed a shadowy organ described as the 'general assembly'. Possibly, the word organ is over-sophisticated, since the general assembly seems to have been in fact simply the gathering on the main square of the town of all the members of the collective who wanted to (it is not clear if every member of the collective was sometimes included, even women and at any rate working children, or whether, as is more likely, only workers were expected to attend). At any rate, there are instances of the general assembly electing the *consejo de administración* (for example at Grandella in the province of Lérida and at Alcázar de Cervantes—the old Alcázar San Juan).[2] The collective of Cervera del Maestre (Castellón) was clearly set up by decision of an 'open assembly' in the main square. In some places the general assembly was probably an active body where the entire population was able, at least for a time, to guide the policy of the collective. At Ademuz (a dramatically beautiful town of Moorish origin in the extreme north of the province of Valencia), for instance, the general assembly met every Saturday to discuss 'future orientations'.[3] In Masroig the assembly had the power to expel *malas colectivistas*, and also to decide what should be imported and what should not.[4] In the collectives at San Mateo (Castellón) and Serós (Huesca) it was provided that the general assembly could expel members for 'immorality'—though apparently this power was never used, nor is it obvious what 'immorality' meant in these communities.[5] No account seems to have been made of a meeting of a general assembly.

It appears that in practice nearly everywhere power remained in the hands of the *consejo de administración* and that the members of this body never felt it necessary to have their mandate renewed. This was an obvious threat of petty dictatorship, though it was one which rarely became patent: the most outrageous case appears to have been in the collective at the Pyrenean frontier town of Puigcerdá, where the anarchist mayor Antonio Martín used the collective as a centre of smuggling, false passport manufacture and bribed escapes.

[1] *Campo Libre*, September 11, 1937. Members of the Tomelloso consejo got 11 pesetas less per week than ordinary workers—i.e. 28 pesetas instead of 39 for a childless couple, a drop of 25 per cent.

[2] *Campo Libre*, January 29, 1938.

[3] Peirats, I, p. 336.

[4] Ibid., p. 308.

[5] Peirats, I, pp. 334–5. Whether general assemblies could sack *consejos* if necessary is also uncertain; some collective managements in *industries* were apparantly elected annually, but I have not found reference to a similar or indeed any other period where agriculture is concerned.

Although the collectives were supposed to function separately, almost as if they were little sovereign city states of an imagined mediaeval utopia, they were in fact linked, as Dr Issac Puente had provided in his blueprint adopted at the Saragossa conference, with the provincial and the regional organisation of collectives. The administrative *delegado* of each collective was supposed to tell the 'comrade accountant' of the region of the balance of imports and exports into the collective and hand over any surplus to the *caja de compensación* of the region, to help towards the general economic equilibrium of the area. The *caja de compensación* was expected to help collectives which could not cover needs and costs with their own production. In many cases money was given over to collectives, though there is no national estimate of this aid: it was a gift and not a loan. It was natural with this system that rich collectives would tend to consume more than they absolutely needed, rather than hand over their profit for the benefit of others, and several collectives were reproached in anarchist newspapers for this.[1]

The persons who formed the collectives were usually previously landless labourers, apart from a small number of professional men such as barbers, vets, doctors and so forth. But there were many exceptions: in Alcázar de Cervantes, the president of the collective was a farmer, Vidal Cruz, who brought with him six fanegas of his own land, together with three others which he had rented.[2] He was reported 'very satisfied with the economic and social rhythm of his new life'.[3] In Miralcampo (Guadalajara), a collective formed on land taken over from the old monarchist politician, the Count of Romanones, two members of the five-man *consejo* were, in the past, Romanones's overseer and agent.[4]

How far private or tenant farmers were forced into membership of the collectives is hard to judge. In the early days it was often hard for a private farmer, if he held out, to market his goods without selling to the collective. Tenant farmers and peasant proprietors were usually denied the use of the collective shops. Thus a number of anti-collectivists probably joined collectives either for fear of being forced in anyway or because the economic conditions of life outside were intolerable. Other people left, the bakers of Calaceite (near Tortosa) simply abandoning their shops; no replacements seem to have been found for a long time, if ever.[5] After a while, the championship of the small farmer by the Communists, and to a lesser extent by the right-wing Socialists and the government parties, gave new heart to independent agriculture: small

[1] For the complaints against the Almagro collective, see below.

[2] A fanega is a piece of land large enough to sow a bushel and a half of wheat: usually about an acre and a half.

[3] *Campo Libre*, January 29, 1938.

[4] Loc. cit., July 30, 1937.

[5] Souchy, *Entre los Campesinos de Anagón*, p. 85. At least the bakers had not been replaced when Souchy visited Calaceite. One of the difficulties of studying the collectives is that people who visited them often did not say when they went and often there is no evidence as to whether the practices they described continued for long.

farmers began even to be able to compete with collectives, except in Aragón, where the collectivist hold was very strong (until August 1937). In some places, after a while, separate facilities were provided for *colectivistas* and *individualistas*; at Calanda the German anarchist, Agustin Souchy, noted two cafés, one for the private farmers, one for members of the collective.[1] It was usually provided that people could withdraw from the collective to the value of the goods and machinery they brought with them, but if they did this after having been members for a year, there would be a deduction in the compensation they could take out. In some places too it became possible for a *colectivista* to keep a limited quantity of livestock in his backyard: at Piedras Menaras (Guadalajara) this was allowed because of the remoteness of the town and its bad weather in winter; members of the collective there could keep eighteen chickens and three goats.

The anarchists themselves, in their examples of a selected number of collectives, admit several defections: in Iniesta (Cuenca), for instance, the *individualistas* appear to have been very strong, *not Communists but anarchists interested not in communal farming but in the reparto, redistribution of land.* After the large landowners' properties, 13,913 hectares (about 33,000 acres), had been made the basis of the collective, the *individualistas* insisted on the *reparto* and succeeded in getting, by agreement, three-fifths of this land, together with half some of the stock and farm implements, three-fifths of others. Eighty families remained in the collective afterwards, and evidently they prospered, borrowing 13,000 pesetas from regional headquarters, so that 200 families were members of the collective at the end of 1937.[2] In Peñalba (Huesca) the outcome was a good deal less satisfactory. To begin with, in August 1936, the whole population of 1,500 became part of the collective. But evidently this was not popular, almost certainly because one of the collective's chief tasks was to feed the Durruti column then quartered nearby. As a result, the majority of the population, when they had gathered sufficient courage, or perhaps when they realised that they would have Communist backing, announced their intention to resume independence and reclaim their property. A commission was entrusted to supervise the act of demolition, and apparently did so satisfactorily. Five hundred persons were left to carry on the collective. Even so, there are further mentions of '*malas colectivistas*' who, when everything was provided free, tried to accumulate goods and then either sell them or let them go bad.[3]

The economic life of different collectives is difficult to disentangle. Figures exist for total production in the Republican zone of Spain, in respect of some commodities. The Ministry of Agriculture[4] gave overall figures for the

[1] Souchy, *Entre los Campesinos de Aragón*, p. 45. Peirats also describes Calanda (vol. I, p. 324).

[2] *Campo Libre*, December 18, 1937.

[3] Peirats, I, p. 321–2.

[4] *Economía Política*, no. 60, series C no. 33, reprinted in *Campo Libre* of October 9, 1937.

increase of the production of wheat: production in Catalonia and the Levante went down in the years 1936–7, but up in Aragón and Castille. The overall increase amounted to 609,000 metric quintals, an increase of about 6 per cent. However, Aragón and Castile were in 1937 the main centres of collectives and Catalonia and the Levante the main centres of peasant proprietors; Castile, the main wheat-growing zone, grew 5.2 million quintals of wheat in 1936 and 6 million in 1937—an increase of 850,000 quintals, or 17 per cent. The fact that the area where there were collectives showed an increase was naturally seized upon by the anarchists: 'Peasants of Castille', wrote N. González in *Campo Libre* of October 9, 'here you have conclusive proof that the agrarian collective is not a folly; it is a system which . . . leads to maximum production! This, dear comrades, is the road to follow.'

The fact that the figures indicate a drop in production in Catalonia and the Levante suggests to some extent their veracity, since they would hardly have been actually invented or twisted by a ministry of agriculture, dominated by a Communist minister and Communist officials, with greater Communist Party strength in those areas than in Castille or Aragón. But a large number of peasant proprietors continued in the areas where there were collectives and it is of course possible that they played a part in the increased wheat production. Nor is it clear on what basis the 1935–6 figures were constituted. Though overall Spanish wheat production had gone down in the years before the war, they reached their lowest level ever in 1936, and might have been expected to increase in 1937 anyway, with a better harvest. Finally, even if it were proved that the collectives did show an increase in their first year, it is of course impossible to judge the superiority or otherwise of any system of agriculture simply on the strength of a single year. It is obvious that there were places where the collectives did introduce striking agricultural reforms, however: there is often mention of deep tilling with tractors (Montblanc), of modern chicken farms (Amposta), of irrigation (Monzón, Huesca).

In a limited number of collectives, some accounts for production are available (and, in even fewer cases, for the general financial structure). Production figures exist for Miralcampo (Guadalajara province). Of this collective (the one where Count Romanones's staff stayed on), we hear that 'during the period of effervescence, not to say madness, which dominated many places

---

The Ministry's figures were:

Metric Quintals

	1936	1937	*Difference*
Catalonia	1,968,228	1,550,000	−417,628
Aragón	1,349,999	1,620,000	+270,001
Central Zone	5,236,721	6,090,238	+853,517
Levante	1,293,942	1,197,216	−97,726
	9,848,890	10,458,054	+609,164

in Spain at the beginning—those days during which everything was out of control and when thrift, as a result, was not the outstanding characteristic—our comrades kept all the cattle on the farm—while in other places, such as in Santos de la Humosa, the Communists sacrificed even the heifers about to calve.'[1]

Production figures of Miralcampo are as follows: Wheat, in 1935–6, 3,000 fanegas[2]; 1936–7, 7,000; barley, 500 fanegas in 1935–6, rising to 2,000 in 1936–7; wine moved up, in the same years, from 3,000 arrobas[3] to 'over 4,500'. Melons rose (*in value*) from 196,000 pesetas' worth to 300,000. These increases were explained by as due to an important piece of irrigation, achieved by diverting a stretch of the River Henares. Taken at face value, the increase seems considerable: an increase of 130 per cent in wheat, of 200 per cent in barley, of 50 per cent in wine. Now, probably, there was a genuine increase, though whether it was quite this much is doubtful. But it is not clear if, even given the continuing presence of Count Romanones's staff, the pre-revolutionary figures were the accurate ones. Is it not more likely that they were in fact the figures kept for the purpose of tax, while the real ones might have been closer to those achieved by the collective? This seems a matter which will never really be known, and it is an uncertainty which hangs over most of the collectives in Spain in the civil war.

The most complete general account of a collective's finances is that of the 300-family collective of Almagro, in the province of Ciudad Real, a town with a population of 8,592 in 1930. Assuming that the average size of the family was five, which is possibly a little high, it would appear that about one-sixth of the municipality was enrolled in the collective. (There was, however, an anomaly in that in the town there also existed an anarchist flour mill, run collectively but not as a part of the town collective.) Almagro is known for its mule fairs and its lace. Its wine is reportedly delicious. The accounts consist of an estimation of the value of the livestock and farm machinery and tools in 1937 as opposed to 1936, an inventory of goods held by the collective in 1936–7 in comparison with 1935–6, and a statement of incomings and outgoings into the town during the first year of the life of the collective. The town was, we hear, notable for being free of 'disorderly Communists' and for good relations between the parties. The old municipal council survived in a kind of supervisory role, the CNT and FAI having 6 seats out of 15—the others being presumably 6 for the UGT and 3 divided among the Republican parties.

The first group of figures are not really conclusive, though they suggest the value of the stock of the collective rose in the year October 1936–October 1937 by about 17 per cent from just under 300,000 pesetas to just over 355,000.

[1] *Campo Libre*, July 30, 1937. Livestock is almost always slaughtered for food in the first stages of revolutions. Almost the only other collective where production figures can be compared between 1936 and 1937 is the tiny one at Villas Viejas (*Campo Libre*, July 25, 1937).

[2] A fanega, when used as a dry weight measure, is about a bushel and a half.

[3] An arroba is 32 pints, or 4 gallons.

The account is tabulated as follows[1]:

	Estimated value of goods at date of formation of the collective (Sept. 1, 1936)	*Estimated value of goods* (Oct. 2, 1937)
GOODS:		
	pesetas	pesetas
Mules	68,080	91,150
Pigs	19,750	26,700
Sheep	70,000	74,000
Farm Implements	140,000	150,405
Road Work Implements	—	4,965
Carpentry	—	5,125
Value of Goods:	298,830	356,686
PRODUCTS:		
Barley	3,400 fanegas	5,955 fanegas
Wine	500 arrobas	2,050 arrobas
Oil	600 "	1,700 "
Rye	80 fanegas	139 fanegas
Peas	60 "	310 "
Wheat	1,700 "	900 "
Maize	35 "	—
Algarrobilla (bean)	160 "	335 "
Chick peas	4 "	20 "
Yeros (vetch)	70 "	30 "
Haba (bean)	20 "	160 "
Value of Products:	100,953 pesetas	158,726 pesetas
Value of Goods:	298,830 "	356,686 "
Total Value of Goods and Products	399,283 pesetas	515,412 pesetas

Imports into the town, 1936–7: 375,577.84 pesetas
Exports from the town, 1937–7: 371,242.10 pesetas

Difference: 4,335.74 pesetas

(Difference between value of 1936 and 1937: 116,129 pesetas.)

[1] *Campo Libre*, October 2, 1937. An abbreviated account is in Peirats, I, pp. 345–7.

In each of the main items considered there has been a small increase varying from a 5 per cent increase in the value of the farm machinery available to one of 26 per cent in the value of the mules retained in stock. Unfortunately nothing appears to be known of the numbers of animals held by the collective of Almagro in 1937, as opposed to 1936, though this is the sort of information quite often known in respect of other collectives. And of course these figures do not take into account any variation in the value of money between 1936 and 1937. In fact, the size of the stock and its real value probably stayed the same in the course of this year; *the 17 per cent increase in the alleged value of the stock is probably a rough indication of the fall in the local buying power of the Republican peseta between these two years.* Both in 1936 and 1937, far the biggest single investment in the collective was farm machinery, though their percentage of the total was slightly less in 1937 (40 per cent of the whole as opposed to 45 per cent).

The next set of figures in Almagro refer to products, not, unfortunately, to production. Thus it is only possible to compare the quantity of goods in store owned by the collective when it was founded with that existing a year later. But this is not without interest. There was 75 per cent more barley in 1937 than in 1936, 500 per cent more wine, 200 per cent more olive oil, 80 per cent more rye, 400 per cent more peas, 300 per cent more chick peas, about 90 per cent more beans of varying sorts. At the same time, there was 50 per cent less wheat, no maize at all, and 60 per cent less vetch in 1937 than in 1936. The total value of the products possessed by the collective was about 50 per cent higher than in 1936. Meat, milk, eggs, clothing, do not figure at all in the list. Overall, the collective estimated that it was worth 116,129 pesetas more in 1937 than in 1936, a sum equivalent to about £3,000 by the rather misleading 1936 rate of exchange, a nominal increase per head, therefore, among the 300 families, of about £10.

The collective also gave figures for its 'exports' and 'imports' and, however anarchist the delegate for accounts was, he evidently had a nice sense of classical economics: imports were 376,000 pesetas, exports, 371,000: a trade gap of a little over 4,000 pesetas.

How far were these figures accurate and how far can they be regarded as representative? The figures were purportedly given to an anonymous anarchist reporter by the officials of the collective. His article appeared in Madrid, without much prominence and at a time when the war was mainly concentrated in a different zone. The anarchist collectives in Aragón had been repressed by the Communists, but Communist activity was not specially strong in the region of Almagro. The likelihood that someone solemnly sat down and worked out a series of bogus figures for Almagro seems remote. The probability is that this was a fairly accurate picture of the economy in the Almagro collective in the first year of the civil war.

The fact that statistics were not generally published in the anarchist papers, and that these were, would suggest that they were generally more favourable than usual.[1] It would certainly seem obvious that Almagro was better off than most places. The reporter who visited it commented rather sharply that the collective ought to try and save, 'not for itself, but for others in the region less prosperous'. 'The collective of Almagro has almost forgotten', says the reporter, 'that it is part of a federation.' The comrades who formed part of the administrative council in Almagro were too proud. On the other hand—and this was something which apparently by late 1937 could be said of few leaders in collectives—none of them smoked or drank.

Some figures are also given of the consumption of the collective. In the year September 1, 1936–August 31, 1937, the 300 families used 3,000 arrobas of olive oil, 30,000 kilos of potatoes, 110,000 pesetas' worth of bread, and 7,000 arrobas of wine. The average family in the Almagro collective thus drank just under 750 pints of wine a year; 320 pints of olive oil; and ate 3,000 kilos of potatoes and 300–350 pesetas' worth of bread. The bread, potatoes and olive oil were apparently distributed free to the families of the collective, as in many, though not all, collectives, and wine was also distributed free to workers during the day. A consumption of wine of just under two pints per day per family would seem rather low (if it is free), since many families had more than one worker.

Almagro was obviously a fairly well-off collective. The fact of its prosperity illustrates the chief weakness of the whole system of collectives: that the poverty or wealth of the town at the beginning determined the poverty or wealth later: nowhere is this shown more than in the enormous variation of wages in the collectives for which data is available. In the first weeks of the war, money was abolished altogether in many places, but after a few months it reappeared either as cash or in the form of *vales* or *bonos*, which was, in fact, simply a credit note for getting goods in the collective. Real money replaced *vales* or *bonos* as the war went on—in some places, as at Montblanc (Tarragona), on the firm demand of the *colectivistas*.[2]

The wages paid, either as local or as real money, varied inside the collectives according to needs. Thus almost everywhere there was a separate scale for a working husband and his wife, with a bonus for each working son, a different bonus for each minor, a different bonus again for invalids living with the family, a separate wage altogether for bachelors, for widows and for retired couples. There were also a number of additional payments in different places specifically provided for, that is, quite apart from what might be got by good luck or personal arrangement. But this seems exceptional. In the Madrid region, collectives were paid very highly (higher than anywhere else) and were also given a ration of greens per day, valued at 2 pesetas (in a 270-strong collective just by Madrid) and at 3 pesetas (at Villaverde). The highest wage seems in fact to have been in these two collectives: 12 pesetas per day per working couple, with (most unusually) another 12 per working son; at the

[1] These are the only detailed accounts given by Peirats in his survey of some forty collectives.

[2] Peirats, I, p. 311.

Madrid collective, another rate quoted is 10.20 pesetas per day for workers between 16 and 18, and 7.20 for workers between 14 and 16. At Villaverde, there is no quotation for minors, but there was one for widows and retired couples—the same one, inequitably surely (though there is no discussion of the reasons for the quotation), of 7.20 pesetas.[1]

Against these high rates of pay in Madrid, the lowest appears to be that at Iniesta (Cuenca province) where the wage was only 4 pesetas per working couple, i.e. only 25 per cent of the highest wage in the prosperous collective at Villaverde. In Iniesta the bonus for a working son was 1 peseta, and 50 centimos for minors. Now of course Iniesta is poor and remote, in comparison with Villaverde, though presumably real living costs in the latter were higher being near Madrid than elsewhere, despite control of prices. The variation in the wages in the collectives does not, as might be thought, derive from the fact that in the low wage areas essential goods were distributed free and in the high wage areas not; in Iniesta, food (wine, oil, meat, farm produce) was *sold* in the collective at a price admittedly a little lower than the official rate. Significantly, it was at Iniesta that the *colectivistas* insisted on the redistribution of 3/5 of the land. The wage rate before the Revolution was 5.50 pesetas (higher than the wage ultimately paid to a married couple without children after the formation of the collective).[2]

In fact, wages simply had to vary according to the wealth of the collective itself. Any national wage even guaranteed by, for instance, the regional peasants' committees, would have meant an acceptance of the idea of national organisation—a matter so foreign to anarchist doctrine that it does not seem even to have been discussed, at a time when, after all, anarchism was under such heavy fire from its enemies. There does not seem to have been adequate machinery for the treasury of a collective to be emptied at the end of the year, and so quite large surpluses were piled up unused. In at least one collective—Villaverde—50 per cent of the profits were divided up among the 400 families, the other 50 per cent being divided up between 'general expenses', widows, and hospitals.[3]

The average payment in all the collectives is not possible to estimate accurately for lack of data. A rough estimate would seem to place the average at something close to 7 pesetas a day, or 42 pesetas a week. This would compare with 10–12 pesetas a day received by militiamen and ordinary soldiers at the front, and 12 pesetas a day which seems to have been the average wage in factories. The most elaborate variation of wage in a single collective seems to have been that at Dosbarrios, a collective with 610 members out of a total population of about 1,000, owning about 17,000 acres, in the province of Toledo. Bachelors got 32 pesetas a week. Childless couples got 45. Couples with children under age got 45, plus 1 peseta a day for each child, i.e. presum-

[1] *Campo Libre*, November 20, 1937 and December 4, 1938.

[2] *Campo Libre*, December 18, 1937.

[3] Op. cit., November 20, 1937.

ably seven days a week, not simply the six working days. Couples with working children got 45 pesetas plus 15 pesetas a week for each producer. Couples who had to keep elderly invalids got 45 pesetas plus 12 per invalid. Widows without sons got the same as bachelors (32 pesetas) if they worked, and if they did not they got 25 pesetas. Widows with sons who did not work got the normal widows' wage, plus 1 peseta a day, and widows with working sons got the widow's wage plus 15 pesetas per son—though, if there was only one working son, the widow and the son would get 45 pesetas, the same, that is, as a childless couple.[1]

In some places wages would be further supplemented by the provision of a communal restaurant where bachelors could eat free or passers-by for the cost of a peseta.[2] Barbers were sometimes free, as at Calanda.[3] Extra money was made available if visits to other places were necessary—to a family in another town, or to a doctor; applications for this extra expense had to pass through the appropriate *delegado*. But of course there was 'no money for vice'.[4] When a collective member wanted to marry he might be given a week's holiday, furniture and a house—at least this occurred in Graus.[5] A wife might get a trousseau.[6] There are many different provisions where wine is concerned. At Alcázar de Cervantes, wine was free during harvest time, afterwards the ration being a free litre a day (though this privilege was sometimes withdrawn).[7] As has been seen, wine was always free at Almagro[8]; in Castro del Río, there was no wine[9]; at Mebrilla, the *colectivistas* got 3 free litres a week,[10] at Calanda, 3 quarts a week.[11]

Life in collectives had of course changed, but not perhaps out of all recognition from that existing before the Revolution. Hours of work were usually the same in the country—almost always from sunrise to sunset, though in some collectives an 8- or 7-hour day was agreed. Festivals were generally ignored, except for those new ones of the revolutionary tradition, such as May 1, the anniversary of the death of Durruti, or the start of the war. A 6-day week was normal. The absence of young men at the front—300 or so out of a town of 10,000, as at Amposta—obviously made some difference. Another difference was the presence of refugees from other parts of Spain who had fled in the wake of advancing Nationalist armies, from Extramadura or Andalusia. In a town such as Villajoysa (Alicante), the refugees had increased

[1] *Campo Libre*, January 29, 1938.
[2] This was at Seros (Peirats, I, p. 307).
[3] Souchy, loc. cit.
[4] Kaminski, p. 122.
[5] Prats, quoted Peirats, I, p. 318.
[6] Peirats, I, p. 321.
[7] *Campo Libre*, January 29, 1938.
[8] Ibid.
[9] Borkenau.
[10] *Colectivistas: l'Oeuvre constructive de la révolution espagnole*, p. 239.
[11] Souchy, p. 45.

the population of the town from one of 9,000 to one of 14,000. Schools had undoubtedly multiplied,[1] and the thirst for education by both young and adults was at least partially satisfied, in converted convents or palaces, by new schoolmasters, themselves finding learning difficult. The school-leaving age was raised, at Amposta, to 15.[2] At Calanda, advanced pupils were sent at the collective's expense to the Liceo at Caspe.[3] Hospitals and health services generally were improved—we hear of the doctor at Villaverde having given 200 vaccinations and 400 other injections in six months in a 400-strong collective.[4] For the vast majority of workers, the death, absence or, in some instances, retirement, of the old master class, of the priest, of the church, of the whole complicated apparatus of traditional catholic living, and of all the things that went with it (such as the subordination of women) was enough to sustain a persistent exhilaration, making up for shortages and inconveniences caused by war, even for the triumph of the Communists in the machinery of the State. Traditional life in Spain had been, in so many instances, in the small towns of Castille or Aragon, extraordinarily limited. Now the windows at least seemed open; the conquest of power by the workers had created problems, but at least some of the obstinate tedium of the old life had vanished in a wealth of slogans, encouragements to harder work, revolutionary songs, old songs rewritten with modern words, and wireless broadcasts. It is clear that in many places 'the poor lived as in a dream', as Prats put in when describing Graus.[5]

From the government's point of view, the immense disadvantage of collectives was that they did not pay taxes; and though they 'judged it a sacred duty to take food directly to the front'[6] this arrived at irregular intervals, so that it could not be counted upon, and was therefore sometimes wasted. Also the industrial cities needed food as well as the front and here the duty seems to have been regarded as less sacred. Further, despite the presence of UGT representatives in most Councils of Administration, the collectives could not be counted on to carry out governmental directives. This was partly a question of organisation. The collectives were organised locally, with responsibility for all activities resting with the Council of Administration. It was therefore difficult for the Ministries of Agriculture or Industry even to communicate with local agricultural or industrial officials without going first to the collective's nominal leadership—much less give them orders. By December 1936, the chief officials of the Ministry of Agriculture from the Minister downwards were Communists.[7] But this Communist control over yet another department

[1] Discussed elsewhere.

[2] Peirats, I, pp. 305–6.

[3] Ibid.

[4] *Campo Libre*, November 20, 1937.

[5] Prats.

[6] Peirats, I, p. 320 (here speaking of Alcolea de Cinca, in Aragón).

[7] The then Communist, Castro Delgado (*Hombres Made in Moscú*, pp. 379–82), says his three priorities on taking over the Agrarian Reform Institute were to destroy the agrarian

of State did not bring victory in agriculture. On the contrary, the collectives persisted in their separate way, and not even the Communist military occupation of Aragón, in August 1937, was enough to ruin the collectives there completely. The main change in the course of the first year of war was the removal of the judiciary powers assumed by collectives in the first weeks; under the anarchist but conformist Minister of Justice, Garcia Oliver, this removed the trappings of total sovereignty from the collectives, even though the state-backed revolutionary tribunals in the different towns seem often to have been composed of the same persons as would have been the case before.

The fate of collectives if the country had been at peace is impossible to speculate upon. For the very existence of the war and of the other revolutionary parties—perplexing and frustrating though both these seemed to the anarchists—may have been responsible for some of the success the collectives had. The war sustained anarchist discipline and the sense of communal service. At the same time, the government's and the Communists' backing of the small farmer and *individualista* meant that all such people were certain of an ally in need: the local village *consejo de administración* could thus not go too far in bullying individuals to make them join or conform. The Communist Minister of Agriculture made many speeches promising the *individualista* that his interests would be served by the Communist Party and the message seems certainly to have gone home: 30.7 per cent of Communist Party members in Republican Spain were peasant proprietors in February 1937. The Peasant Federation of small farmers, organised by the Ministry, and Communist-led, became the bulwark of defence against the collectivists.

It is possible to draw a few conclusions: First, the data is not available to prove whether or not the collectives were an economic success, if this is measured in terms of production, though the absence of overall planning possibilities makes it very difficult to see how national production could have been increased over a long term.

Secondly, even if total figures were to become available for every collective, no moral could be drawn about the merits or demerits of the collectives as agricultural experiments. War conditions are unlike those of peace. Communist pressure on the collectives may have given them the necessary urge to survive, otherwise they might have disintegrated. Anyway a period of a year or two is not enough to judge an agricultural system.

Thirdly, the success or failure of the collective depended economically overgreatly on the situation before: it was thus possible for Amposta to build a 200,000 peseta chicken farm, but this would not have been possible in places where that sort of money was not available—even allowing for gifts from regional headquarters. Thus, in respect of redistribution of wealth, anarchist collectives were hardly much improvement over capitalism. No effective way

---

reform teams staffed by Socialists; to force employers to accept that the rhythm of war was different from that of peace; and to enrol as many people as possible into the Communist Party.

of limiting consumption in richer collectives was devised to help poorer ones.

Fourthly, the independence of the collectives probably was a handicap to the Republic, measured simply in terms of economics. It was not possible to impose, for instance, a national production plan. On the other hand, the fact that the collectives survived at all, in such adverse circumstances, testifies to the strength of the hold they must have had on their members. Their morale must have been high, and certainly in a civil war morale of the rearguard is important. Anyway, the Republic was chiefly handicapped not because of lack of food or lack of agricultural planning, but because of lack of weapons.

Fifthly, whatever the economics of the collectives, there is a good deal of evidence for thinking that they were a considerable social success. The pains-taking apportionment of wages according to needs in Dosbarrios is immensely sympathetic: and of course the payment to widows, the maintenance of orphans, the care of invalids, was a genuine breakthrough into a new world. From the accounts of most of the collectives, even if they are written by anarchist sympathisers, there does radiate a considerable spirit of generous co-operation without many complaints at breach of privacy and at local tyrannies, though, as at Puigcerdá, there were certainly some. On the other hand, the possibility of leaving the collective and being politically protected by the Communists if one did, may have been an essential factor in this. It is not clear how a large-scale rural or small town community of such collectives could work alongside a differently organised urban society, and the survival of such communities would not seem likely in the long term, though in ideal circumstances they might have lasted during a few years while primitive misery was being overcome.

EDWARD CRANKSHAW

Revisionism and Reform in the Soviet Union since 1953

EDWARD CRANKSHAW

Revisionism and Reform in the Soviet Union since 1953

IN discussing change and reform in the Soviet Union we must first make a bow to those who insist that there have been no real changes at all, only tactical retreats and concessions which may be reversed at any time. But retreats and concessions from and to what?

Reluctance to admit that there has been any fundamental change since the death of Stalin appears to be due not to deep-rooted ideas about original sin, but to certain professions of Lenin, Stalin, Krushchev, about the unchanging aims of Bolshevism and the permissability, the desirability, the imperative necessity, indeed, of dissembling those aims on occasion in order to effect temporary alliances with individuals, groups, parties—by implication governments too—opposed to Bolshevism and marked for ultimate destruction on the way to world revolution. It is odd to find historians, diplomatists, and politicians, who, of all people, should be conscious of the everlasting gulf between the expressed aspirations of statesmen, even left-wing statesmen, and their actions, being taken in by this sort of thing.

A classic text occurs in Lenin's pamphlet, 'Left-wing Socialism: an Infantile Disorder', dedicated, appropriately enough in more ways than one, to David Lloyd George:

'It is possible to conquer a powerful enemy only by exerting the most intensive effort, by taking thorough, attentive, meticulous and skilful advantage of each and every split among the bourgeois of the various countries, and by taking advantage of every opportunity, even the most trivial, to gain a mass ally, though this ally may be temporary and unstable, vacillating, conditional and unreliable.'

These are the words of a man intoxicated with his own cleverness and ruthlessness. Apart from the invocation of the masses, there is not a word in that exordium which has not been thought and put into practice by every statesman since the world began. Lenin shared Bismarck's weakness, a compulsion to spell out, with the air of a man making a great discovery, truisms known to and acted on by others in their sleep.

Bolsheviks profess to think that there is no morality except class-morality, therefore what is moral is what advances the interests of Bolshevism, seen, with a high element of fantasy, as the voice of the working-class. Duplicity is in order provided it serves the ends of the working-class. 'Who tells a lie as for Thy laws. . . .' And so on. There is nothing new about this, just as there was nothing new about Stalin's homicide, except in the matter of scale. The one has been practised in the name of patriotism or religion for a great many centuries; the other was adequately summed up in Machievelli's anecdote about Castruccio Castracani of Lucca: asked how he could bring himself to murder his old friends, Castruccio replied: 'I do not kill old friends; I kill new enemies.'

Perhaps, more than anything, it has been the unhappy example of *Mein Kampf*, which still fascinates in a hypnotic manner so many who did not take Hitler seriously when they should have done. Indeed, it is a common thing to find Hitler's programme and the open statement of it equated with the Bolshevik programme and the open statement of that. We discounted the one, the argument runs; we must on no account discount the other. Nobody wants to discount the Bolsheviks. How is this possible? They have created the climate of our existence. *Mein Kampf* (without at all going into scholastic details about Hitler's intentions) was offered as a straight account of a plan of action, of what one man intended to do, and, more or less, how. There was no theory about this: it read like an operation order. At no stage, at no time, have our Russian comrades ever issued an analagous manifesto. All they have done is to state that a certain interpretation of history works, therefore it must be true; a projection of this interpretation into the future shows that such and such events will occur, involving the communisation of the globe; the Soviet Union, being the first country to conduct a Marxist (*sic*) revolution, has the right and the duty to assist, by whatever means, other countries to achieve their own revolutions; only when all the world has achieved Marxist revolutions will universal peace be guaranteed and justice and equity be established on earth.

I have put this statement in simple words because it is high time that it was put in simple words. The first point to be made is that the spirit behind this statement, which sums up fairly accurately the position of Lenin, is wholly different from the spirit behind *Mein Kampf*: the first is a declaration of faith, the second a declaration of will.

We know what happened to the will: after a promising start it was frustrated. This is what usually happens to declarations of will. What has happened to the statement of faith?

In the first place we may, perhaps, agree that to take Lenin's statement of faith at its face value is to admit the validity of that faith. Most of us do not make this admission: what then are we worrying about? What we are worrying about is a perversion of the faith. When a faith is perverted it loses its virtue and immediately dissipates itself into a collection of expedients cloaked by holy words and calculated to serve an ulterior purpose. But we, to magnify the deadliness of the Bolshevik purpose, assist in maintaining the camouflage. Thus when Mr Khrushchev, paying lip-service to a faith long abandoned, declares 'we shall bury you', we hasten to take him at his word.

In discussing change, there is no need to go back to Marx. The man we are first concerned with is Lenin, who owed his inspiration to Marx and Engels but, to justify his own conduct in carrying through a *coup d'etat* disguised as a proletarian revolution without a proletariat, had to do some quick *ad hoc* thinking, including the brilliant mental switch which transposed, in effect, the proletarian revolution outside Russia into an anti-colonial revolution. What we are dealing with today is not Marxist-Leninism but the heritage of Leninism, which owed a great deal to Marx as a 'starter' and then abandoned him to the Mensheviks.

At no stage did Lenin or any of his successors declare that they intended to conquer the world in the name of the Revolution. When, at one stage, it looked very much as though Stalin had in mind to conquer at least a good deal of the world, he was acting not in the name of the Revolution but in the name of Great Russia, which happened to be the headquarters of the Revolution. By the time Khrushchev arrived on the scene this process had shot its bolt, and when he announced 'we shall bury you'—in the name of Lenin—the phrase was already absurd. Who was 'we' and who was 'you'? Did 'we' include Yugoslavia? Did it include China?

Marx was a great one for lies, but he did not believe in the unlimited lie: Lenin did. Marx was not above using force to overthrow the enemy, but he did not believe in the continuing use of force by a self-perpetuating group of rulers to terrorise workers and peasants into obeying their commands for half a century. Lenin did not believe in this either, but he created the conditions in which it became possible, even likely. The Soviet Union has been ruled since 1918 in the workers' despite, and since 1929 by precisely such a self-perpetuating group interested first in preserving its own power, then, in varying degrees, in using that power to build up a strong Soviet Union and extend its dominion or influence by whatever means, from military occupation to long-range political subversion. Stalin, most cautious in extending his power, savage and irresponsible in the exercise of it once it was won, was careful—to ensure that there was no revolution anywhere which he could not physically control—except in the case of the Chinese revolution, which was not his fault: Yugoslavia was a simple error of judgment; Stalin had reckoned without the Southern Slavs. Khrushchev, more of a gambler, tried to cash in on Cuba, seen not as an outpost of revolution but as a military base in the Russo-American conflict: he forgot about sea-power, and he soon lost interest in Castro when Cuba ceased to be a rocket-carrier.

What people mean when they say that nothing has changed in the Soviet Union is roughly the following: Lenin's revolutionary aims still dominate the minds of his successors; the domestic Terror may have been relaxed, but it can be restored at any time; the Soviet system and all its institutions, perfected by Stalin for the convenience of his personal dictatorship, have been preserved intact by his successors in order to maintain theirs; this system and these institutions, so long as they survive, preclude any possibility of fundamental reform. There are two lines of argument here, and they cancel each other out. How can men concerned above all with their own power be regarded as dedicated crusaders for universal brotherhood?

Obviously a great deal has changed in the Soviet Union since Lenin's day: some of the changes may appear to fall under the head of what the Chinese call revisionism; some do not. Some may be regarded as permanent in an evolutionary sense; others may only be provisional and impermanent.

It is worth considering this matter of revisionism. Revisionism is one of those loaded words which can be used to mean whatever you want it to mean —or nothing. The Chinese use it in just this way, so that, at first glance, it tells us no more about Soviet or Yugoslav, or Italian CP policies than any other word of simple abuse. The Russians until a few years ago were no better than the Chinese: in the Moscow Declaration of December 1957, drafted by Russians and Chinese and signed by all the Communist parties of the world (by some reluctantly), revisionism, as opposed to dogmatism, was singled out as the chief evil of the moment. This was a demonstration against Marshal Tito, who had been irritating the Russians and scandalising the Chinese, and against all those fraternal parties, above all the Polish Party inside the *bloc* and the Italian Party outside, which had shown signs of taking too literally the promise of the 20th Congress of the Soviet Communist Party about differing paths to socialism. It also stood for a closing of the ranks in face of certain disruptive consequences of the de-Stalinisation campaign.

But the word still has a technical meaning, and both the Russians and the Chinese know what it means. It was first applied to the reformist ideas of Bernstein, when he broke away from Marxism and insisted that Social Democracy should 'find the courage to emancipate itself from a philosophy which has, in fact, long been outmoded, and be willing to show itself for what it really is—a democratic socialist party of reform'. What Bernstein had in mind about the Marxist philosophy being outmoded was what was later to become a general criticism of Marxism—namely that in his insistence that capital would come to be concentrated in ever fewer hands, and that the misery of the workers would increase throughout this process, Marx had been proved wrong by events. Seventy years ago this in fact was not a watertight argument. Marx himself had allowed that under capitalism there could be false dawns, and the only thing that could be said for certain at the turn of the century was that the inevitable process was moving more slowly and erractically than Marx had predicted. Bernstein was a good prophet, but for the wrong reasons.

Nobody wants to accuse the Russians of Bernsteinism. On the other hand, for some time past they have been revising their attitudes fairly drastically. To find out what this amounts to and the extent to which Marxist, or Marxist-Leninism, has been changed or undermined by Kremlin policies the best thing to do is to stop using Marxist-Leninist terms and try to discover in plain English what has been going on. What has been revised, and how?

Lenin had already distorted Marxism out of all recognition when he decided to go for a proletarian revolution without waiting for the bourgeois one. The Chinese have never criticised him for this, nor have they criticised themselves for carrying out a peasant revolution—in Lenin's name. The reason for this is that the term revisionism in the pejorative sense is applied only to those shifts in doctrine which are calculated to lead to a slowing down or cancellation of revolution, never to those shifts which are calculated to hasten revolution.

Thus, although the Chinese are now using the term revisionist as a generalised term of abuse, when they argue seriously they attach the revisionist label above all, and on the face of it correctly, to certain Soviet actions, leading to doctrinal changes, carried out in response to historical developments not foreseen by Marx or Lenin and calculated to postpone world revolution, or even to substitute for violent revolution reformist methods of achieving socialism throughout the world as once advocated by Bernstein.

The main Soviet offence is discovered in certain important departures from the Leninist canon made at the 20th Party Congress: specifically, the adoption of the thesis that war is no longer inevitable and that in some countries socialism, then communism, may be achieved without violent revolution—e.g. by parliamentary means. The Chinese also see in co-existence a retreat from the proper business of undermining and destruction in the interests of revolution. The Chinese accepted these departures at the time, early in 1956. Perhaps they felt compelled to do this, so great was their need for Soviet aid at that time. Perhaps, like many in the West, they imagined that Khrushchev was merely indulging in Leninist trickery, pending Soviet supremacy in long-range ballistic missiles, and only later discovered that he meant what he said and was shaping his policies accordingly; if so they displayed deep ignorance of Soviet ways. Perhaps, inwardly, they already despised post-Stalin Russia so profoundly that they already regarded a Soviet Party Congress as a local affair, not binding outside the Soviet Union.

Be that as it may, the cry of co-existence (which, in Russian eyes, means only physical co-existence: the ideological war, for what it is worth, is still on) was not a confidence trick, and the resolutions about the non-inevitability of war and socialism without violence were not part of a calculated attempt to lull the West into a sense of false security. There is all the difference in the world between the formal resolutions of a Soviet Party Congress concerning doctrinal modifications and the innumerable deceptions, blessed in principle by Lenin, practised both by Stalin and Khrushchev, in their efforts to augment the security and influence of the Soviet Union, to weaken the unity and resolution of the 'enemy camp' and to seduce the non-aligned.

Khrushchev and his successors can no longer believe in the simple certitudes of Lenin, who, at the time when he was most actively theorising, was an internationalist, expecting that revolutionaries in Germany and elsewhere would soon triumph and come to the aid of the Soviet Union. They know very well, as Lenin never foresaw, that if every country in the world were to carry out its own revolution of whatever kind, in the name of Marx, or Lenin, or Mao Tse-tung, the world would still be fragmented and divided into mutually hostile groupings: in the last decade they have seen that the Communist world cannot even hold together in face of what it calls the threat of war from the strongest power on earth. In a word, there is no future in world revolution for the Soviet Union as a power. And the prime interest of the current successors to Lenin must be the preservation and further development of the Soviet Union as a power: it is the only base of their own power.

Knowledge, however, does not invariably condition behaviour, which may be affected by irrational dreams originally projected from premises long seen to be false, nostalgia for lost certitudes, and simple habits of thought. In a word, we all do things which are not good for us, and which are bound to lead to the very consequences we most seek to avoid. There is no doubt at all that the imagination of many highly placed Russians is still sustained by antique dreams of global revolution which will not bear looking into for one moment. In the first place their own state is itself a contradiction of those dreams: should it ever succeed in imposing its pattern on every other state, it would show itself as the antithesis of everything Lenin desired. In the second place—but need we go on? This is not necessarily an expression of total cynicism: an Anglican bishop proclaiming the virtues of meekness, humility, poverty, and enlarging on the camel and the needle's eye, is not, as a rule, perpetrating a conscious fraud.

We all have to rationalise our behaviour or go mad. The current Programme of the Communist Party of the Soviet Union is the rationalisation of the behaviour of men who cannot pretend to derive their authority from a supernatural source—e.g. God—or from the people over whom they rule. Owing their power to nothing but trickery and force and the favour of a discredited dictator, they have to pretend to some authority outside themselves. Lenin is the answer. The Lenin mystique still holds throughout the Soviet Union, and there is no doubt that it also affects in some degree the present incumbents of the Central Committee and its organs as well as the Council of Ministers. Everything they do has to be justified in terms of Lenin's teaching, which is also intermittently a useful guide to policy and conduct: at any rate, they have no other guide, and men cling to what they know, even when it is clearly leading them up the garden-path.

Every departure from Lenin's teaching also has to be justified in terms of Leninism. Lenin believed, for example, that the path to revolution led through war: war created the conditions most favourable to revolution, therefore long live war! The comrades bore this doctrine like a mill-stone round their necks long after the atom bomb had made it absurd: it had always been obscene. Stalin tried to escape from it shortly before he died when he put forward the view in his celebrated thesis for the 19th Party Congress that although there must be wars, as Lenin had taught, the balance of power was now such that with good luck and good management the Soviet Union could hold aloof from them, leaving the capitalist powers to tear each other to pieces. Stalin never got the credit for his essay in revisionism because it was soon forgotten in the excitement over the doctors' plot, then over his death. Malenkov during his brief premiership announced that another war would mean the ruin of the Communist as well as the capitalist world; but this was not put forward as Party doctrine. It was left to Khrushchev, who had attacked the Malenkov view, to formulate this truism as new doctrine, to embody it in a resolution of the 20th Party Congress, and to justify it in quasi-Leninist terms.

It is now part of the canon, and will remain part of it. The same applies to the possibility of some countries achieving communism without violent revolution. There was no question of Khrushchev monkeying about with the Leninist canon in order to deceive the enemy. This is not done: deception is practised by other, so to say secular, means: peace fronts, popular fronts, lying propaganda of a thousand kinds. There is in intention a difference in kind between the principles which, as it were, legitimate the progress towards communism and the expedients resorted to for the fulfilment of those principles. A resolution formally passed at a Party Congress lays down the law to the Party. It cannot be changed except by another formal resolution. On the other hand specific actions within the framework of the general principles, whether proposals for a Summit conference or for co-operation with social democratic parties in Europe, or offers of increased trade or cultural exchanges, or whether, at home, toleration of unorthodox writers, concordats with churches, concessions to peasants, and so on—specific actions of this kind must, on Lenin's own showing (Trotsky's too), be regarded as tactical expedients designed to strengthen the Soviet Union *vis-à-vis* the outside world and the power of the leadership at home. Nevertheless, what may begin as a tactical expedient may imperceptibly be transformed into an enduring custom, may, indeed, become institutionalised. A number of Russia's most abominable institutions had their genesis not in action taken from conviction but in a tactical expedient introduced in an *ad hoc* manner with no thought of permanency: the development of Lenin's Cheka is a case in point.

Domestic reform in the Soviet Union has, in fact, nothing to do with revisionism, because the customs and institutions which need to be reformed have nothing to do with Marxist or Leninist theory. The persecution of minorities, religious and racial, the suppression of free speech, the prohibition of contact with the outside world, the disciplining of artists of all kinds, the eccentricities of Soviet law—these, together with the situations which have developed as a result of the collectivisation of agriculture and the over-stressing of heavy industry, owe little to ideology and everything to the Party's determination to retain power for itself and to strengthen Russia against the outside world. What happens, of course, is that the leadership strives to lend to such expedients what can only be called a moral justification by attaching to them a quasi-ideological value. In so doing they end by deceiving themselves and make necessary change that much harder to effect. Modification, indeed, is accomplished only with extreme reluctance and much half-heartedness only when the ruling circle finds modification immediately necessary for its own survival. As everybody knows, however, such modifications are in fact arrived at, and some are bound to stay. If a harsh expedient resorted to by the Soviet leadership to solve an immediate specific problem can harden into a custom or become institutionalised, there is no reason at all why an ameliorating expedient should not enjoy the same transformation. As for motives, it by no means follows that the man who falls back to jump the better will be given time to execute the manoeuvre as planned.

Khrushchev gave as his reason for abandoning the thesis about the inevitability of war the vastly increased strength of the socialist camp (which then included China), which, he said, was now (1956) sufficient to deter the imperialists from starting a war. Lenin he said, in effect, could not have foreseen this situation. What he really meant was that that the advent of nuclear weapons and intercontinental rockery made war unthinkable. And a few years later, in his polemic against China, he was in fact admitting just this. Then he went further: even local wars must be avoided for fear that one of these might escalate into a major war, ending in universal destruction, Russia not excepted. By implication local wars included any war of liberation, any civil war, indeed, which might give cause for intervention by major powers. Similarly, the new concept of different ways to socialism and the possibility of achieving socialism without violent revolution quite clearly arose from Khrushchev's realisation that it was beyond the power of the Soviet Union to impose itself and its system on at least a large part of the world.

Once these tremendous leaps of the imagination had been made, it followed that, for its own good, the Soviet Union had better come to some sort of an accommodation with the enemy, specifically, the United States. Logic is one thing, action in obedience to it quite another. To abandon Lenin was unthinkable (so unthinkable that it was never even contemplated). Under sheer irresistible pressure of events—e.g. the development of nuclear weapons—it was possible to jettison some of Lenin's teaching with only a perfunctory attempt to justify this action in Leninist terms. But where events were not so pressing it was inevitable that refuge should be sought in odd corners of the dear old doctrine. And when China started making her bid for Lenin's mantle at the very moment when the Russians were disentangling themselves from its folds, while urgently pretending to be doing something quite different, it was too much. Leninism might be in some particulars outworn, but the Soviet Union knew no other authority: if it were to be seized by another power before the Soviet Union had time to grow a new skin the results would be too terrible to contemplate. Hence these tears.

Hence, also, the profound misunderstanding on the part of so many in the West of the processes which are now under way in the Soviet Union. The

Russian leadership is being forced by China to justify in ideological terms attitudes and actions which have nothing to do with ideology. China accuses the Kremlin of revisionism, and the Kremlin feels inevitably constrained, though not consistently, to fight back in these terms. The force of the old magic of the Leninist ideology is thus in a measure revived. It inhibits the Soviet leadership from straight thinking and it alarms the West.

The West should not be alarmed. No matter what the Russians may say they are long past revisionism. Revisionism is the move from conviction from one way of achieving universal socialism to another: e.g. from violent revolution to gradual reform. Socialism is the aim. Lenin, like Marx, thought that it had to be achieved through violent revolution; Bernstein, taking another look at the world, decided that reformism was the better way. But socialism on a global scale, international brotherhood between equal peoples, was the aim, never the greater glory of a single power. Who would dare say that the international brotherhood of workers was Stalin's aim, or Khrushchev's, or Kosygin's?

When Khrushchev introduced his amendments to the Leninist canon in 1956, he dressed them up in ideological camouflage. But, in fact, far from revising Leninism he was abandoning Leninism. He was concerned wholly and solely with the security and prosperity of the Soviet Union—as Stalin had been before him. His act, if not his intention, was on the level of all these internal reforms, usually half-hearted and incomplete, often half withdrawn when made, carried out by his government first to loosen the strait-jacket imposed by Stalin on the Soviet people, then to satisfy, however reluctantly and incompletely, the great hidden pressure of popular demand which followed as night follows day the first loosening of the bonds. In partially freeing the Soviet people so that they could hold up their heads and work better, Khrushchev was responding to the pressure of reality in precisely the same way as he responded to the pressure of reality when he announced that war was no longer inevitable, and in precisely the same way as Kosygin in responding to the pressure of reality when he experiments with the profit motive in industry or scientific inquiry into the way people live and work in the Soviet Union. Conversely, in resisting popular demand—for more personal freedom, for more butter before guns, etc.—the Soviet leadership is responding to reality in precisely the same way as the Tsarist governments responded to reality—attempting to contain popular demand by police action, lest it should gather sufficient momentum to sweep them away.

All these actions, whether liberal or reactionary, still have to be justified in Leninist terms—because the leadership knows no other terms. But the Russian people are not deceived (though they may be muddled, because Lenin was a saint), and we should not be deceived.

The day may come when a government in Moscow will apply itself to some hard thinking about socialism, using elements of Marx, perhaps of Lenin too, as well as lessons from Russia's own experience, to develop a blue-print for society which will capture the imagination of the world. That would be revisionism indeed! But that day is not yet. The Soviet Union now is a great power struggling to escape from its own past, hampered by fears which are no longer relevant, ambitions which are outmoded, dreams which it has confused with reality and a sense of mission without a goal.